To Hillary

Thanks for your help

Love & best wishes

Mike

KILLERS ON THE MOOR

KILLERS ON THE MOOR

The Case of the Dartmoor Ponies and Beyond

Mike Freebury

Book Guild Publishing
Sussex, England

First published in Great Britain in 2011 by
The Book Guild Ltd
Pavilion View
19 New Road
Brighton, BN1 1UF

Typesetting in Garamond by
YHT Ltd, London

Printed in Great Britain by
CPI Antony Rowe

A catalogue record for this book is available from
The British Library.

ISBN 978 1 84624 584 8

To Jill

Contents

PART III THE DARTMOOR SHEEP ATTACKS

PART IV FURTHER INVESTIGATIONS

Prologue

Inspired by a BBC Radio broadcast in 2000, Mike Freebury began investigating a bizarre incident that took place in 1977 when fifteen ponies were horrifically slaughtered in a remote valley on Dartmoor.

Obtaining the only known photographs of that shocking event and tracking the few remaining witnesses to the aftermath, the author painstakingly investigated the strange circumstances of the incident: the gruesome injuries the animals suffered, the rapid decomposition and why details of the incident were not reported for two months.

As his inquiries broadened the author found that the terrible episode on Dartmoor was not the only strange event to take place in the south-west of England. Messages from space, unaccountable explosions and UFOs were all considered as the author's investigation widened, until he stumbled across the animal mutilation problem.

This sinister and disturbing issue first came to light on the open ranges of Colorado and spread across North America leaving ranchers, police and veterinary practitioners dumbfounded. The author explores the facts behind this problem from its first recorded case to the present day. He reveals that no creature is safe from the mutilators: mice, hedgehogs, badgers, foxes, deer as well as every pet and farm animal, they are all vulnerable to the dazzling but sinister technology that is used by the perpetrators of these crimes.

As the author searched through various archives for more and more evidence a shocking truth emerged and it became apparent that the threat is not confined to the United Kingdom, or indeed, the USA, it is worldwide! What had started as an investigation into a bizarre attack on fifteen ponies on Dartmoor in 1977 now mushroomed into a wider inquiry that led across several continents.

As the author's research brought him back to England, he uncovered a series of macabre sheep killings on Dartmoor. He was the first to recognise the true nature of these killings and with a calm logical approach he dismissed the claims of an occult conspiracy. Gaining the confidence of the farmers and working with them, Mike found himself centre stage in this horrifying series of attacks that baffled the police and left the local farming community in terror.

In a bid to catch the mutilators in the act, Mike and his colleague Dave Gillham carried out a programme of all-night surveillance operations on Dartmoor. The nights of cold discomfort on the desolate moor are vividly described. As a sinister presence stalks the area, there are confrontations with another reality, eerie interdimensional entities, strange lights and missing time, revealing further clues about the origin of the attacks.

As the authorities use every means to monitor the investigation the author finds himself in an arduous struggle for the truth. This struggle is detailed in full in the account of his three and a half year legal battle through the Freedom of Information Act to obtain release of astonishing photographs taken by scene of crimes officers for the Devon and Cornwall police.

This book strips away the cloak of government secrecy surrounding the animal mutilation problem and reveals how the Department for the Environment, Food and Rural Affairs (DEFRA) and their forerunner, the Ministry of Agriculture Food and Fisheries (MAFF), have attempted to keep the lid on this explosive issue and to track the activities of the author.

This book methodically examines every potential suspect for these clinical attacks, using calm logic and relying on facts, not supposition. The evidence, and there is a great deal of it, points to a terrifying scenario. The author presents case after case in support of his belief that this issue is real, ongoing and poses such a potential threat to the nation, and the world, that it should be at the top of the UK government's agenda.

Based on a prodigious amount of research this book may read like a crime whodunit. But the stakes are much higher, as Mike Freebury sets out to unmask the ultimate serial killers.

Introduction

Working most of my life in finance has required me and people like me to be realistic, down to earth and to follow a cold logic in assessing a particular situation. I'm someone who prefers to keep his feet on the ground and carefully weigh up situations. I am intrigued by mysteries and the logic needed to solve them. Despite this I have a very open mind to most subjects.

During the summer of 2000 I was sitting at home alone, deep in thought, and began to consider whether I should turn the radio off, which was tuned to the BBC. The programme was conducting a phone-in on government secrecy and how various matters were covered up and withheld from public scrutiny. A caller, a man who I would judge was in his mid to late thirties, began talking about a BBC producer whom he much respected. The man then made an amazing comment to back up his point in the discussion. The BBC producer, a lady, had told him that the British public didn't know the half of what was going on and that one incident in particular – the deaths of fifteen ponies on Dartmoor in 1977 – was the cause of a major cover up by the United Kingdom government.

I was stunned to hear this, as I had been interested in this incident for many years. I remembered the headlines and how, curiously, the story had disappeared from the newspapers just when things began to gain momentum. Mangled bodies, very rapid decomposition and UFOs. What a mystery! There seemed to be a cover up. But why did no one write a book about the case? I had made some enquiries through the years but had seen or learnt nothing about the Dartmoor ponies case. Basically, I was relying on someone else to do all the hard work and write a book about it.

I decided there and then that I would investigate this case and do all that I could to bring out the truth. I would carry out the investigation with the same cold logic by which I earned my living. This book contains the results of my research into this incident and the cases I have uncovered during the investigation.

The book is in four parts and begins with the infamous case of the fifteen Dartmoor ponies and a variety of other strange happenings in the West

Country, in 1977 and 1978. Thirty years is a long time and you will see how attitudes have changed during that period, a time when there were no mobile phones or Internet.

Part II contains an overview of the animal mutilation problem, here and abroad, and discusses numerous case histories, many of which have never appeared before in print. The cases revealed in this book are only the tip of a very large iceberg and represent only some of the incidents known to me and a handful of other researchers. I know the animal mutilation problem is far more widespread than is suggested in this book, and it is my hope that a wider awareness will bring to light more cases and information.

Part III relates my personal investigation into the Dartmoor sheep killings that began in 2005, my thoughts, tribulations with authority, my mistakes and the important breakthroughs in this complex case. I believe the investigation into this series of killings has produced some vital information that should benefit other researchers, as well as warning those who are currently unaware of the problem.

The final part contains a review of the principal cases discussed. I do not claim to have produced the 'smoking gun' evidence demanded by the carping sceptics and the closed minds of established science. However, I believe I have produced sufficient evidence, and the logic to support it, that makes the argument I have put forward difficult to answer.

I began the investigation with the deaths of fifteen ponies in a remote valley on Dartmoor. I have become involved in another major case on Dartmoor involving so many disturbing incidents that I have been compelled, once again, to reappraise my own attitudes to life, the universe, the UK government and some of its institutions. In effect, I have uncovered evidence of the very subject that the radio phone-in was discussing back in the year 2000, together with a sinister and disturbing issue that confronts the whole of mankind.

Dartmoor

Dartmoor is the largest of three major moorland areas in the south-west of England, the other two being Exmoor and Bodmin moor. The lush and fertile county of Devon is dominated by Dartmoor which is also a national park.

However, Dartmoor was a very different place six to seven thousand years ago, being highly forested and with a large population of hunter gatherers. During the Neolithic period, around 4500 BC to 2200 BC, settlements were founded and arable farming began shortly afterwards. The technique known as 'slash and burn' where clearings were made in the woodland had a profound effect on the area. These early settlers did not understand soil fertility and when the soil deteriorated they moved on to another section of woodland. The consequence of this early farming was that large parts of Dartmoor became deforested and the impoverishment of the soil led to the large deposits of peat across much of the moor. Dartmoor's wild beauty was thus formed.

Today there are reminders of Dartmoor's ancient past with stone rows, circles, track ways and reaves (a local dialect word for boundary), which lie within the shadows of the high granite outcrops known as tors.

Dartmoor has been the source for many legends and was the setting for Sir Arthur Conan Doyle's masterpiece, *The Hound of the Baskervilles.* This desolate and remote area is the backdrop for many of the events that I am going to discuss in this book.

Acknowledgements

My research into the incidents on Dartmoor would have been far more difficult had it not been for the incredible support and encouragement from my great friend Dave Gillham, who shared those difficult, cold surveillance nights on Dartmoor. I would also like to thank him for making the Joan Amos archive available to me.

I must extend grateful thanks to Mary Alford and her family for working with us during the sinister Dartmoor sheep attacks. Their help, friendship and hospitality is much appreciated.

It is appropriate that David Cayton, a UK pioneer in this difficult area of research, should be acknowledged for the important work he has done in this field and I thank him for his contribution.

From the United States, I would like to thank Linda Moulton-Howe for allowing me to quote from Doctor John Altshuler's account of the *Lady,* a horse mutilation case in Colorado. Linda has also been a source of help and encouragement.

I should also thank Edwin Joyce of *Flying Saucer Review* for allowing me access to the archive from the oldest UFO publication in the world.

My thanks to Chris Cole for taking the time and trouble to show me the January 2005 crime scene and to his son, Adrian, for providing images of the scene.

I must also thank Nicola Holdgate of the *Western Morning News* Library department for her help and assistance, and Rosa Hill of the *Western Daily Press* for supplying me with a copy of the article 'Terror on the Tor'.

Photographic analysis was vital and I must thank Darren Rudge for his contribution to this important area. I should also thank Peter Martin for video analysis and Hillary Porter for her maps and contribution.

Thanks also to James Bird, Chris Boswell, Brian Damerell, Valerie Hellemink, Steve Jones, Dr Terence Meaden, Pamela Penfold, Peter Preston, Steve Poole, Sallie Scott, PC Steve Saunders, Robert Tudge, Joanna Vinson and Chris Warren.

Importantly, there are those whose identity I must protect and thank for their help, assistance and contribution – you know who you are.

This is my first book and I have received enormous help and support from a great team of people at The Book Guild. My thanks to you all for guiding me through the publication process.

Finally, I must thank my wife for her support, without which this book would not have been possible.

Glossary

ABCs	Alien big cats
ACPO	Association of Chief Police Officers
APFU	Animal Pathology Field Unit
BEAMS	The British Earth & Aerial Mysteries Society
BUFORA	The British UFO Research Association
CUFORG	Cornwall UFO Research Group
DEFRA	Department for the Environment, Food and Rural Affairs
DLPS	Dartmoor Livestock Protection Society
FoIA	Freedom of Information Act 2000 (UK)
FSR	*Flying Saucer Review* UFO magazine
ICO	Information Commissioner's Office
MAFF	Ministry of Agriculture, Fisheries & Food
MI5	Military Intelligence 5 (UK interior intelligence)
MI6	Secret intelligence service
MoD	Ministry of Defence (UK)
NFU	National Farmers Union
NORAD	North American Aerospace Defense Command
NSA	National Security Agency (USA)
PUFORG	Plymouth UFO Research Group
RSPB	The Royal Society for the Protection of Birds
RSPCA	The Royal Society for the Prevention of Cruelty to Animals
UFORM	Midlands UFO Research Group (UK)
VLA	Veterinary Laboratories Agency

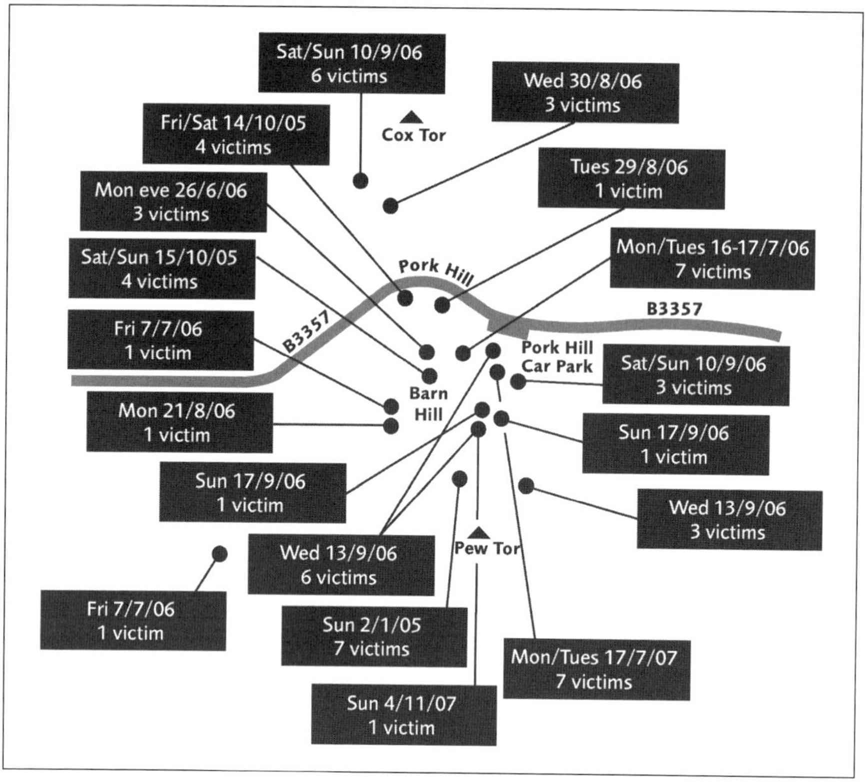
Sat/Sun 10/9/06
6 victims
Wed 30/8/06
3 victims
Cox Tor
Fri/Sat 14/10/05
4 victims
Tues 29/8/06
1 victim
Mon eve 26/6/06
3 victims
Mon/Tues 16-17/7/06
7 victims
Sat/Sun 15/10/05
4 victims
Pork Hill
B3357
Fri 7/7/06
1 victim
B3357
Pork Hill
Car Park
Sat/Sun 10/9/06
3 victims
Barn
Hill
Mon 21/8/06
1 victim
Sun 17/9/06
1 victim
Sun 17/9/06
1 victim
Wed 13/9/06
3 victims
Wed 13/9/06
6 victims
Pew Tor
Fri 7/7/06
1 victim
Sun 2/1/05
7 victims
Mon/Tues 17/7/07
7 victims
Sun 4/11/07
1 victim

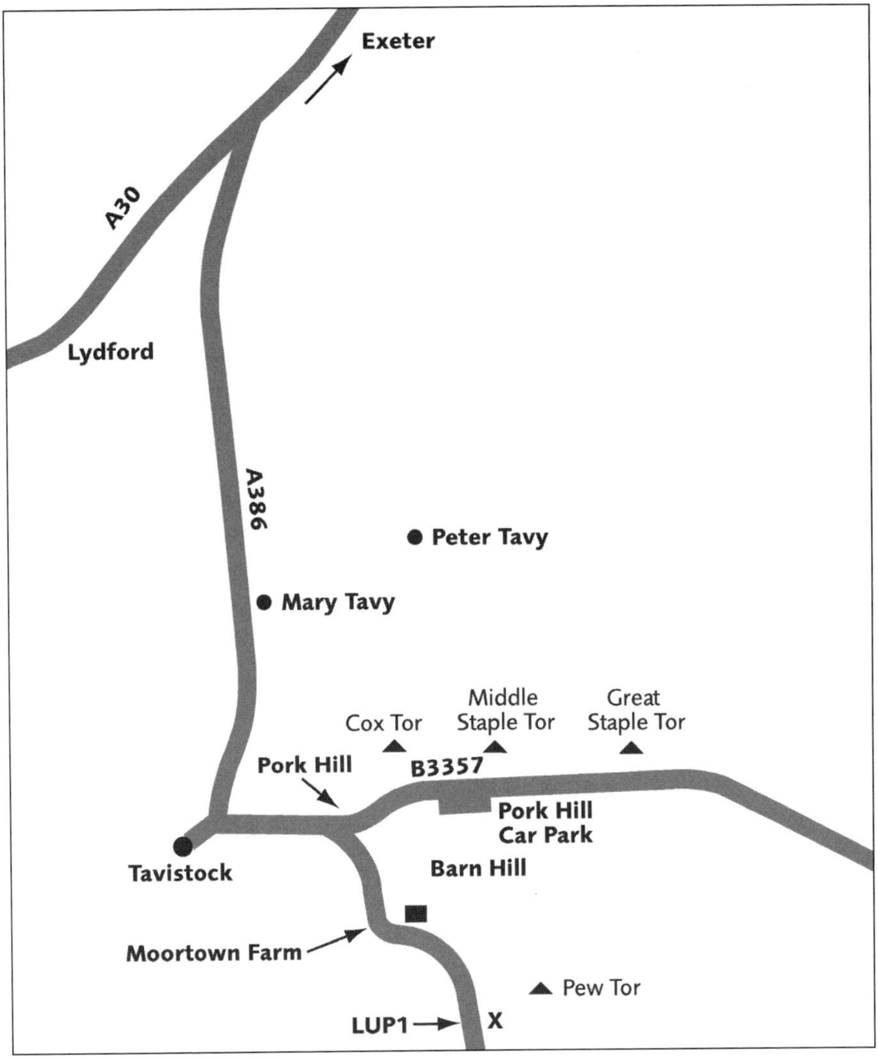
Exeter
A30
Lydford
A386
Peter Tavy
Mary Tavy
Middle Staple Tor
Great Staple Tor
Cox Tor
Pork Hill
B3357
Pork Hill Car Park
Tavistock
Barn Hill
Moortown Farm
Pew Tor
LUP1
X

Part I

Dartmoor Ponies 1977

1

The Dartmoor Ponies Incident

On Easter Monday, 11th April 1977 Mr Alan Hicks, his wife and two children were walking on Dartmoor. As they approached a small remote valley called Hollocombe Bottom, situated below White Tor, they came upon the twisted and mangled bodies of four Dartmoor ponies. The bodies showed evidence of remarkable violence such as broken necks and backs. A hundred yards further on lay an even greater carnage as more bodies exhibiting similar injuries were found. In all, fifteen dead ponies and a sheep lay in this remote area two miles from the small village of Postbridge and the nearest road. Alan Hicks was interviewed by the press and gave the following account:

'They were all grouped together within a hundred yard section of the valley. There are no cliffs or anything at that spot where the animals could have fallen.' He also said, *'I counted twelve, four of them were freshly dead, and they were still seeping blood. Others were submerged in the brook and others had their bones showing through.*

'My first reaction was that they were a potential health hazard. Somewhere along the line that water was going to be used by someone. So I called the police.' Mr Hicks had regularly walked the moor for some twenty-five years and had never seen such a sight in all that time.

The horrifying state of the corpses prompted Alan Hicks to report the matter urgently and, in addition to the police, the RSPCA, The Dartmoor Livestock Protection Society and the Animal Defence League also became involved. The RSPCA investigated the deaths within the first couple of days and their investigation highlighted another bizarre fact. It appeared that many of the bodies decomposed within forty-eight hours. Tony Booth, the RSPCA Chief Inspector sent to investigate the killings, said, *'Decomposition was unusually fast – that in itself is a mystery.'*

The Dartmoor Livestock Protection Society and the Animal Defence League launched a joint enquiry into the incident. Mrs Joanna Vinson, Secretary of the DLPS and Mrs Ruth Murray, Devon President of the Animal Defence League, visited the crime scene many times in their search for an explanation. Joanna Vinson told reporters, *'We have spent many hours dissecting and examining what was left of the carcasses. The ponies had broken bones and torn arteries. Whatever happened was fairly violent. We are keeping an open mind.'*

Strangely, the incident was not reported in the local press until the first week in June 1977, nearly two months after the ponies were found, and it was a further six weeks later that the story eventually made the national press. Lurid headlines such as 'Dartmoor death riddle of 15 mangled ponies' (*Daily Mail*, 15th July 1977) were fairly typical. There was wide coverage given to this macabre event not just in the UK, but across the world.

During all this media frenzy there was no mention of the fact that this incident took place on 10th April 1977. All the national newspaper reports were dated between 13th July and 19th July 1977, three months after the bodies had been discovered. If you were unaware of the true facts you would have assumed, as I did for some time, that the ponies had died on or about 13th July 1977. This curious fact regarding the timing and release of the story to the media has made me much more aware of how news is reported and fed to us by the media. Why was the story reported by the national press so long after the event?

The incident would not have been reported at all had it not been for the investigation by the Devon Unidentified Objects Centre based in Torquay. This organisation sent a four man team, headed by Mr John Wyse, to Cherry Brook Valley to scan the area with Geiger counters in the hope that evidence might be found that a flying saucer was responsible. It was suggested that a vortex from an extraterrestrial craft could have thrown the ponies into the air and inflicted the terrible injuries. The UFO angle made the story a tabloid dream and catapulted the event into the national press.

The *Daily Mirror* dated 15th July 1977 carried the story on page nine with the headline 'UFO probe into dead ponies riddle'. John Wyse, who had founded the Devon UFO Centre, was quoted as follows, *'We are seeking proof that extraterrestrials were responsible.'*

Joanna Vinson of the Dartmoor Livestock Protection Society said of the UFO investigation, *'I am fascinated by the UFO theory. There is no reason to reject that possibility, since there is no other rational explanation.'*

The UFO headlines reached far and wide. 'Were these ponies killed by UFO invaders?' asked the *Durban Mercury* in South Africa. 'Outer space theory on deaths of moor ponies' was the leader in the *Western Morning News* in Plymouth.

Among the various reports, there was a small reference to the animal mutilation problem in the United States of America. In particular, there were similarities between the injuries suffered by the ponies and the horrific mutilations of horses and cattle in some USA cases. It is a pity that no one investigated this clue any further. During the 1970s North America was gripped by a wave of unexplained animal deaths.

As often happens in a case where there is no apparent explanation there are always people willing to put forward a theory that could solve the mystery. In July 1977 the *Western Morning News* combined coverage of the UFO investigation with the theory put forward by Major John Parkinson of Yelverton. Major Parkinson, who had been a vet in the Dartmoor area for thirty-four years, suggested that the bodies had been dumped there by owners who were unwilling to go to the inconvenience of burying their dead animals. Major Parkinson said, *'What was stumbled across was simply a moorland knackers yard. Anyone with any real knowledge of Dartmoor will appreciate this is fairly commonplace. It is not unusual or uncommon practice on the Moor.'*

Major Parkinson was referring to the obligation of the ponies' owners to remove dead animal carcasses from the moor. He added, *'You need to dig a damned big hole to bury even a small pony. You don't lose a dozen or fifteen ponies without being aware of it. Nothing can be proved or disproved, I suspect.'*

Mrs Ruth Murray of the Dartmoor Livestock Protection Society was particularly dismissive of the Major's opinion. For a start, it did not explain the injuries, or the fact that the ponies appeared to have died at about the same time. The logistics of transporting the fifteen dead ponies to this remote knackers yard beggars belief.

Top prize for unusual theories went to a Devon botanist who suggested that the ponies might have eaten a plant called bog asphodel, Latin name *Narthercium ossifragum*. This plant contains a poison which is believed to cause brittle bones. The ponies, it was suggested, might have consumed this plant and perished. It seems highly unlikely that ponies would consume a plant that was potentially fatal to them. Why was this not a recognised danger for the ponies' owners? Because ponies do not eat the plant and such deaths by poisoning have not been previously recorded.

More down to earth theories were promulgated in the press. Miss Lillian Martin, a member of the DLPS, suggested that the ponies had drowned when the valley became flooded following a cloudburst. Miss Martin had a bungalow that overlooked the general direction of Cherry Brook Valley and she noted a large black cloud over the area. There was severe flooding in Ashburton that seemed to coincide with appearance of this dark cloud. She told the *Western Morning News*, *'My theory is that the ponies were in a very enclosed valley. There was a waterfall at the head of the valley, and they may have been caught in a sudden burst of water and knocked against the boulders.'* This theory does not explain all the injuries or the alleged rapid decomposition of the bodies.

It was suggested that the ponies all died of redworm but, as Joanna

Vinson said, that does not explain the broken backs or, for that matter, the torn arteries and rapid decomposition.

Mrs Ruth Murray believed the ponies could have been stampeded down the valley by vehicles and that the killings were the result of a grudge. She claimed to have found a skid mark on the ground near to the scene.

There were forensic tests on the bones and flesh taken from the animals in May by Ruth Murray and Joanna Vinson. When this little known fact was reported in the *Western Morning News* on 19th July 1977, the DLPS were still awaiting the results. As far as I am aware these forensic tests have never been made public.

For all the wrong reasons, this terrible and disturbing incident might well have been buried and forgotten, had it not been for the surge of media interest following the involvement of John Wyse and his team of investigators. The true facts of this incident were lying dormant behind an incorrect date and lurid headlines.

2

The Dartmoor Ponies Investigation

My early research into the Dartmoor incident was hampered by the fact that not a single reference to the deaths of these fifteen ponies seemed to exist anywhere on the Internet. That in itself was very curious. I spent many hours in Birmingham Reference Library, laboriously turning the microfiche pages of various newspapers dated between 1971 and 1979. The investigation, it seemed, couldn't get going. Then I had a breakthrough. One night as I scanned the Internet, I came upon a reference to the case. A guy called Steve Gamble had written an article about the ponies for BUFORA magazine and had listed it in a bibliography on his website. The article, written for the *BUFORA Journal No 7*, was entitled 'Those Dartmoor ponies' and gave the date 15th July 1977. At last I had the necessary information to focus my research. I sent Steve Gamble an email, but got no response. However, I soon obtained copies of various newspapers and the investigation started in earnest.

My efforts to obtain a copy of the BUFORA magazine with Gamble's article were singularly unsuccessful as BUFORA were transferring their records from London to Exeter. In early January 2007 the researcher, John Hanson, kindly sent me a copy of the article. It briefly gave details that several newspapers had carried the story of the dead ponies in July 1977 and that a Devon UFO organisation had suggested the deaths might have been caused by UFO activity in the area. A main supporting point of this claim was the rapid decomposition of the bodies.

The responsibility for investigating the incident for BUFORA was given to Randall Jones Pugh, MRCVS, who was the BUFORA Physical Data Section's veterinary expert. Pugh had co-written a well-researched and informative book, about the wave of UFO and associated strange events on the coast of south Wales between 1974 and 1977, called *The Dyfed Enigma* (Pugh and Holliday, Faber & Faber Ltd, 1979). However, the investigation into the Dartmoor ponies incident appeared to consist of a solitary telephone call made by Pugh to a local Dartmoor vet. I quote Pugh, directly from the article: *'I spoke to M... P... (name on file), the vet involved with the examination of the ponies. The report was to me quite logical. In effect, they had died of a very heavy worm infection following the effects of the previous year's prolonged drought.'*

Stephen Gamble then stated that this was a plausible explanation and pointed out that the soil on Dartmoor tended to be quite acidic and that this would aid, and presumably explain, the rapid decomposition. The event was dismissed as a potential UFO incident and until further evidence came to light the case should be regarded as closed.

Both Pugh and Gamble missed a great opportunity to bring the true circumstances surrounding this incident into the open, and several errors were made in their brief enquiry. The first mistake was the actual date of the incident: the misinformation about that date, conveyed by the national newspapers, was to lead me astray too, as we shall see.

Pugh had telephoned M... P... This was almost certainly Major John Parkinson, a vet on Dartmoor for many years and it was he who proposed a quite bizarre reason for the deaths of the fifteen ponies, a reason that contradicted his comments to Pugh. It should also be noted that Major Parkinson did not examine the bodies of the dead ponies. As a vet, Pugh should have known that for all fifteen ponies (and one sheep) to die almost simultaneously from worm infection was extremely unlikely, and in any case, the ponies had not been up on that part of the moor for all that long. Stephen Gamble's suggestion that the decomposition (in some cases within twenty-four hours) was accelerated by acidic soil, defies belief – was the soil 90% sulphuric acid? Nonetheless, the article gives an impression of how easy it was for this incident to be conveniently buried.

Initially, I too fell into the trap of thinking that the date of the killings was around 13th to 14th July 1977. It was only when I obtained copies of the *Western Morning News* articles on the event that I realised the true date was three months earlier.

In late 2004 I wrote to the BBC South West Library in Plymouth, asking if they had any footage relating to the incident in their archives. Unfortunately, their librarian could find only a catalogue entry, curiously dated 1st June 1977. The catalogue entry stated, *'Hugh Scully talks to Mrs Joanna Vinson about mysterious deaths of Dartmoor ponies being investigated by RSPCA' No film exists.*

On Wednesday 1st June 1977, the *Western Morning News* had carried a small report, on their front page, about the incident. Written by their environment correspondent, the article stated that an RSPCA investigation had been carried out between five and six weeks before. It was further stated by the RSPCA spokesman that *'The four bodies that were found were so badly decomposed that it was impossible to determine the cause of their deaths. We will go out and look again in the area and, if necessary, we will call in a veterinary surgeon.'* The article said that the bodies could have been there for up to six months, and concluded with the suggestion that redworm, which tends to flourish in hot summers, might have been responsible for the deaths.

I find it rather strange that the RSPCA could have gone to the scene of the incident and, given the scale of the carnage, found only four bodies. Considering the long trek to the scene and the fact that the corpses were lying within an area one hundred or so yards long, within a small valley, I have to say that the RSPCA statement does not ring true. The *Tavistock Times* stated on 3rd June 1977 that the RSPCA would soon be issuing their report on the incident and, as far as I am aware, no such report was ever made public.

I found out that the ponies' story was first given prominence in the *Tavistock Times* in the first week of June 1977. The paper had sent reporter Tom Utley and photographer Jim Thorington to the scene of the incident. This was a major story for the *Tavistock Times*, which carried the story on its front page on Friday 3rd June 1977 with the headline 'How did 15 ponies die?' They also showed two pictures, taken by Jim Thorington, of dead ponies at the scene. The fact that the paper despatched two of its reporting staff to this very remote part of Dartmoor shows how important this story was. Intriguingly, they appeared to have ignored the story for two months before splashing it across their front page. Why was this? Alan Hicks reported the incident to the police and the RSPCA as soon as he got home. This delay in reporting the incident suggests that, possibly, some other agencies might have been involved and that some sort of cover up might have taken place.

I decided to try and track down some of the people mentioned in the newspaper reports. Tony Booth of the RSPCA and Ruth Murray of the Animal Defence League had both passed on and I could not locate John Wyse of the Devon UFO Centre. However, I had some luck with the Dartmoor Livestock Protection Society, who kindly put me in touch with Joanna Vinson who was the secretary of the DLPS at the time of the incident.

Joanna Vinson was no longer connected to the DLPS, and ran a smallholding in south Devon. On 23rd October 2004 I spoke to her about the case. She told me that her first visit to the crime scene was on Wednesday 13th April 1977 and that she and Ruth Murray visited the scene every day for a week. Joanna told me that the killings had taken place off the normal moor walkways and that extreme violence had occurred. She confirmed that the bodies had decomposed quite rapidly, although forty-eight hours was, in her words, *'Pushing it a bit.'* The weather at that time was very hot and sultry and there were large numbers of midges, which were a constant nuisance. *'I can still smell the bodies!'* she said.

I asked whether any photographs had been taken and Joanna said that there were none taken by her or Ruth Murray. However, she thought there might be some photographs in Ruth Murray's files, which had been held in a bank since Ruth's death.

I asked about the identity of the ponies, as they all belonged to someone. Apparently there were no identifying marks and Joanna further elaborated on the grudges that could occur between livestock owners in that part of the moor. In fact, the area was sometimes referred to as 'Indian country'.

In 2005 I received information that gave me the identity of the ponies' owner. There was a possible dispute over grazing rights involving this person, a dispute made more acrimonious by a broken love affair, which resulted in her ponies being evicted onto a part of the moor with which they were not familiar. Because of this the ponies, already undernourished, were thought to have eventually died of starvation. However, I do not believe this to be the cause of the pony deaths.

I inquired about the possible involvement of the Ministry of Defence but received an unequivocal response. The army were not involved, and in any case they did not train on that part of the moor. However, despite Joanna Vinson's reply, I believe the army was involved. During my investigations into the Dartmoor sheep killings, in early 2005, I received some interesting information. I was approached by a local resident, from the Tavistock area, who told me that the army was, most certainly, involved in the incident. Unfortunately, they would elaborate no further on this startling piece of information.

I asked Joanna about alien big cats, such as a puma. ABCs as they are sometimes called, were not responsible. They might kill the occasional animal, but only for food.

Joanna said that the case was highly unusual and that no similar incidents had been noted. She referred me to a book called *Dartmoor Legends* that had an account of the pony killings incident as well as other bizarre mysteries from the Dartmoor area. Although it was twenty-seven years after the event Joanna Vinson retained a clear memory of the incident and I was grateful for her input into this cold case.

In October 2004 I wrote to the Royal Society for Prevention of Cruelty to Animals. My letter to their South and South West Headquarters, based in Exeter, was passed to Jonathan Silk, Regional Manager, who responded. He told me that Tony Booth, who had investigated the case, had died a couple of years previously and that the RSPCA had no records from 1977.

I asked about the RSPCA database and whether they had any records of similar cases in the south-west. Mr Silk said that the RSPCA did not computerise its records until 1992 and that there was a basic system until 1999 so they had no helpful database. Curiously, he added the following: *'I doubt whether we could release anything, even if we did apart from bland statistics.'*

I was surprised that the RSPCA were so reticent about giving information about specific cases, particularly if information could lead to the apprehension of the perpetrators. As we shall see later, the RSPCA may have preferred to keep a database of information about animal mutilation cases to themselves, rather than share it with other agencies – a policy that would be counterproductive.

In February 2005 I contacted Tavistock police and asked if they had any files on the Dartmoor Ponies incident. My letter was passed to the Devon and Cornwall Constabulary Force headquarters at Middlemoor, Exeter. On 23rd February 2005 I received a reply from Mrs J. Moon, the Force Assistant Data Protection Officer, who informed me that they no longer held any files from April 1977. I called Mrs Moon a couple of days later and she told me that only serious crimes were retained and subjected to ten-year reviews.

Due to other pressures it was not until April 2006 that I made an application to the Ministry of Defence, under the UK Freedom of Information Act, for information about the Dartmoor Ponies incident. I did not have long to wait before receiving a response from Mr Peter Francis of Info-AccessOps5 of the Ministry of Defence in Whitehall, London. The incident, he wrote, was not MOD related and as a consequence the MOD held no information about the pony deaths. However, Mr Francis was extremely helpful, and went out of his way to give a possible explanation of the incident. I quote from his letter dated 27th April 2006:

> *Discovery of the incident can apparently be recalled by a member of the National Park Staff and the word of mouth on this is: During a cold period in early 1977 the badly decomposed remains of a group of Dartmoor ponies was found in a dell on the moor; they appeared to have taken shelter in that place. Enquiries were made as to their ownership and no one came forward. The then Ministry of Agriculture Fisheries and Food (MAFF) sent a veterinary surgeon (possibly a Mr Cunningham) to the scene and he is thought to have been of the opinion that the ponies had been killed by lightning. The remains were reckoned to be over one month old and it was therefore difficult to determine precisely how the deaths had occurred. No doubt a record of this incident would have been made at the time but you will need to make a request to DEFRA, the department of state now responsible.*

I had heard this explanation before. On 1st April 2005 while travelling back from my first visit to Moortown to investigate the mysterious deaths of seven sheep, I called in to the National Park tourist centre at Postbridge. The lady in charge was most helpful and rang the local park warden and asked if he recalled the incident. The story he told me was basically as above, but without mentioning MAFF or Mr Cunningham.

There were a lot of holes in this explanation. What about the state of the mangled bodies? How could Mr Cunningham deduce that it was a lightning strike when the bodies were so badly decomposed? Joanna Vinson never mentioned any burn marks and she was one of the first on the scene. I had to ask myself why MAFF would send a veterinary surgeon to the scene at all unless there were some highly unusual circumstances surrounding the incident.

I was amazed that Mr Francis had been so helpful, and wrote thanking him for his reply. In the same letter I asked if there was a possibility that Porton Down, the UK's biological weapons establishment, had been involved in the incident. His reply was perfunctory and stated in two lines that there was no involvement.

The involvement of MAFF gave me a new line of enquiry and in June 2006 I wrote to the Department of the Environment, Food and Rural Affairs in London, asking for information on the incident. About a month later I received a letter from the State Veterinary Service in Clyst St Mary, Devon. Mrs Catherine Harper wrote on behalf of the Divisional Veterinary Manager and explained that records were only kept for twenty-five years. Therefore, they were unable to help.

The interesting question here is this. Where did Mr Francis get his information regarding the involvement of MAFF and Mr Cunningham's name? I very much doubt it was from the National Park Ranger, who had already given me his explanation.

The most intriguing line of inquiry involved the identity of the BBC producer who had been mentioned on the radio phone-in. This, after all, had been the one thing that had sparked off my investigation. There was so much she could tell me! I checked the biographies of a number of well-known television news personalities to see if they had worked in the south-west. One such candidate was the BBC news correspondent Kate Adie, who had worked in the south-west at the time of the incident. I eventually managed to contact her, but unfortunately she had no recollection of Dartmoor pony deaths.

In November 2006 I put an advert in the BBC house magazine *Ariel*. It was a shot in dark, but if that TV producer was still working in the industry, then there was a chance I might contact her. Anyway, it was worth a try and I placed an advert in the classified section of four weekly issues of *Ariel*. Unfortunately, there was no response.

In October 2006, while making enquiries about the ponies incident, I learnt that there was a chance that there were original photos of the crime scene, taken by photographer Jim Thorington, and that they might still be in existence. I was given the name of a photographer who had all the negatives taken by Jim, as far back as 1976. I managed to track him down and to my amazement and joy he had four negatives of the scene. I asked for copies of the four pictures and was told they would be with me in a week. I could hardly wait! I had always thought that photographs of the crime scene would be the holy grail of this particular case, more so considering the fact that there was hardly anyone still living who could give me the kind of detail that might be revealed by the pictures.

The photos arrived as promised and I was not disappointed. Three of the images were terrific and disclosed a great deal of information while the third, which appeared to show the body of a sheep lying on a rock, near a stream, was inconclusive. The best photo of the four showed the body of a dead pony, its head twisted backwards, lying partly in a stream, with Bellever Tor about two miles away in the distance. The most incredible thing about this image is the fact that the entire head of the pony has been stripped of skin and tissue and the animal's skull is bleached white. Why had the head decomposed and not the rest of the body? I immediately thought of the numerous photographs I had seen taken in the United States, where the skin and tissue from the head had been removed and that same weird, bleached appearance was evident. This was the most compelling evidence I had found and suggested that there was a definite link between the pony deaths and the large number of killings reported in the United States at that time and since. The question is, how is this done to the animals, and why?

It had taken more than five years to get the investigation to this stage and despite the fact that there were some issues that needed further research I considered that the truth about this case might not be far away. One of the issues I needed to look at was whether there had been any similar cases or strange events that might be connected to the killing of the ponies. I was soon to find out that there was quite a lot of bizarre goings on in the West Country in the late seventies.

3

The Newquay Zoo Affair

During 1976 and 1977 Newquay Zoo lost a number of animals and wildfowl in a series of bizarre attacks. The zoo's owners suspected there was a rational explanation for the livestock losses, so the police were not notified. In 1978 the attacks began again and initially they were put down to animal predators and not thought to be connected. However, as the circumstances surrounding the killings were examined more closely it became apparent that the attacks were serial and the perpetrators possessed some extraordinary capabilities.

The 1978 incidents appear to have started in February, and on 9th February a Muscovy duck was decapitated. On 16th February a Bar Head goose was killed in a similar manner. On 26th February another Muscovy duck was decapitated. Although these deaths were unusual (the bodies had little or no blood around them and the heads were never recovered) it appears that the police were not initially notified.

During March there were no further attacks, then, on 12th April another Muscovy duck was decapitated. There seemed to be a further pause in the killings until 3rd June when a wallaby was found dead in its paddock by staff opening up early in the morning. The animal had been beheaded, although there was no trace of the head and there seemed to have been no blood spilt. The removal of the head appeared to have been carried out in a very clinical manner and the staff were at a loss to explain how the perpetrators could have accessed the enclosure without leaving any marks or tracks.

On an unknown date between 3rd June and 17th August, a Chinese goose was killed and its body, minus the head, was found tightly wedged into a confined space away from its enclosure. No other animal could have possibly put it there and the head was never found. On 17th August there was another attack, this time a Black swan was killed and had its head and neck removed in the same surgical manner as the wallaby. There appeared to have been no struggle and no blood was found at the scene. A search of the area revealed the neck within some undergrowth, but the head was never found.

On 23rd September there was a further attack on a young wallaby, which was removed from its enclosure, carried some fifty yards over several other animal pens and dumped, minus the upper part of its body, into another enclosure. Again, there was no trace of blood at the scene and the decapitation had been carried out in a very precise manner. The grass around the body had marks indicating that it had been flattened by someone or something and, in addition to this, there were several particles of meat found by the body. A further puzzle was, how did the perpetrators manage to remove the wallaby from the enclosure? At the end of each night the pathways around the enclosures were raked over and yet no tracks were found.

All the attacks appeared to have taken place in the early hours of the morning and neither the zoo staff, nor any security personnel heard or saw anything. In each attack the security fence remained intact.

Mr Marshall, the zoo manager, informed Joan Amos, who was investigating the killings on behalf of the Plymouth UFO group, that immediately after the attack on the second wallaby the remaining wallabies exhibited strange swellings on their jaws and sides and that the skin on their feet had turned white. Curiously, this revelation was not disclosed to the police.

The zoo's Consultant Veterinary Surgeon, Mr W. Clifton Green carried out a post mortem on the remains of the dead wallaby. I have obtained a copy of the post mortem report, which has some interesting observations on the killing of the wallaby. The backbone had been deeply severed in a clean and precise manner, and I quote directly from the report as follows: *'The carcass appeared to have been cleanly transected by a sharp appliance, the round edges were even clean. No evidence of bite wounds were present, nor was there any interference with muscular tissue. The bladder and rectum were absent from the pelvis, but the pelvic girdle and muscular skeletal system of the hind legs appeared undamaged. At the time of examination there was no evidence of any great haemorrhage having occurred at the time of incision. Nor, judging by the transection, was there any struggle.'*

Mr Clifton Green concluded his report as follows: *'It is possible that the division of the carcass occurred after death, and was not its cause. The subject inflicting the damage is uncertain, but the possibility of human involvement cannot be excluded following this post mortem examination.'*

The clean and precise manner of the injuries suggest that the killers had total control over their victim and were able to carry out what, to all intents and purposes, was a surgical operation, requiring anatomical knowledge and some very advanced equipment that was easily portable. How else could the decapitation have been carried out without spilling any blood and leaving the edges of the cut skin clean? The removal of the rectum is a classic symptom of an animal mutilation attack, of which we will hear in more detail later.

Mr Clifton Green's assessment of the killers, though displaying the usual caution shown by all veterinary pathologists, states that human involvement cannot be ruled out. This said, we can certainly rule out the possibility of a natural animal predator attack, as there were no bite marks or frenzied splattering of blood as would be expected in such an attack.

The police investigating this series of attacks had ruled out the possibility of local occultists, despite the suggestion, particularly in the press, that occultists might be responsible. The police checked the attack dates with the occult calendar to see if there was any correlation and none was found.

There is a little-known fact concerning the police investigation into these attacks. Earlier in the year some lambs had been attacked and killed in a field, barely half a mile from the zoo. Although dogs had been seen in the field where the attack had taken place the victims had been killed in the same manner as the animals and wildfowl at the zoo – all the dead lambs had been beheaded! The police saw the link between the two crimes but did not make any further comment on this connection. It is worth mentioning here that in 1981 at Rossendale, Lancashire, twenty-five sheep were found beheaded and mutilated on a remote hillside. As we shall see later, sheep appear to be a favoured prey of the mutilators.

The Plymouth UFO group (PUFORG) investigated the attacks, and their representative Joan Amos made an appointment to see the Head of CID, Chief Inspector Fouxes, and the investigating officer, Detective Constable Hulme. It goes without saying that such cooperation from the police would be unheard of today, in fact there is a distinct impression that Joan Amos's involvement brought a 'Miss Marple' feel to the investigation. Joan was given a copy of the official police report into the investigation at that time. Parts of the report were censored, most probably because certain individuals may have been named as possible suspects and the police, while involving Joan in their investigation, were hardly likely to disclose any names they might have 'in the frame'. During her meeting with the police and zoo staff, Joan was told that earlier in the year several reliable witnesses had reported seeing a puma walking along the railway track that ran behind the zoo gardens. Some unidentified paw prints had been found at different locations within the zoo. An abandoned mine near the zoo added further to the theory that a big cat could have been involved. However, it appears highly unlikely that the puma noted by the railway line, or any other large cat, could have been responsible for the sinister attacks

The bizarre killings had several unusual and disturbing features, not the least of which were the traces of radiation found in the wallaby compound and where the body was discovered. The use of Geiger counters and other such devices by private individuals for recording radioactivity was plainly more prevalent in those years, before the fear of radiological terrorism hung over the United Kingdom and restrictions on obtaining such equipment were introduced. Joan Amos was given a Radiac Survey meter by PUFORG, which unfortunately did not work. Not to be denied in her investigations, Joan managed to borrow a Radiac Survey meter No 2, measuring in roentgens. Joan's radiological survey gave the following results: wallaby compound 0.2 roentgens, site of wallaby carcass 0.2 roentgens, all other sites 0.0 roentgens. It is possible that the higher readings in the compound and crime scene are the result of the mixture of tin and granite in the area (granite has a higher radiation level than most other rocks in the UK).

In 2003 there was an eerily similar case to the Newquay killings, this time in the north-east of England. Two wallabies at the Hope animal sanctuary in Loftus, on the north-east coast of England, were beheaded and the heads were never found. In each case the attacks took place overnight and there was little or no blood at the scene. The security fencing had not been damaged, although it was suspected that the assailants had gained entry by climbing over it. Cliff Spedding, the owner of the sanctuary, buried the first wallaby but kept the body of the second victim in a freezer to await a post mortem.

This case was investigated by the Crypto Zoologist Foundation run by Jonathan Downes, who sent Richard Freeman to Loftus as their representative. By chance a television crew from the company that produced 'Scream Team' (a programme based on paranormal investigations) were there at the same time and it appears they agreed to join forces.

Simon Beck of the Beck Veterinary practice at Whitby agreed to carry out the post mortem with Freeman and the 'Scream Team' in attendance. I can only think that the lure of television was too much for him to resist as the onlookers packed into his surgery to witness the autopsy. The wallaby's head had been cleanly severed and the heart and lungs were full of blood, indicating that the animal had struggled with its killers and was alive at the point of decapitation. No organs were removed and it was suggested that the killers had put the head into a polythene bag immediately prior to the beheading, thereby avoiding any blood spilling onto the ground. I have to confess that I find this speculation on the lack of blood at the scene to be highly unlikely.

Freeman, who enjoyed the cooperation of the local police, suggested it was likely that three men had been involved and that the killings had been carried out as some sort of grudge against Mr Spedding. PC O'Hara and WPC Rachel Dick appeared to concur with that view and were also of the opinion that people from outside the area had come to Loftus and carried out the attacks. I find this logic quite incredible. For a start, why bother to be so careful about not spilling blood when killing the animals? Why not vandalise the sanctuary buildings if it was a grudge, and why did they kill just two wallabies on different nights? I personally find it difficult to believe that a group of individuals would travel any distance out of their way, let alone to some backwater such as Loftus, to carry out the precision killings of two wallabies. The case remains unsolved.

Joan Amos's report, though quite thorough, was inconclusive and a number of questions remained to be answered, such as were there any unusual aircraft reported during the nights when the attacks took place? Had any medical equipment or animal sedatives been stolen from the Newquay area? Joan was plainly unaware of the sheep attacked and beheaded only half a mile away, a few months previously – a fact surprisingly not disclosed by the police. I believe that if Joan had been made aware of the attack on the lambs, the two cases could have been profiled, leading to a much clearer conclusion as to the possible identity of the perpetrators. The references quoted in Joan's report are quite illuminating as to who or what she thought was responsible for the attacks – *Mystery Stalks the Prairie* by Robert Donovan and Keith Wolverton, *Mysteries of Time and Space* by Brad Steiger and *The Mothman Prophecies* by John Keel – books that dealt with the animal mutilation problem!

Joan made a very interesting observation during her investigation into the Newquay Zoo killings. She stated that there were unsubstantiated reports that a herd of Dartmoor ponies had been killed a year previously and that there were similarities between the zoo attacks and the Dartmoor case. I believe that Joan had 'hit the nail on the head' and that the zoo killings were indeed connected, not only to the Dartmoor ponies case but, as we shall see, to other attacks in the south-west of England as well.

I would like to quote from Joan's handwritten notes from the report: *'In view of the Dartmoor case I am still trying to locate the investigating officer on that case, if I succeed details will be forwarded in a separate report.'* From the use of the word 'still' it would seem that Joan was not having much luck in contacting the police officer dealing with the Dartmoor ponies case – not surprisingly. Despite a systematic search of her archives, I have been unable to find the separate report she hoped to do and, as a consequence, I must assume she failed to get any information on that notorious incident. Joan became interested in UFOs and strange animal deaths after she witnessed a UFO while in Tavistock hospital in April 1978, a year after the Dartmoor incident. It is a great pity that her undoubted investigative tenacity and intelligence was not focused on that sinister incident on Dartmoor on 11th April 1977. A year later the trail had gone cold.

4

The Message from Outer Space

On 26th November 1977, Southern Television, a commercial station covering the south-west of England, was broadcasting a news bulletin. The news reader was Ivor Mills and at 5:12 pm GMT the newscast was interrupted by a bizarre voice that appeared to override the sound transmission. Mills was still on the screen but his words could not be heard, only the eerie, deep, sonorous voice, which seemed to echo and sounded as if it was coming from under water. The five and a half minute broadcast caused consternation and Southern Television was inundated with calls from concerned viewers.

The following day both the press and television claimed the message was a hoax and only the first thirty seconds or so was re-broadcast, curiously with the second sentence of the original broadcast omitted. This gave the message a more sinister tone and there was a clamour for the full transcript. It seemed that only a few private individuals were able to react to the situation and they only managed to record the back end of the message. However, a full recording was made, not least by the television company themselves – how else could they broadcast the first thirty seconds the following day? Eventually, a full recording came into the public domain and the transcript was published by *New Life* magazine. There are variations to the exact text of the message due to the distorted nature of the voice. The identity of the being delivering the message is given as Glon, Vrillon, Gillon or Gramaha, of the Ashtar or Ashtron Galactic Command. In the transcript I am going to quote here, I have used the latter.

> *This is the voice of Gramaha representative of the Ashtron Galactic Command speaking to you. For many years you have seen us as lights in the sky. We speak to you now in peace and wisdom as we have done to your brothers and sisters all over this your planet Earth. We have to warn you of this destiny of your race and your world so that you may communicate to your fellow beings, the course you must take to avoid the disaster which threatens your world and the beings on other worlds around you. This is in order that you may share in the great awakening as the planet passes into the New Age of Aquarius. The New Age can be a time of great*

evolution for your race but only if your rulers are made aware of the evil forces that can overshadow their judgement.

Be still now and listen, for your chance may not come again for many years. Your scientists, governments and generals have not heeded our warnings, they have continued to experiment with the evil forces of what you call nuclear energy. Atomic bombs can destroy the Earth and the beings of your sister worlds in a moment. The wastes from atom power systems will poison your planet for many thousands of years to come. We, who have followed the path of evolution for far longer than you, have long since realised this – that atomic energy is always directed against life. It has no peaceful application. Its use and research into its use, must be ceased at once or you will all risk destruction. All weapons of evil must be removed. The time of conflict is now past and the races of which you are a part may proceed to the highest planes of evolution if you show yourselves worthy to do this. You have but a short time to learn to live together in peace and goodwill. Small groups all over the planet are learning this and exist to pass on the light of the dawning New Age to you all. You are free to accept or reject their teaching but only those who learn to live in peace will pass to the higher realms of spiritual evolution.

Hear now the voice of Gramaha, the voice of the Ashtron Galactic Command, speaking to you. Be aware also that there are many false prophets and guides at present operating on your world. They will suck your energy from you – the energy you call money and will put it to evil ends giving you worthless dross in return. Your inner divine self will protect you from this. You must learn to be sensitive to the voice within that can tell you what is truth and what is confusion, chaos and untruth. Learn to listen to the voice of truth which is within you and you will lead yourselves onto the path of evolution.

This is our message to you our dear friends. We have watched you growing for many years as you too have watched our lights in your skies. You know now that we are here and that there are more beings on and around your Earth than your scientists admit. We are deeply concerned about you and your path towards the light and will do all we can to help you. Have no fears seek only to know yourselves and live in harmony with the ways of your planet Earth. We of the Ashtron Galactic Command thank you for your attention. We are now leaving the planes of your existence. May you be blessed by the supreme love and truth of the Cosmos.

This message with its dire warnings for mankind's reckless exploitation of nuclear energy both as an energy source and as supreme weaponry, has a familiar ring and you would have to wonder what the Ashtron Galactic Command would make of our world, thirty years on, with its climate beginning to lurch out of control and beset by war and strife.

The message was also allegedly transmitted on LBC, a regional radio station covering London, at precisely the same time as the television broadcast. I have not found any reference to how this could have been done because, as far as I am aware, they did not share the same transmission resources. The speculation surrounding this bizarre occurrence was centred on the five television transmitters that had been subjected to a simultaneous override.

The Sunday Times from 4th December 1977 claimed that the equipment required to override five television transmitters would only cost eighty pounds (the equivalent sum today would still be considerably less than a thousand pounds) and a car battery. Furthermore, they claimed that students were responsible. I would suggest that if students were able to cut into television transmissions so easily, and for so small a cost, then British television viewing would be quite a mixture of bizarre programmes. The message and the way it was delivered was written off only too easily, but a closer look at the circumstances suggest that there was something really strange going on.

There are a number of facts surrounding the 'space' message that suggest this broadcast may not have been the hoax that the establishment claimed it was. To break into the Southern Television programme required not only the ability to override the five television transmitters simultaneously, but also the Independent Broadcasting Association's monitoring system. The IBA monitoring system has an 'instant switch-off', technically known as an insertion test signal. It has been claimed that the IBA were moving premises at the time and that was the reason their engineers failed to act. I find this excuse too convenient and highly unlikely, as I do not think any UK government would 'drop its guard' and allow any television broadcast to go out unchecked.

Neither the main transmitter at Southampton nor the engineers at Croydon, Surrey were aware that the message was overriding their signal. Because the interruption was not registered it suggests that the electrical system may have been bypassed. On 27th November, the day after the broadcast, the *Sunday Express* reported that a Post Office spokesman claimed a link into the GPO land line had been used to gain access to the transmitters at Rowbridge and Hannington. The day after this revelation GPO experts confirmed that the source of the broadcast was indeed Hannington in Hampshire.

Some of the phraseology used in the message appears pure science fiction, like *'Galactic Command'* and the *'Age of Aquarius'*, phrases that reflect terrestrial perception of extraterrestrial concepts. However, it seems to me that a lot of technological ability was required to get the 'space' broadcast on air and I believe this rules out any possibility of a hoax. It should also be noted that no one has come forward to claim responsibility for the broadcast. You can decide for yourself as to the content and veracity of the message.

It is worth noting another strange incident of television interference which occurred on the evening of 23rd October 1971. Again it took place on a Saturday evening and seemed to affect the south-west and Cornwall in particular. Many television viewers experienced a blackout, with other viewers finding their pictures fading or superimposed. The radio stations in the south-west were also affected and there was widespread Continental interference.

The BBC announced that the interference was due to 'circumstances beyond their control', while the spokesman for Westward TV gave a more detailed explanation that the trouble had been caused by 'propagation of radio waves in the atmosphere which affected the actual micro-wavelengths used in television transmission'.

It is alleged that on the evening in question a large pink and golden ball of light was seen near Plymouth. The object disappeared for a while before reappearing as a cigar-shaped craft. Thereafter it changed shape several times, although maintaining the same colours. After thirty minutes it disappeared completely.

In his book *Flying Saucers Uncensored* (Arco Publishers, 1955) the British writer and scholar Harold T. Wilkins recalls a message received by a lady in the USA, which was forwarded to US Air Force Intelligence, Wright-Patterson Air Force Base, Dayton, Ohio, on 20th November 1953. The message was received by this lady on 6th November with the instruction to pass it on to *'Your Offices of Government'*. No mention is made of how the lady concerned received this communication which was as follows:

Greetings in the light of love and peace, I am Ashtar, Commandant, Vela Quandra Sector, Station Schare. I bring you Zolton, Commandant from the centre of the Sector System of Vela.

I am Zolton. I extend to you, people of Earth planet, the greetings from the combined federation of our people in the Vela Sector System. The information I am about to give you, you shall record to be advanced to your office of Government at the time we instruct you to send it.

Our craft have prepared and charted facilities for landing on your planet in numerous remote areas. We have given sufficient demonstrations of our abilities in speed and performance. We do not expect to convert non-believers at the moment. There is no need to fear of panic among your people at our approach and landings, for we shall previously condition the minds to accept us. The present destructive

> *plans formulated for offensive and defensive war are known to us in their entirety. The surface of your planet is in our photographic records in detail. Through the control of light forces we can instantly terminate production, transportation and communication at any time, at any place upon your planet. Our methods do not require that we destroy any single living thing. Our laws do not permit us to take human life. They do not however, forbid us to control minds. The present trend toward destructive war will not be interfered with by us, unless the condition warrants our interference in order to secure this solar system. This is a friendly warning.*

This 1953 message from 'Ashtar' has similarities with the 1977 broadcast. Note that a hierarchy is used, as Ashtar (is this coincidental with the 1977 broadcast?) introduces Zolton. The content is also similar to the 1977 message.

To the casual reader, these 'messages from space' may seem far-fetched. However, there is no doubt that the broadcast in 1977 occurred and I would suggest that some high technology was used to convey it.

5

The Mystery Explosions

During late 1977 and throughout 1978 the south-west of England was plagued by a strange series of violent 'bumps' and explosions, the origin of which could not be identified. At first, the explosions occurred at exactly the same time on different days, 9.20 in the evening, although after a while they became more sporadic and unpredictable. Complaints from the public flooded in and the phenomenon was experienced as far away as Oxfordshire and across the Bristol Channel in south Wales. The main areas affected by the 'bumps and booms' were either side of the Bristol Channel.

On 3rd January 1978 the *Daily Mail* reported the story under the headline 'All at sea over the mystery bangs.' The article stated that the eastern US seaboard from South Carolina to Massachusetts had also suffered from the strange explosions, which were estimated to be the equivalent of 100 tons of TNT. Sonic booms and freak weather had been ruled out on both sides of the Atlantic. Coastguard Peter Baker suspected it might be gunfire but the Royal Navy stated it was nothing to do with them. Mr Baker gave the following quote: *'I have heard these bangs while on duty at Gwennap Head and St Just (Cornwall) and once the explosion was powerful enough to rock the lookout. There is something going on out there that defies explanation.'*

Auxiliary coastguards around Cornwall heard the blasts too, and personnel at Yeovilton Naval Air Station also felt the effects of the explosions, which were described as a thump, followed fifteen seconds or so later by a double thump. The strange explosions were violent enough to make cracks in plaster and whole buildings would resonate from the effects of these mysterious shockwaves.

In the book *The Welsh Triangle* by Peter Paget, a gamekeeper working at the county council farm institute at Cannington, near Bridgewater, said that the roosting pheasants were being disturbed and that the birds would become restless about fifteen seconds before the boom. Animals and birds have a higher sensitivity to low-frequency noise and it was probably this that alerted the pheasants to the forthcoming boom.

The interesting thing about the pheasants' advance warning is this: if they were alerted approximately fifteen seconds before an explosion, then we must assume that the low-frequency noise they picked up must be part of the boom. This suggests that the boom was not a detonation, but perhaps something travelling at immense velocity towards the area affected by the boom.

Referring directly to Peter Paget's book *The Welsh Triangle*, Thomas Lawson, reader in Industrial Aerodynamics at Bristol University, who had heard the sounds himself stated: *'They could not have been made by a supersonic aircraft because of the long gap between them. I have heard nothing like it before. It sounded like thunder, yet it was not thunder. At the moment I just cannot explain what causes the bangs, and I would like to go into it a lot further.'*

A team of experts from Bristol University set up recording equipment to register the sound and yet they were unable to determine the origin of the booms from the data they collected and analysed.

The regularity of the booms suggested a man-made explanation and it was convenient to blame Concorde. This explanation did not stand up to scrutiny as the booms occurred at times when Concorde was not flying or anywhere in the vicinity. The range for hearing sonic booms is about twenty miles and it appears that Concorde was well beyond that range when many of the booms were heard. In any event, British Airways stated that Concorde did not go supersonic until it was fifty miles south of Ireland, not Land's End.

The Ministry of Defence said that they had no records of any military aircraft being in the area at the time of the bangs, and that the sounds were more reminiscent of thunder than the sharp retort of a sonic boom. The claim of innocence from the MOD is unsurprising as it is highly unlikely they would admit to anything either British or American being tested in the skies of the south-west of England.

Compared to the late 1970s we now have a greater perspective on aircraft technology, so could the booms have been caused by the testing of some highly classified aircraft, like the F117 Stealth fighter? I think this unlikely, given the comments from Thomas Lawson earlier in this chapter. This was also considered unlikely by the Joint Services Rescue Coordination Centre at Plymouth, who said the phenomenon could not have been caused by military activity.

In 1979 there was a newspaper report about mysterious explosions under the sea. The mystery sounds were baffling US Navy scientists who had picked up the sounds from a hyper-sensitive listening network under the sea that was used to track the movements of Soviet submarines. The input from the listening devices was fed through computers, which separated the noise of the submarines. So sensitive was this undersea network that Soviet submarines from thousands of miles away could be detected.

The puzzling thing was that in the residue of unidentified sound there were the mysterious explosions. Incredibly, the scientists claimed that the only explanation they could come up with was that they were echoes of sea battles from the Second World War and that the sounds from that era were somehow trapped under the water. One particularly eerie sound they recorded was that of a baby crying. The theory was that the sound was 'trapped' after the baby drowned in a sinking ship.

Mike Somers, principal scientific officer at Britain's Institute of Oceanographic Sciences was doubtful of the theory put forward by the American scientists. He was quoted as follows: *'There are many earthquakes and volcanic eruptions at sea and the sounds of these can carry half way around the world in a broad natural channel, which dissipates the sound to a million-millionth of its density in twenty-four hours.*

'The strange thing about the mystery underwater sounds is this – surely the American scientists, with all the technology they had available, would know what an undersea earthquake or volcanic eruption sounded like?'

A rather curious phenomenon had been recorded in association with the bumps and booms. On several occasions an orange glow was seen in the sky and some witnesses have claimed to have seen an orange fireball streaking across the sky shortly after a boom.

On 24th February 1981 the whole of Cornwall was rocked by an earth tremor which was registered 4 on the Richter scale. The police were contacted by hundreds of concerned people and it was thought that the enigmatic booms from the 1970s had returned. Concorde was ruled out and the incident was forgotten. In the months leading up to the tremor there were several tremors in the Plymouth area, the source of which were never discovered.

In October 2006 the south-west of England was again shaken by an unidentified explosion and shock wave, the effects of which were felt from Cornwall to Devon. Although it was not heard by everyone, the massive boom caused structural damage to houses that was similar to the damage caused by the 1970s explosions. It also created some consternation across the two counties. This thunderous shock wave was not blamed on supersonic aircraft and the cause remains a mystery, despite the claims by a meteorologist that the shock wave was caused by a large meteorite exploding in the Earth's upper atmosphere.

It is interesting to note that the National Aeronautical and Space Administration in the USA had no comment to make about the large explosion of a meteorite in the upper atmosphere of our planet. Furthermore, Britain's early warning radar system, based at Fylingdales in North Yorkshire, similarly made no comment about the large boom and shock wave, despite having the capability to pick up tiny fragments of 'space debris' circulating around the Earth.

You may ask, what do these enigmatic bumps, booms, explosions, or whatever you wish to call them, have in common with fifteen dead ponies on Dartmoor? Apart from the dates during which they occurred, which ran concurrent with the strange animal deaths on Dartmoor and Newquay Zoo, there were bizarre attacks and the unaccountable movement of farm animals on the Pembroke peninsular, which were accompanied by similar strange bumps, booms and orange glows in the sky. I intend to prove, as you will see in later chapters, that horrific and inexplicable attacks on animals are invariably accompanied by various strange phenomena, of which the strange bumps and bangs are but one.

6

Strange Craft Around Dartmoor 1977/78

The south-west was the centre of many strange happenings during 1977 and 1978 and it should be noted that there was a considerable amount of anomalous aerial activity in the form of UFOs and craft of unknown origin, particularly in the Dartmoor area. While the reports I am going to describe here fall under the generic term UFO, the witnesses in some of these cases are referring to craft of unknown origin, a more specific and appropriate term.

Let us begin with a report from the *Tavistock Times* on 16th September 1977. Under the headline 'Cathy's white light in the night!' a Tavistock lady named Cathy Edgar described how she had gone outside her house at nine o'clock in the evening to call in her cat. Hovering in the sky over her house she saw an unidentified flying object. She described her initial reaction as follows: *'Suddenly I saw a bright light appear in the sky. I called my husband, David, to make sure I wasn't imagining it. It seemed far too large and bright and moving too fast to be a normal plane.'* Mr Edgar ran across the road to fetch two neighbours, Peter and Margaret Carnell. Mrs Edgar stated that all four watched the object fly in a straight course across Whitchurch Down. She added, *'Then it sped upwards, getting faster and faster and changing to a red dot. It winked on and off as it went across the sky.'*

Peter Carnell told the newspaper's reporter, *'While we were watching that one, there was another dot acting in the same way, on the same course.'*

The *Tavistock Times* investigated the matter further and contacted the Marine Commando Air Squadron at Plymouth who stated that two helicopters were doing a naval exercise in the Tavistock area, between 2200 and 2300 hours on the same night. However the Marine Commando spokesman said that the helicopters would have shown two or three red lights and one green. The objects seen by the four witnesses were bright white.

A week or so later, Mr John Chell from Middlesex, who was staying overnight at Mary Tavy, wrote to the *Tavistock Times* and said that he had also seen the lights. The second paragraph of his letter is as follows:

Both moving objects were travelling very fast and no sound came from them and after observing them for some few minutes both lights disappeared. My only other impression whilst watching them with the aid of binoculars was that their course was slightly erratic at times although in every other respect I agree with the views of your informants. I was with four other people at the time and we had only tea to drink!

This interesting incident has some important features: the craft were silent, there was a corroborative witness (who watched with binoculars) and the objects appeared to head across Whitchurch Down, an area of much activity as we shall see.

On 2nd December 1977 the *Tavistock Times* carried reader Joan Amos's account of a series of huge flashes over Blackdown Moor. The headline '"Science fiction" experience on Blackdown' carried the following account:

Last Sunday week (November 20) at 11 p.m., I was driving across the Blackdown Moor. I was returning from my work at the Dartmoor Inn, Lydford.

It was a clear night, cold and frosty. I could see for miles over the countryside, the lights of Yelverton in one direction, to the hills on the other side of the Launceston bypass, on my right.

I know one can see beyond Brentor, Kit Hill and towards Stockland Hill in daylight. Suddenly there was a blinding flash, which illuminated the whole area, a blue, white light as bright as daylight.

It seemed to come from the south west. It gave me quite a shock and my first reaction was: 'What the hell was that?'

I was expecting an explosion or roll of thunder but there was no noise at all.

I had slowed down and was trying to reason with myself that it couldn't have been lightning, as I have often seen sheet lightning in a summer sky, but this was winter and the flash was of far greater intensity than that.

The witness stated categorically that the flashes were not caused by flares and then continued the account:

I suppose a few minutes had elapsed by this time and although the first flash took me by surprise, I can assure you I was watching for the next one.

Zap! There it was again, a bright terrifying flash – as bright as the sun, yet as cold as the moon.

It was all over the sky at once, lighting up all the land in Cornwall, and it was just as bright in the sky beyond Yelverton.

It seemed to come from the south west, and I'd say it was from 'out at sea'.

I felt a shiver go through me. It was like someone taking a photograph with a gigantic space camera.

Again there was no noise, just a weird silence.

It was uncanny and I knew I was witnessing something unnatural.

There were four other witnesses to the disturbing flashes mentioned by the *Tavistock Times.*

On the same night as the flashes, 2nd December 1977, a former Royal Navy Observer who lived in Lydford saw three UFOs in the Blackdown area. He watched the objects through high-powered binoculars for some considerable time before they disappeared.

The next report, which is from Tavistock, involves several witnesses from two different places, sighting the same object. On Monday 10th April 1978, four lady patients at Tavistock Hospital saw an extraordinary craft in the sky over Tavistock. It was about 6.20 in the morning and the weather was bright and sunny. Mrs June Catlow and three other patients in the surgical ward were waiting for breakfast, the day staff had not arrived. June was alerted by one of the other patients who said, '*What is that bright light in the sky?*' The other patients were Thelma Trigger, Betty Gedge and Joan Amos. All four climbed out of their hospital beds to watch a bright silvery cigar-shaped object that was hovering in the sky over Whitchurch Down, which is to the south of Tavistock.

The craft was in a vertical position and apparently was surrounded by a halo of golden light. After a couple of minutes the craft gradually turned left into a horizontal position and the witnesses could now see that the craft was saucer-shaped, with a dome on the top and the bottom. The craft now appeared to be silver-grey in colour and after a few minutes it seemed to move effortlessly away and disappeared behind Cox Tor. Cox Tor and Barn Hill, which it overlooks, is a place we shall hear much of later in Part III. The incident was reported to the *Tavistock Times* by Robert Wyse Junior, who was also involved in the Dartmoor ponies investigation.

The intrepid Joan Amos investigated the incident herself and uncovered two other witnesses to the event. On the day of the incident, at a kiosk by Tavistock bus station, Frank Jago and his brother also saw the saucer-shaped craft and confirmed the incredible sighting.

Was the saucer shaped craft the same one seen four days later by Enid Getson of St Anne's? At 7.55 in the evening of 14th April Mrs Getson saw a saucer-shaped craft with an aura of light around it, on the horizon overlooking Saltash bridge. Brunel's masterpiece of bridge building is on the outskirts of Plymouth, only ten miles from Tavistock.

Another report during the same week, from Plymouth, is worthy of mention here. Nicola Brown, who was aged twelve at the time, was looking out of her bedroom window at seven o'clock on the morning of 13th April, when she saw a blinding white light that came from a UFO the size of a jumbo jet. Nicola watched for several minutes as the UFO moved slowly towards Dartmoor and out of her vision. Her mother reported the sighting to RAF Mount Batten, who were unable to shed any light on the affair.

There appears to have been a lot going on in and around Tavistock during the month of April 1978. A local newspaper reported that three pupils from Tavistock Comprehensive School were out walking with two dogs at about 1830 hours. The dogs began barking and looking upwards, which prompted the boys to look. They saw a green cigar-shaped object at about one thousand feet. It remained stationary for about thirty seconds, before it shot straight up and disappeared. Ian Brookes, one of the witnesses stated, *'We could see it clearly before it shot off.'*

The high number of UFO reports from the south-west, and Tavistock in particular, brought an eccentric proposal from an American scientist. On 21st April 1978 it was reported that Cornwall's Chief Constable, John Alderson, had been asked to approve installation of machines which could record 'flying saucer' movements from police cars, Chief Constable Alderson was quoted as saying, *'I shall be interested to see what the American scientists have in mind. We have an open mind on the subject of UFOs and we are always ready to help science.'* This story is perhaps more suited to 1st April than 21st April, but it was widely reported and I suppose, seriously considered.

Still in April 1978 Mrs D.G. Roberts of Easton near Chagford wrote to a local newspaper regarding a curious incident on Dartmoor. Her letter was in response to reports of UFOs in the newspaper. Mrs Roberts wrote as follows:

> *At about 8.30 on Saturday evening (after dark) my son and I were looking out of my kitchen window which looks right over the Moor and we suddenly saw a large 'ball of fire' which disappeared very quickly.*
>
> *We obviously wondered what it was. The next morning at about 9 a.m. a large fire was raging exactly over the spot where we saw the 'ball of fire' and was still raging when my husband and I went up to Berry Down at about seven o'clock in the evening. Apparently the local firemen could not reach the fire but I believe the Plymouth firemen were called out to the other end of the fire which had reached an enormous length – maybe something dropped and the scientists may like to look at the start of the fire which was running eastwards.*
>
> *I shall be interested to hear if you have any reason for the fire.*

The newspaper commented that Mrs Roberts' sighting coincided with a three-acre gorse fire on Kit Hill, near Callington which, due to its great height, was visible for a great distance. Terry Cox, Devon and Cornwall investigator for *Flying Saucer Review*, stated that on the same night a red flaming object was sighted at Landrake, heading out of Cornwall and into Devon. It is also worth mentioning that once again the area around Kit Hill and Blackdown Moor has played host to unusual aerial activity.

In the middle of June 1978 there was a series of UFO sightings over a succession of nights. Once again the *Tavistock Times* carried the story with the headline 'Mystery of "Star" over Dartmoor'. The article stated that on at least five nights a twinkling sphere of light had been seen near the North Hessary Tor television mast, although the staff that worked there were unaware of any object in the vicinity.

Mrs Julia Bath, who lived in Princetown which is right next to the Hessary Tor mast, gave the following account: *'It was a very bright light, three or four times bigger than a star.'* Mrs Bath, who saw the object for the first time at 11 p.m. on Monday 12th June, had another sighting the following night as she was driving home with her husband. The object was seen at the Devil's elbow moving across the moor.

There were two other witnesses quoted in the article, Brian and Cathy Newsham, also of Princetown. They had seen the object on Sunday 11th June and on the Monday evening as well. Mrs Newsham said, *'When it moved, spikes of light seemed to come from it. It didn't look like a flare.'*

The *Tavistock Gazette* dated 30th June 1978 picked up the story, but from different witnesses. The report stated that a dozen prison officers and a local policeman, Mr Bob Privett, were also witnesses to the strange object. The UFO was brought to the attention of the officers when they were in the Prison Officers Club. They watched the object for an hour and Mr Privett said it seemed to be hovering and was definitely not a star. The article concluded with a mention that Mr Privett's wife had seen a cylindrical-shaped object in the sky, earlier in the year.

In 1982 there was another strange incident near the North Hessary Tor mast. On the afternoon of 19th December 1982 a couple from Princetown saw a strange white ball, hovering over forest land near Hessary Tor. Later, the couple and two young men saw a red ball of fire with a tail travelling very low, in a straight line, over the moor. It was now evening and the two men decided to drive off in pursuit of the UFO. During their pursuit they became aware of another car, apparently chasing the same object. The red ball fell into the middle of the moor and one of the four men in the car quickly got out and clambered over a wall with a torch. After some minutes, the man with the torch returned and the two young men decided to approach the four individuals in the car to ask them if they knew what the object was. The four men in the car said nothing, wound up the window of their car and drove away.

The four strangers were dressed in blue one-piece overalls and all looked alike. The car they were driving was described as being like a new Rover. The notorious Dartmoor prison is situated nearby, but it is highly unlikely that the four strangers were from the gaol.

There was a strange series of sightings in September 1978 and again the area in question is Blackdown Moor, near Lydford. At 2330 hours on 2nd September a stationary starlike object was seen over Blackdown Moor. The pulsating white light and red light eventually moved eastwards, over Dartmoor.

The following night, another object (or was it the same object from the previous night?) was seen to hover over Blackdown Moor. No time was given for this sighting, which seems very similar to the previous night, although on this occasion red, white and green lights were flashing. The object remained stationary for several minutes before moving southwards.

On the third night, 4th September, a witness looking out of a landing window at 0530 hours saw a box formation of bright lights, which apparently looked like floodlighting on a football field. The witness watched the formation move away in a north-westerly direction.

The next report, detailed in the booklet *UFOs over Plymouth* by the Plymouth UFO Group, took place in the Hartley Vale area of Plymouth, but is relevant here as the UFO or UFOs came from, or went in, the direction of Dartmoor.

At 2115 hours on Monday 25th September 1978, two young friends, Ian Stephens, 13, and Sean Memory, 9, were standing in Sean's back garden, gazing at the stars on a cold and bright evening. The two boys saw what they initially thought was a shooting star, but was in fact a flat, bright, disc-shaped object. The craft appeared to come from the direction of Dartmoor and as it passed directly overhead the boys could see a clearly defined circle of light blue mist, with a slightly darker blue rim around the outside edge of the craft. The object, which exhibited a 'jerky' motion in flight, headed out across Plymouth Sound and out to sea.

Within two minutes of this extraordinary event another object, identical to the first, headed towards them from the direction of Dartmoor. The craft showed the same strange movement in flight and the same flight path until it was over the Sound, when it veered off along the coast of Cornwall. Another two minutes elapsed and, incredibly, a third identical craft appeared from the direction of the moors. This time, as the craft passed overhead it turned left and headed up the Devon coastline. Two minutes later a fourth and final UFO, identical to the previous three, flew over the two witnesses and upon reaching Plymouth Sound, doubled back on its flight path and returned in the direction of Dartmoor.

This extraordinary sequence of sightings raises an interesting question, was this four UFOs or one? If it was the same craft on each occasion then it must have been capable of fantastic speeds.

The next report of a UFO includes some unusual side effects. Kathleen Willcocks and her husband were driving to their home at Lamerton, near Tavistock on Sunday 1st October 1978 at about 2300 hours. As they were travelling down Barleymead Hill, not far from where they lived, Mrs Willcocks saw a very bright light that was approximately two hundred yards to their right. The light was very low and it illuminated the branches of nearby trees. The light passed over Longford Farm and disappeared beyond some trees. The sighting did not last more than thirty seconds and there was no sound whatsoever from the mystery object. In addition Mr Willcocks, who was driving, noted that the car headlights dimmed inexplicably and both the petrol and temperature gauges suddenly went to zero.

The effect some UFOs have on motor vehicles is well known and there are numerous reports of cars being stalled when within close proximity to a UFO or craft of unknown origin.

It is perhaps appropriate to close this list of reports with another visit to the area by Blackdown Moor and a sighting, not of a UFO, but a strange 'being'. In November 1978 at a pub at Peter Tavy, near Blackdown, it was just after closing time when a customer, a Mr Cox of Plymouth, came into the bar from the outside toilet and told the landlord, Paul Sommerfield, that he had just seen a silver-suited figure walking down a pathway next to the pub. The figure was wearing a helmet with the visor down and was approximately seven feet tall. The landlord, realising that there was no exit down that particular bridlepath for a motorcycle, dashed out to look, but could not see the strange 'being'. The lane ends in a field which has an electricity substation located next to the River Tavy. A search of the area allegedly revealed evidence of a landing site.

The majority of the sightings detailed here are multi-witness accounts and come from a cross-section of people who had nothing to gain from reporting what they had seen. It is plain that there were a lot of strange things going on in the late 1970s in the south-west of England, and Dartmoor in particular.

However, while these strange events were unfolding, the ranchers of the

United States of America were experiencing a sinister wave of animal mutilations that no law enforcement agency could stop or explain. In Part II we shall look at the animal mutilation problem.

Part II

The Animal Mutilation Problem

7

What are Animal Mutilations?

I feel it is appropriate to give some sort of definition to a phrase I will use a great deal – animal mutilation. To those unfamiliar with the huge problem in the USA and the numerous cases in Britain and worldwide, animal mutilations suggest some sort of barbaric ritual carried out by depraved individuals on farm or domestic animals. The word 'mutilate' has the following Oxford Dictionary definition: 1 a) deprive (a person or animal) of a limb or organ. b) Destroy the use of (a limb or organ). 2. Render (a book etc) imperfect by excision or some act of destruction.

The Oxford Dictionary definition is very accurate in the context of animal mutilation attacks, although the public may perceive a frenzied attack on the victim. This perception almost certainly comes from the description of hapless victims of human serial killers, such as Jack the Ripper. The reality, though, is that the attacks, no matter how apparently savage, are measured, precise and purposeful.

The attacks are carried out predominantly at night, in darkness, although some mutilations have been done in broad daylight. The perpetrators operate covertly and prefer remote locations, although there have been numerous attacks on livestock situated in or near farm buildings. The attacks often occur in conjunction with other strange events, such as the appearance of the enigmatic black helicopters and UFOs.

The animal mutilation problem came to prominence in the USA in 1967 and became a major issue there during the 1970s. In the UK, however, the problem received little or no publicity at this time and it is likely that attacks that took place in Britain were misidentified as natural predation or the work of warped human occultists.

However, there is evidence to suggest that animal mutilation attacks in Britain go back a long way. That great ambassador for the unexplained, Charles Fort, drew attention to mysterious sheep deaths at Hexam, Northumberland in 1904. The newspapers attributed the killings to an escaped wolf.

On a farm near Newcastle, late in 1904, there was a series of attacks on poultry. Mr White, the farmer, lost the majority of his chickens, some two hundred and twenty-five birds, to the mystery attackers. Mr White stated: *'They have all been killed in the same weird way. The skin around the neck from the head to the breast has been pulled off, and the windpipe drawn from its place and snapped. The fowl house has been watched night and day, and whenever examined four or five birds would be found dead.'*

There are a number of recurring factors that will give an indication that the animal or bird has suffered a mutilation attack. The following list, which may not be comprehensive, details many of these injuries and strange after-effects:

1. The removal of the tongue, which is invariably cut smoothly and precisely at the back of the mouth with little or no blood loss.
2. A small hole in the top of the head. On larger animals, this injury gives the impression of a bullet wound. Animals as small as mice have been known to have this injury.
3. Puncture marks on the neck and face. These can be up to two centimetres in diameter on larger animals such as sheep.
4. Rectal coring, this injury often appears to have been done 'mechanically' and there is little or no blood loss.
5. One or both eyes are removed, together with all tissue, leaving the eye socket completely empty.
6. The removal of precise circular, eliptical or rectangular patches of skin. This is done without cutting into the lower skin tissue and there is no apparent blood loss.
7. One, sometimes two, ears are removed. In the case of sheep, the ear with the number tag is invariably taken.
8. The 'surgical' removal of limbs.
9. Decapitation. In the case of birds they are always beheaded and the heads are never found.
10. The removal of reproductive organs.
11. The removal of skin and tissue from the jaw area exposing the jawbone which has a 'bleached' appearance.
12. The removal of some internal organs through small neat holes in the carcass.
13. Complete blood loss and lack of blood at the death site.
14. Strange substances found on some bodies include a bluish gel, a yellow powdery substance around the wound area and, in one case, a white cobweb substance that was identified as petroleum distillate.

15. In some cases there is very rapid decomposition and the body can be reduced to a skeleton in a few days.
16. Deterioration of the liver.
17. Sometimes the carcasses are 'treated' with some substance that kills blow flies and keeps natural scavengers away.

In many animal mutilation attacks there may be several injuries corresponding to this list. Some of these injuries, such as the removal of the tongue and eyes, and the hole in the top of the skull, occur in a very high percentage of cases.

In the following chapters I will detail further features of the animal mutilations and review some cases from the UK and around the world.

8

The Black Helicopters

A strange feature of animal mutilation attacks, particularly in the USA, has been the appearance of black helicopters that have so often been seen before and after an animal mutilation attack. The term 'black helicopters' is, however, rather misleading, as the enigmatic 'helicopters' have been noted in a variety of colours.

The mysterious helicopters appear to have no markings to identify them, which is illegal in the USA and the UK, and they are invariably silent and flying at a very low level. They are usually seen singularly, but as many as nine have been seen at one incident. The helicopters are not always black and have been reported in other colours, which suggests that there may be incidents where aircraft with an innocent purpose have been involved. These strange planes have a long history, one that predates the modern era of animal mutilations which gained notoriety with the attack on an Appaloosa mare called Lady in 1967. There are apparently records of black helicopters being seen in the 1930s, before helicopters had been developed.

The USA has been plagued by the black helicopters, which have terrorised some ranchers. One rancher in Alabama stated that he saw a helicopter, using its searchlight, forcing forty-two of his cattle into a corner in his pasture. Another rancher, Mr John Strawn, said that he had seen helicopters land in pastures at night, and that he and a group of other farmers had been able to identify three turbine helicopters, one light blue and white, one dark blue and the other black.

There have been numerous incidents of ranchers firing at the strange craft and it has been claimed that the occupants of some of the strange craft have confronted some farmers.

It is further alleged that the occupants of the helicopters are dressed in black, with no insignia to identify them. This suggests that they may have a military origin and might be part of some covert military operation to monitor, or even carry out, the animal mutilations. Further evidence of such a clandestine programme lies in the numerous eye-witness accounts, claiming that the area around the animal mutilations is sometimes sprayed by the craft. What is being sprayed we can only guess. However, as we shall see later, the spraying has been known to keep natural predators away from the bodies.

The occurrence of black helicopters in the United Kingdom has been far less documented than in the USA. However, there have been some interesting accounts of black helicopter activity in this country.

On 22nd February 2005 I attended a lecture on Welsh UFO activity, organised by the UFORM UFO group in Stourbridge. The talk was given by Gary Rowe, a researcher with many years of experience in investigating UFO incidents in the area around the north Wales coast. His talk was extremely interesting and informative and contained some exceptional case material that Gary had built up over some fifty years. Gary showed an extraordinary photograph of a circular craft of unknown origin, flying below treetop level, near to the north Wales coast and then suggested that the anomalous traffic was heading towards the remotely populated corridor that stretched down to the Berwyn mountains.

Gary stated that there had been numerous animal mutilations within this remote area and made a further astonishing revelation. A witness had described seeing a black helicopter and, having heard no sound coming from it, was intrigued by the sighting. The witness kept the aircraft under surveillance as it approached his position at a remote farm. To the astonishment of the witness, the black helicopter underwent a metamorphosis that transformed it into a saucer-shaped craft of unknown origin. This metamorphose stunned and terrified the witness. Apparently, mutilated animals were found in the area of the sighting.

It should be noted that in this sparsely populated part of Wales, where the strange craft had been seen, it was not unusual for military manoeuvres to be carried out at night.

Another case of metamorphosis comes from the USA. It concerns a Mr John Cumby and his family who lived in Littleton, Colorado. One evening in September 1980 Mr John Cumby was on the telephone, the time was about 1900 hours and he was looking out of a window that gave him a clear view of the local pasture and foothills and mountains west and south-west of Denver. As he looked out of the window he saw what appeared to be a helicopter, flying at no more than a hundred feet from the ground. The helicopter seemed to stop about a mile from his house and was silhouetted against the western sky (the sun had set only a few minutes previously). Mr Cumby could not make out visually if there were rotor blades on the craft. The helicopter, after appearing to hover in mid-air, then began to rise slowly. The helicopter had the appearance of being black initially, but as it began to rise the craft took on a silver colour and, incredibly, turned into a ball-shaped object, which seemed to be smaller than the 'helicopter'. The object rose upwards and out of Mr Cumby's view. However, he alerted his mother-in-law, who ran to the back of the house as Mr Cumby looked for his binoculars. At a height estimated by the witness of approximately four thousand feet the craft now took on a 'square shape' with an elongated appendage hanging from the one side. The strange appendage appeared to be fluttering as the craft reached an estimated climb of three thousand feet per minute. Suddenly the craft completely disappeared then re-appeared a few seconds later several hundred feet to the witness's right, still with the fluttering appendage. The object was visible for only a few seconds before it shot up into the sky vertically, disappearing completely in a couple of seconds. Unfortunately, Mr Cumby did not have time to train his binoculars on this strange craft.

This curious incident is reminiscent of an experience I had on 5th November 1970 in the presence of a co-witness, Mr Ron Buck. On the date in question Ron and I were sky watching from a hill below Barr Beacon, near Aldridge in Staffordshire. Nothing had been seen until about 2100 hours, when we noted a red pulsing object approaching from Barr Beacon. It was flying at very low level and looked as though it was going to fly under the power-line cables that crossed the lower part of Barr Beacon. The object rose suddenly and 'hopped' over the power lines and approached our position, no more than twenty to thirty feet from the ground. We were both deeply concerned as the object headed towards us. At a range of about one hundred and fifty metres, it rose steeply and went straight over us on a flight path towards Birmingham. The object, which moved in complete silence, appeared to be bell-shaped and had a red glow. However, when the object had passed over us, it took on the appearance of a small plane – I assure you it was not one! In his book *The Mothman Prophecies,* John H. Keel reports a similar experience where a strange object appeared to change into a more conventional craft.

There are two interesting accounts from Yelverton, on the western edge of Dartmoor and, incidentally, only a few miles from Postbridge, scene of the notorious pony deaths, and Moortown near Tavistock, where a series of unexplained sheep deaths began in 2005. On November 18th 1993 at 4.30 in the afternoon, two witnesses were in a line of traffic approaching Yelverton's main traffic roundabout. Both witnesses saw a large, brilliant light approximately half a mile from the road and around this light there were four red, unmarked helicopters with black windows. The red helicopters were apparently hovering 'like bees' around the huge white light, which suddenly went out, following which the four red helicopters made off at great speed in the direction of Cornwall. The stunned witnesses, who had stopped near the island to get a clear view of the event, could not see where the large white light had gone to, it had simply disappeared.

Virtually two months later, on 19th January 1994 at 1.30 in the afternoon, one of the witnesses to the previous incident was approaching the same roundabout at Yelverton when he saw a similar red helicopter, this time on its own. The helicopter flew very low and around the roundabout, making several passes over the witness's car. Both sightings had lasted nearly five minutes and enquiries to Plymouth Airport and local flying clubs failed to solve the mystery.

Another strange case, this time involving a 'helicopter' sound, occurred near Callington, Cornwall. On 5th September 1994 at about 9.30 in the evening a teenage girl was at home watching television when she heard a loud whirring noise, which sounded like several helicopters. The noise became deafening and continued for more than a minute. She was prompted to look out of the window to see why the 'helicopters' were hovering so close to the house. The girl looked out and across to her father's garage which was no more than twenty feet or so from her window. She was totally shocked to see a triangular craft hovering over the garage. On each corner of the craft there was a brilliant light, as bright as a floodlight and along each side there was a row of smaller, dimmer lights. The craft was equivalent in size to the garage and was hovering only a couple of feet above it. The object remained motionless for thirty seconds or so, before moving upwards about six feet then taking off at great speed. The witness claimed the craft had left a white trail and sparks as it zoomed away at great speed. The departure was likened by the witness to be *'like when you wave a sparkler'* (firework). As the craft disappeared, so the deafening sound receded. Curiously, neither the girl's mother (who was asleep), nor the two dogs the family owned, heard anything.

There is definitely something strange going on with the enigmatic 'helicopters' that have no markings, that are sometimes silent and which have the ability to change from, or into, a 'helicopter'. Despite the high incidence of black helicopter activity, especially in the USA, there are few close-up photographs known to exist of this phenomenon.

9

The Crop Circle Connection

Crop circles have attracted huge interest worldwide and there are many who dedicate themselves to researching the enigma. Although crop circles have been recorded far back in time, interest in the strange circular patterns in the crop fields of southern England began in the late 1970s. It may be just coincidence that the crop circles began to appear at a time when many other strange things were going on, as detailed earlier in Part I.

The circles, which first appeared around Stonehenge and megalithic sites in Wiltshire, attracted terrific interest and as more people were drawn to the area to view the puzzling patterns in the crops, so the circles became pictograms and increased in their complexity. In comparison, the earlier crop circles seemed quite crude in design.

Needless to say there were many theories as to the origins of the crop circles and how they were created. There are a number of researchers who claim there could be a natural explanation, and that the crop circles could be created by atmospheric vortices. Despite all-night vigils, there have been few witnesses to the creation of a crop circle. It appears that some circles are formed in seconds, while large, complex pictograms can be created in a few minutes.

There have also been claims that all crop circles are faked and that two individuals in particular were largely responsible. I do not wish to become involved in the controversy surrounding the crop circles in this book, however, while I accept that there are many faked examples, some of which are quite complex in design, I believe there are many genuine crop circles or pictograms that are not man-made.

Researchers have found that in the genuine crop circles there are certain characteristics that are difficult, if not impossible, for hoaxers to replicate. Physiological changes to the crops inside the formation and an increase in electromagnetic activity are two such features.

In an excellent article entitled 'High Heat' for *Western Spirit* magazine, published in 1998, the American researcher David Perkins propounded the theory that the apparent use of microwave energy originating in the electromagnetic spectrum at crop circle and animal mutilation sites suggested that the phenomena might be linked, furthermore, that similar energies had also been detected at alleged UFO landing sites.

In 1991 the British crop circle researcher Pat Delgado asked the American bio-physicist, Dr W.C. Levengood to analyse plant samples from crop circles in England. In the first batch of plants he examined, Dr Levengood found that the majority of seed husks from within the circle were empty, and on further examination, he found an uncommon genetic aberration where there is a multiple formation of embryos within a single husk, the endosperm does not form and consequently they are not seeds.

Dr Levengood had found in other samples from the English crop circles that the seeds were malformed, and explained that the deformations were caused by '*premature dehydration of the seeds*'. The crop stem nodes (the apparent joints along the stems) were also affected and he found that the bending of the stem nodes was often in conjunction with cavities in the nodes where holes had been blown from the inside out. The crops within the formations had been subject to high heat and Dr Levengood stated, '*We're seeing a lot of indications of microwave damage, a transient, very rapid, high-heating energy.*' Dr Levengood postulated that an atmospheric phenomenon known as an ion plasma vortex might be responsible and that these vortices might exist in the unstable upper reaches of the Earth's atmosphere.

Dr Levengood expanded his programme of crop circle sampling to formations in the USA and Canada and learned that shiny black spherules of magnetite were being found in the soil within crop formations and that the concentrations were up to forty times that found in control samples. In 1996 similar magnetite beads were found at animal mutilation sites. In one cattle mutilation site in Colorado the concentration was found to be a staggering five hundred times higher than in a normal soil sample.

In 1994 the American animal mutilation researcher and documentary film maker Linda Moulton Howe began submitting plant and soil samples to Dr Levengood. These samples were taken from animal mutilation sites in the USA and the results corresponded with those from the crop circle sites. In 1995 Dr Levengood issued a series of reports on his findings on the samples from five cattle mutilation sites. He concluded his reports as follows: '*These studies clearly suggest that microwave energy is a major component of the energetics involved in the plant alterations at bovine excision sites. These findings are in agreement with crop formation results, which also point to a microwave energy component.*'

At some animal mutilation sites in the USA and in the United Kingdom the mutilators appear to have left circular marks in the grass. Dr Levengood investigated these curious markings and uncovered another strange feature of the animal mutilation sites. He found that the radiation levels detected at these sites increased outwardly and the greatest concentration of energies was in the outer ring. The reverse was true of crop circle sites, where the energies were concentrated at the centre. Dr Levengood suggested the astonishing theory that at the animal mutilation sites the energies were being emitted from the outer ring of the craft and that the energy ring on the ground was dependent upon the size and altitude of the craft from which the animal had been lowered or dropped!

It should be noted that Dr Levengood also examined plant samples that had come from alleged UFO landing sites, and had similar findings to the results obtained for the crop formations and animal mutilation sites.

There appears to be strong scientific evidence to suggest that micro-wave energy has been used in the animal mutilation attacks, as the incisions on the animals appear to be cauterised, and where magnetite spherules have also been found. With similar evidence of high-heat energy being employed in the crop circles and at alleged UFO landing sites, there would seem to be a connection between these three mysteries.

10

The Dead Cow Experiment

In 1975 Sheriff Herb Marshall of Washington County, northern Arkansas, began investigating a series of cattle mutilations in Washington County. Being at a loss to identify the perpetrators, Sheriff Marshall came up with an unusual and innovative approach to the investigation. He decided to see if the precise excisions on the victims' bodies could be replicated by natural means.

A dead cow was donated by a local farmer and the corpse was laid out in an empty field. The Sheriff's Department then set up a tent nearby and mounted a round-the-clock monitoring operation on the carcass of the cow. This operation apparently lasted for several days. Within forty-eight hours the body of cow, subjected to the strong daytime heat, began to expand and became quite bloated. The cow was infested with maggots, which began their customary feeding on the putrefying flesh. After several days the maggots had pupated into blow flies and left the body of the cow. The outer skin of the corpse had split in some places as the putrefying gases had expanded and the maggots, which need both the heat of the sun and air, fed along the seam of the splits in the outer skin. The maggots were also very efficient at consuming any blood around the corpse.

In the opinion of Sheriff Marshall and his department, the resultant look of the cow's carcass, with the lack of blood around the corpse and the precise splitting of the skin, was reminiscent of the cattle mutilations that they were investigating and thus the mystery of the cattle mutilations was solved. Or was it?

Sheriff Herb Marshall's experiment must appear very convenient and welcoming to those who deny there is a problem with the animal mutilations, or wish to prevent further investigation into the subject. However, there are numerous errors with the tidy explanation put forward by the Washington County Sheriff's Department

Although it has been difficult to fully establish the time of death for the thousands of cases of animal mutilations in the USA, and elsewhere, it is known that the majority of cases have been discovered within forty-eight hours and many inside twenty-four hours. This puts the timing of events surrounding the corpse used in the experiment well outside animal mutilation cases. There are numerous cases where an animal, previously healthy, has been found twenty-four hours later with the flesh from various parts of the body completely removed.

In the 1975 experiment there is no mention how long the cow had been dead, or if the animal had died of natural causes before it was donated to the Sheriff's Department. In a suspicious death of a human being, the length of time a body has been left at a crime scene can be ascertained by a pathologist studying the blow flies around a body and identifying which stage of their lifecycle they have reached – this is called forensic entomology.

Blow flies are attracted to recently deceased animals and lay their eggs on the carcass. The resulting maggots infest the corpse for between five and ten days, before leaving to pupate, emerging as blow flies after a further five to seven days. This timescale alone rules out the assertion by Herb Marshall that the mutilations are caused by maggots, as the experimental carcass was monitored for several days and may have been dead for more than a day to begin with.

It also appears that Herb Marshall failed to speak to any pathologist about the nature of the cattle mutilations, which are invariably very precise and selective about both the flesh and the organs that are removed. The edges of the cuts found in animal mutilations have been found to be cauterised and the American pathologist, Dr John Altshuler, and others, have stated that the process has been carried out by high heat, in the region of 350 degrees centigrade. Furthermore, I don't think that maggots can be held responsible for the 'cookie cutter' style of precise and serrated excision, or the circular cuts found in many mutilation cases. How can maggots guillotine part of the head of an animal? Can maggots surgically remove the spinal cord from a dead animal? Can maggots remove the vertebrae from a dead animal? Can maggots cleanly cut and remove an animal's tongue? I also doubt that maggots can be responsible for rectal coring. There is a great deal of other forensic evidence that the Sheriff's Department appear to have ignored in order to substantiate their theory of natural predation.

I wonder what Herb Marshall would make of the mutilated sheep discovered on Dartmoor and put into the back of the farmer's Land Rover – the blow flies found the corpse, but the perpetrators had left a substance on the carcass that killed all the flies.

The 1975 dead cow experiment was an interesting attempt to get to the bottom of this enigmatic and sinister problem, but the efforts of Sheriff Marshall and the Washington County Sheriff's Department were fatally flawed and ignored much forensic evidence. Therefore it is not surprising that the theory that the mutilated corpses are the result of natural processes have been discounted, quite rightly, by all serious researchers into the animal mutilation mystery.

In late 2006 the National Geographic Channel ran a documentary about the Chupacapras (goat suckers), a strange creature that has been terrorising parts of South America for over ten years in a campaign of unexplained animal attacks. A part of the documentary migrated to North America and inevitably brought the cattle mutilation problem into the story. They then showed the 1975 dead cow experiment and gave it sufficient prominence to suggest a plausible explanation for the cattle mutilations. It seems that the makers of the film were only too willing to include the experiment to prove their argument of a terrestrial, natural explanation for the thousands of mutilation cases recorded in both the USA and elsewhere.

11

A Strange Harvest

One name has become synonymous with long-time field investigations of the animal mutilation phenomenon. That name is Linda Moulton Howe. Linda is an Emmy Award-honoured TV documentary producer; investigative reporter for Premiere Radio Networks in North America; and reporter and editor of the award-winning science, environment and Real X-Files news website, *Earthfiles.com*, founded in 1999. Through her groundbreaking documentaries, books and *Earthfiles.com* website, she has brought more information about the troubling problem of animal mutilations into the public domain than anyone else. Yet her name is not widely known in the United Kingdom, other than within the UFO and crop circle community.

Linda Moulton Howe graduated from Stanford University in Palo Alto, California, with a Masters Degree in Communication and began a career in television producing film documentaries about science, medicine and the environment. She has received numerous awards and nominations from within the USA and internationally for her TV productions.

In 1979, as Director of Special Projects at KMGH-TV, the CBS affiliate in Denver, Colorado, Linda began research into the animal mutilation problem, which at that time was reaching epidemic proportions in the USA. The resulting production was *A Strange Harvest*, a documentary film that had terrific impact in the United States and was awarded a Regional Emmy.

A Strange Harvest related one animal mutilation case after another and interviewed a number of ranchers and law enforcement officers about their research and conclusions of who or what was killing and mutilating animals ranging from cattle and horses to deer, elk, rabbits and even cats and dogs.

It was a provocative film that posed many difficult questions. *A Strange Harvest* is the first television documentary to have law enforcement say on camera, on the record, that the animal mutilation perpetrators are *'creatures from outer space'*. Those were the words spoken to Producer Linda Moulton Howe, when she was interviewing Lou Girodo, Chief Investigator for the Trinidad, Colorado District Attorney's Office, in October 1979. Mr Girodo was in charge of animal mutilation investigations and had seen with his own eyes the large, fiery, red-orange spheres come down from the skies over ranchlands, split into two fiery spheres travelling in opposite directions, and return to the same spot, merge and go straight down into the ground. *'Every time those red-orange spheres showed up, Linda, we had animal mutilations!'* Lou Girodo told Linda.

For some people the suggestion that alien life forms might be responsible seemed far more rational, and palatable, than the allegation in some quarters that the US military were carrying out the mutilations, as part of a programme of clandestine sampling – the purpose of which could only be speculated about.

Despite the film, the United States government and state institutions remained unmoved and maintained their stance that all the animal mutilations were explainable as predator damage, disease and satanic cults – even though a Catholic priest told Linda that satanic rituals always involved blood. The mysterious animal mutilations reported in both hemispheres around the world since at least the middle of the twentieth century are notable for the lack of blood or tracks on the body and ground around the mutilated animal.

The film had a stunning impact on the American public and Linda was awarded an Emmy for the production, which so far has not been aired on terrestrial television in the United Kingdom – I wonder why?

In March 1983 Linda left her position as Director of Special Projects at the CBS station in Denver in order to produce and direct an hour special for Home Box Office (HBO) entitled *UFOS: The E.T. Factor.* But the US government blocked the completion of that production and Linda decided she would work independently for CNN and other media while she produced a book, *An Alien Harvest: Further Evidence Linking Animal Mutilations and Human Abductions to Alien Life Forms.* That book was published in 1989 and detailed ten years of research into the animal mutilation issue. In 1994 she published *Glimpses of Other Realities, Volume I: Facts and Eyewitnesses,* followed by *Glimpses of Other Realities, Volume II: High Strangeness* in 1998. These books provided forensic lab information about the hard evidence of high heat at the excision lines of mutilated animals, whether cattle or cats, but also provided eyewitness and human abduction testimonies that link the animal attacks with other phenomena such as UFOs and alien life forms.

During the course of her investigations, Linda established that many animal mutilation attacks, quite apart from their inexplicable nature and modus operandi, were invariably accompanied by sightings of UFOs, strange black helicopters and bizarre confrontations with apparently alien life forms. Linda has concluded from her research that numerous UFO-related phenomena are inextricably linked to the animal mutilations and has pursued all areas of UFO research, including abductions and crop circles, in order to find a clear motive for the attacks. Linda has speculated, from the research she has carried out and from information provided by sources within the US military, that mutilations are being undertaken by EBES (extra-terrestrial biological entities) that need certain genetic material for their survival.

Linda continues to investigate and report about a wide range of environmental, scientific, and medical issues for Earthfiles and radio, while she also investigates the persistent animal mutilations both in the USA, England and around the world, has archived more than a hundred animal mutilation cases at *Earthfiles.com* and has appeared on many television shows and spoken at many university and other conferences about the disturbing phenomenon that continues to this date.

12

The APFU

In 2001, former British Aerospace Chief NDT Engineer David Cayton, and a small group of other like-minded individuals, intrigued by the animal mutilation problem, formed a small research group called the Animal Pathology Field Unit or APFU as it is more generally known. The mission of the APFU was to gather information about the animal mutilations and to investigate who or what was responsible. Despite its limited resources the APFU have been successful in investigating a number of animal mutilation cases that might never have been recognised for what they were.

David Cayton was established as director of the APFU and it was he who successfully unmasked the animal mutilation unit within the DEFRA establishment at VLA Preston, otherwise known as Barton Hall. David Cayton invariably fronted the APFU in its dealings with the media and also presented an excellent video documentary about a sheep mutilation case at Stroat, Forest of Dean in Gloucestershire, during 2002.

The APFU have had some setbacks too, and have lost some of their forensic resource. I was warned to be careful, keeping details of any vet I used as confidential as possible and to keep my cards close to my chest. We shall see, later in this book, how effective the government can be when it comes to identifying and dissuading vets and scientists from involvement in this sinister and disturbing subject. The APFU have a very professional approach to the animal mutilation problem and have produced leaflets and videos, directed principally at farmers, to highlight the situation.

I joined the APFU on some of their survey trips into the remote farming areas west of Shrewsbury. These had varying success, but occasionally our visits would trigger a memory of a sheep death that had puzzled the farmer at the time, but had been dismissed as something mundane. It was not unusual for a farmer to say something like, *'I couldn't understand why there was no blood,'* and *'I thought it strange that the tongues were missing.'* I have to say that not every visit we made was welcomed. There were some farmers who viewed the APFU with suspicion and seemed to think that we were some sort of government agency. At every call we would leave the customary leaflet.

On one such visit, in early 2006, we called at a smallholding, where we were intrigued to see some rather exotic animals. We did not expect to see any llamas in this particular part of Shropshire, but that is what we saw as we drove carefully down a narrow track and parked our car near to the owner's cottage. It was obvious that this was no farm, but more of an animal sanctuary. After our arrival had been announced by the repeated barking of two large dogs, the lady owner somewhat aggressively demanded to know the reasons for our visit. We said that we were investigating animal attacks in the area. The lady (I am withholding her name), I suspect, thought we were some sort of branch of the RSPCA. It soon became apparent that she was now retired and had a keen interest in animal welfare. We explained the aims of the APFU and then showed her some photographs of mutilation cases which had occurred in Shropshire. The lady was shocked angered and only too willing to assist us. She apologised for the initial climate of suspicion that had greeted us on arrival and offered us a cup of tea.

During our now convivial discussion, the lady related a very strange incident that had occurred in November the previous year. A dead sheep had been left near a fence on a neighbour's field and the lady had reported it, thinking that the animal had died due to mistreatment. She heard nothing more until the following day, a Sunday, when a police inspector arrived at her property at four o'clock in the afternoon. Taken aback by the seniority of the lone policeman, she asked why he was visiting her. The inspector began by asking the lady about the dead sheep, when did she see it and was she aware of any other dead sheep in the area? The lady asked what the cause of death was and then received an astonishing reply. The Inspector told her that the government vet from Anglesey had been summoned to inspect the animal. This was an amazing revelation, as Anglesey was approximately sixty miles away! Just as curious was the fact that no local vet had been contacted, despite the fact that there were six practices in the surrounding area, known by the lady as she had worked for each of them at some time in her life.

There are some curious elements to this story, the first of which is, what was a relatively high-ranking policeman doing investigating a sheep death on a Sunday afternoon? And why bring in a government vet all the way from Anglesey, when there were local vets available? We were unable to find out more about this puzzling episode, but on the same day we had visited the animal sanctuary we also visited a farm in the same area which was to provide details, at a later date, of an equally strange incident.

On Thursday, 17th August 2006 I took a phone call from David Cayton, who told me that he had received a call from a Mr Rob Price, a farmer from Rowley near Welshpool, (this was one of the farmers we had visited). Mr

Price had rung David Cayton and told him that a week previously he had found a dead yearling ewe on his farm, the tongue had been removed and there was no blood. David rang me and asked if I could contact Rob Price and get further details.

I rang Mr Price straight away and soon found out that there were more strange elements to this incident. He was unable to give a precise time or date for the death, but was of the opinion that the ewe had been killed on either Friday 11th August or Saturday 12th of August, which coincidently was the time of a full moon phase. The sheep had been killed less than fifty metres from a bungalow, yet nothing was heard or seen. Furthermore, the body had not been attacked by the usual natural predators. Mr Price then told me that there had been a bizarre incident on a neighbour's farm, which might be more than coincidental with the killing of the sheep. He gave me the telephone and name of the farmer concerned, a Mr Webster, and I rang him for the details.

Mr Webster told me that during 9th or 10th August, in a field not far from Rob Price's bungalow, a row of twelve hay bales were slashed in a very precise manner. The bales, which were on the upper row of a stack of one hundred bales, had been cut in circular fashion, to a depth of approximately two inches. The bales had been cut open at the top and Mr Webster surmised that an extremely sharp knife must have been used in order to cut through the plastic netting. He also mentioned that the cutting appeared very measured and precise, not frenzied. The stack of bales was not visible from the road and nothing similar had occurred on the farm before. The police were informed but the perpetrators were never caught. It is highly unlikely that anyone from this remote community was responsible and this inexplicable incident remains unsolved.

13

Animal Circles

A curious phenomenon, that may be linked to the animal mutilation attacks, is the animal circles. This strange phenomenon involves the gathering together of a group of animals, forming a circle or semi-circle. These circles, which are rarely seen, suggest that the animals are under some outside influence, as the forming of a circle is not a natural behavioural instinct of domestic, farm or wild animals. It has been suggested that animal behaviour can sometimes be influenced by the magnetic forces found at some crop circles, and there are numerous instances of dogs, cattle, sheep and horses becoming agitated by the energy fields in such places.

I would like to give some examples of this phenomenon. We will start in Dorset, England with a very disturbing case.

In July 1993 there was an animal mutilation attack in north Dorset, involving the deaths of two calves belonging to Mr Brian Cherrett. More details of this case are to be found in Chapter 17, but there was a bizarre event that occurred after the killings.

Mr Cherrett was interviewed by Linda Moulton Howe during her August 1993 field trip to England that was included in her book *Glimpses of Other Realities, Vol. I: Facts & Eyewitnesses.* When Linda asked Mr Cherrett if anything unusual had occurred around the same time as the killings and mutilations, he gave the following account. A couple of days after the mutilations, he heard a terrible bellowing from some cows in an adjacent field. He described the sound as being similar to the sound made by cows when they are in the slaughter house. When he looked into the field he saw half a dozen cows standing in a circle with their heads towards each other. Suddenly, the remaining cows in the field, about forty of them, charged towards the cows in the circle. Mr Cherrett ran towards the circle of cows and then swiftly retreated to his tractor when the herd of cows changed direction and stampeded towards him. In thirty years of farming he had never experienced such a strange event as the six cows bellowing in that circle.

In his book *The Eternal Subject*, Brinsley lePoer Trench recounts a strange affair that came to light in the African aviation magazine *Wings over Africa*. The article was subsequently reprinted in *Flying Saucer Review*. There is no precise date given, but this probably occurred in 1968. One evening Mr Anton Fitzgerald, who owned a farm in Natal province, South Africa, was walking towards his homestead with his farm manager Jack Marais. As they walked down a hillside that overlooked the farm with its adjacent runway and large aircraft hangar they both saw an eerie reddish glow on the runway. It was about three hundred yards from the farm house and approximately two hundred yards from their position. The object was approximately a hundred feet in diameter, bright pink in the centre and fading gradually towards the circumference.

It was noticeable that the farm animals were behaving oddly and Mr Fitzgerald said, *'We slowed down involuntarily and as the light improved noticed that the flock of sheep bedded down in the runway paddock were all standing in two one-third circles on opposite sides of the glow and looking intently towards the centre.'* He added, *'From our elevated position the sheep reminded me of iron filings on a piece of paper around a magnet – a sort of orderly pattern but yet following no accepted geometric form.'*

Suddenly, when they were within 'a stone's throw' of the object it rose vertically into the air. There was no sound or rush of air as they watched the object disappear into the mist. At this point Jack Morais shouted. *'Just look at those sheep!'*

Fitzgerald later wrote: *'I also looked at the sheep and noticed with amazement that they all appeared to be standing on tip-toe like ballet dancers with heads held unusually high just as if they were suspended in space with their hooves barely touching the grass. It was then that we both first experienced a peculiar feeling almost of weightlessness.'* A check of the animals revealed that one old sheep was missing.

A year later Fitzgerald was in the USA, trying to buy a replacement for his old Aero Commander. Jake Rugel, a descendant of the Cherokee Indians, was trying to sell him an MU2 turboprop and took Fitzgerald on a test flight from Love Field, Dallas to San Angelo. During their flight they encountered a UFO, climbing at extraordinary speed. It had the same reddish glow that Fitzgerald had noted in the incident in Natal.

On arrival at San Angelo, Rugel had a telephone call from a Texas farmer called Ted Leslie, who claimed that the UFO had landed on his farm. Rugel and Fitzgerald flew to Leslie's farm immediately. Ted Leslie then told Fitzgerald and Rugel a story astonishingly similar to the incident in Natal. Apparently a group of white-face Hereford steers had formed a semi-circle in the night paddock, only half a mile from his house. Leslie had seen an object that gave off a pinkish glow and left in complete silence. He had also noticed the peculiar weightlessness experienced by Fitzgerald in Natal. A count of his animals revealed that one of the older steers was missing.

Rugel told Fitzgerald of an ancient Cherokee legend of the 'red sun' that appeared among the buffalo herds – Indians believed that some of the buffalo were carried away. This Indian legend is remarkably similar to a Zulu legend of the 'red sun' that rises straight up into the sky after devouring some of the tribe's cattle.

We now go back to England where, in 1988, the renowned crop circle researcher, Colin Andrews, saw and filmed a sheep circle at Cheesefoot Head near Winchester. Andrews thought, quite logically, that there might be a possibility that the forces that created the crop circles might be responsible for the behaviour of the sheep.

In 2002, crop circle researcher Brian Damerell wrote an article for *Swirled News* about a strange occurrence that took place in Scotland in 2001, a time of widespread restrictions throughout Britain because of the foot and mouth outbreak. On 17th March 2001, Pamela Penfold and her husband were on a motoring holiday in Scotland and were somewhere north of Inverness on the main A9. Most of the lay-bys were cordoned off due to the restrictions, however, they came upon one that was open. Mrs Penfold, who was a keen photographer, immediately noticed that the sheep in a nearby field had gathered in an enormous semi-circle. Realising the strangeness of this event she took two photographs and some video footage of the sheep circle.

I spoke to Pamela in 2010 and she clearly recalled the incident, saying that she counted 103 sheep in the circle, 50-51 on one side, 51-52 on the other, and that the animals appeared so still that she initially thought that they might be rocks or sculptures!

The field was wet and muddy and vehicle tracks were plainly visible, going left to right and right to left. If food had been dropped off from a farm vehicle (a theory that has been used to explain this phenomenon) then such circular tracks would have been clearly seen.

Pamela noted that some stragglers appeared to move in to the circle and others wandered out. The circle itself remained constant. This incredible spectacle did not change from the moment they arrived at the lay-by, until they departed (after a picnic) some 30 to 45 minutes later!

The next report comes from the *Journal of Meteorology*, 14:54, 1989, by G.T. Meaden, in which a Mr M. Belcher gave a very detailed account of not just one sheep circle, but two. The event occurred on Sunday 21st August 1988 and this is Mr Belcher's account:

Out on an afternoon drive M Belcher parked his car near the trigonometric survey point on Baildon Moor, near Leeds, in Yorkshire, at approximately 14:30 GMT facing north-east. His wife suddenly exclaimed: 'Look at that circle of sheep in that field!' That was sheep circle 1 on the plan where a hundred or so sheep were in a circular formation, each sheep being more or less equidistant from the next. At the north end of the field some 20 or 30 cows were standing, grazing and chewing cud in the usual haphazard manner. The circular formation of these sheep was so unusual that I thought I was looking at bales of hay set out in the field by the farmer. Indeed, a stone-age stone circle might have been appropriate on this occasion. I looked around from north-west to north-east, and then espied a similar sheep circle (2) on a plateau opposite. In the sector between north and north-east, flocks of sheep were in other fields but in no case exhibited the circular formation, being in typically haphazard groups.

In a second letter to Mr Meaden, Mr Belcher stated that the sheep in the circles were variously standing, lying down or grazing, but nevertheless maintaining this highly unusual formation.

Animal circles, or to be more precise, sheep circles became national news in January 2008. Estate agent Russell Bird came upon a sheep circle at a farm near Kington, Herefordshire and was able to take a photograph of the spectacle. The photograph and story surrounding the circle appeared in numerous national and regional newspapers. Mr Bird stated, *'I was quite taken aback. I couldn't believe what I was seeing,'* adding that the circle only broke up when the farmer entered the field on a tractor with some food.

Incredibly, just a few minutes later Mr Bird saw another sheep circle three fields away but unfortunately, he was unable to take a picture of this second formation.

Mr Bird mentioned in his statement to the press that he had seen a dog worrying sheep in a nearby field beforehand. This may be significant, as an interesting theory was propounded by Andrew Richards, an NFU senior policy advisor, who himself had witnessed an example of this strange phenomenon. On 30th January 2008 Mr Richards was interviewed by *The Shropshire Star* and gave the following account: *'A year or so ago, I was lucky enough to see a similar scene one morning when looking out of my bedroom window at first light. On that occasion some thirty sheep, all heavily in lamb, had formed a defensive circle surrounding a fox in the centre. The fox clearly took the view he was heavily outnumbered and managed to slink away through a small gap in the ring of the sheep, leaving the flock completely unharmed.'*

Andrew Richard's theory that the sheep may be forming a defensive formation against a potential threat has some logic to it. However, many eye-witness reports (such as Mr M. Belcher's account in Yorkshire) do not mention any familiar, or potential, predators, within or near the circles.

This behaviour by sheep is very unusual, and some farmers claim never to have witnessed such a sight. However, it does happen and there is photographic and video evidence to support this. The question is: what is making animals form these circles? It does suggest manipulation from some outside force, as sheep, particularly, rarely indulge in any sort of group coordination, even when disturbed by potential predators. The question of 'outside control' of sheep is an issue we shall encounter in Part III.

14

Attacks on Pet Animals

There have been numerous mutilation attacks on family pets and very often these are blamed on savage dogs or mindless vandals. However, this may not always be the case. There have been many serial attacks on both cats and rabbits that I feel have not been adequately explained. In this chapter I am going to give details of some of these as I fear the mutilators may not be interested only in farm animals.

In the autumn of 1998 there was an epidemic of cat killings and disappearances in the London area. The victims were invariably decapitated with one half of the body missing, and there was no blood at the scene. The tails were often missing. Many of the victims were found close to their owner's homes and the bodies were often found with the heads placed beside the corpse with the brains removed. The killings caused consternation amongst pet owners right across London and on Monday 23rd November 1998 the BBC news carried the story.

The police, the RSPCA and the Cat Protection League were all baffled as the killings began to escalate. Initially, a single individual was thought to be responsible. However, as the scale of the attacks grew and spread across the capital, it was thought that a gang of individuals was responsible. A researcher contacted the RSPCA and was told by a lady that the killings were being carried out by people.

Cats were not the only victims in this horrific series of killings. Rabbits were also killed in a similar manner. Needless to say, no one was caught and charged with the slaughter of these pets, and furthermore, this was not the first or an isolated series of attacks. In the USA during 2006 and 2007 there were more cat mutilations that were similar, if not identical, in execution to the London killings of 1998.

In January 1994 the mutilators turned up in Vancouver, Canada and dismembered a cat belonging to Pearl Perehudoff. The only way that Miss Perehudoff could identify her pet was by the markings on its tail. The vet who examined the corpse stated that the animal had been cut cleanly in half and that it was unlikely that another animal could be responsible.

Vancouver pound-keeper Vic Warren said that many half cats had been found and blood was never found on the bodies. He further stated that the back halves were left at the scene, to be found by their owners or passers-by, and that the front halves were never found. Warren also claimed that a dog had been killed in a similar manner. Once again Satanists were suggested as the perpetrators although no one was charged.

Back to the UK and a series of strange attacks in Blythe Bridge, Staffordshire that appeared to start in December 1991 and continued until 1994.

Early in January 1992, the *Stoke Evening Sentinel* reported that thirty pet rabbits had been killed in the Blythe Bridge area of Staffordshire. The killer or killers always struck at night and it seemed that no pet was safe. Inevitably, the local press came up with the title 'the beast of Blythe Bridge'. The Evening Sentinel interviewed Dave Sutton of Cheadle police, who made the following statement:

> *Whoever is doing it is a perverted individual – not caring how many children he upsets.*
>
> *The dead rabbits have all been pulled out of their cages at night, strangled, then left nearby. In one incident seven rabbits were left in a line on the lawn.*
>
> *We are doing our best to catch this warped individual, but we need information from the public. Anyone who sees anything suspicious should ring us immediately.*
>
> *The killer must be stalking the gardens to find out where pets can be found.*

Dave Sutton's statement mentions that the dead rabbits were placed in a line on the lawn and I feel it is appropriate to give details of an attack in the USA that took place in May 2007. Local gardener Jeff Kyle found eleven dead rabbits on a lawn near the college of English and Language Arts building at Long Beach, California. He was shocked to discover that one rabbit had been cut in half, an operation carried out with precision and without spilling a drop of blood. I should mention that the mutilators have often laid out their victims in a line – it's almost as if they were making some kind of statement.

Back to Blythe Bridge, during January 1992 the mutilators turned their attention to guinea pigs and, following one such attack, local vet Mick Statham claimed that indentations on the back of the necks of the victims suggested that an animal had been responsible. It was alleged that a black dog with a rabbit in its mouth had been seen near the scene of one of the attacks.

On 23rd January there were five more victims and one pet owner, a Mrs Underwood, described what she found. *'I opened the living-room curtains at about 7 am and saw the rabbit laid out on the lawn near the front door. There was no blood, just two small puncture marks on the back of her neck. Whoever has done this wanted us to find her – they must be sick.'*

On 3rd February two more guinea pigs were killed and laid out on their owner's lawn and on 7th February two rabbits suffered a similar fate. After these attacks, the 'beast' appeared to take a break in its activities until the middle of April.

A married couple were disturbed in their sleep at 0200 one night as the 'beast' caused a commotion while demolishing a cage to get at the couple's two rabbits. By the time they had got downstairs, the 'beast' had gone. The strong wire on the cage had been cut, allegedly by wire cutters, and there were teeth marks on the wooden handle of the cage. The couple's intervention had been in the nick of time and both rabbits were shaking with fear. The previous night to this incident a neighbour's rabbit had been killed and, in the words of a local man, *'The rabbit was laid out like a trophy on my neighbour's lawn.'*

In May 1992 a pet rabbit was attacked and killed in an enclosed yard. The attack drew the following astonishing comments from Chief Inspector Charles Jones of Longton police: *'Someone or something broke into the yard, took the rabbit away, savaged it and returned the body. The rabbit had been bitten by an animal – but this was not the work of animal alone. There must have been human involvement.'*

Here we have a high-ranking police officer suggesting that 'something' broke into the yard, removed the rabbit, killed it, then returned it! What evidence did he have for this incredible speculation?

It appears that there was a lull in the series of killings from July 1992 onwards.

In March 1993 two guinea pigs were snatched from their hutch by a pair of stray dogs. However, the police stated that the two dogs were not the notorious beast of Blythe Bridge. I have to wonder what evidence the police could have had in order to make such a definitive statement.

In September 1994 the 'beast' returned and claimed another ten victims, including rabbits, guinea pigs and a goose. The goose was found on the lawn after being taken from its pen in a shed and beheaded. Remember the attacks at Newquay Zoo in 1978 mentioned in Part I, where wildfowl were beheaded?

There was a curious twist in the series of attacks when a dog called Queenie was found covered in blood in a six-foot high pen with five dead guinea pigs and four dead rabbits. Queenie was an eleven-year-old miniature Collie/Alsatian cross breed and her owner stated that the dog suffered from arthritis and was a very friendly animal, certainly not a vicious killer. If the dog had arthritis, how did it jump over a six-foot fence? It seems to me that it is possible that Queenie may have been placed in there – by whom, and for what purpose?

The attacks stopped in 1994 and, as far as I am aware, there have been no further pet killings in this area of Staffordshire since. There are a number of questions that are raised by this bizarre series of attacks. Whatever or whoever carried out these crimes did so over a long period of time. They had the ability to locate the victims and force open the pens and hutches, cutting through strong wire if necessary. They operated in a covert manner and invariably struck at night. They had a predilection for laying the bodies of their victims on grass. They had a preference for rabbits and guinea pigs and ignored other pets such as cats or dogs. I would suggest that the facts indicate it is very unlikely that any known animal could be responsible for these killings. We now move to the south-west of England for another curious series of events involving cats.

There had also been large scale disappearances of cats and during March 1995 in the small town of Clevedon in Avon, and nearby Portishead and Nailsea experienced a sinister happening as hundreds of cats went missing. Three-quarters of the lost cats were black and the local RSPCA administrator, Helen Dallow said, *'It makes you wonder whether there is something funny going on.'*

There were some of the usual theories put forward, such as the occult and, rather bizarrely, one resident claimed the cats were taken for their fur in order to make hats for the Eastern bloc! The disappearances invariably happened at night and no bodies were found. Despite a huge local advertising campaign it appears that only one cat was returned – he was black and white.

It's worth mentioning that in 2006 the Shropshire town of Telford experienced a similar wave of cat disappearances and again, no trace was found of the missing animals. In 2008 there was a spate of similar disappearances in Stourbridge, West Midlands.

The mutilators' habit of laying out the victims on lawns and other places where the remains can be easily found does seem to be an important factor. Are 'they' saying, *'We did this, you work it out if you can?'* Essentially a challenge in a similar vein to human serial killers, some of whom have been known to leave enigmatic clues for the forces of law and order who are pursuing them.

Perhaps the open areas are where they prefer to carry out the killings and mutilations? If this is so, why has no one seen them at work? There were more than seventy killings in the Blythe Bridge attacks and yet on only one occasion were the mutilators disturbed.

15

Animal Mutilations in the USA

During the late 1970s the animal mutilation problem in the USA was out of control, although to be honest, it's a problem that is beyond control or curtailment anyway. The animal mutilation attacks, which involved mainly cattle, were constant headline news in North America. Despite all this, the problem had a longer history and at the time of the American Revolution the native Indians found dismembered buffalo. There had been sporadic reports of animal mutilations on ranches in the USA since the nineteenth century and it has been alleged that according to sources within the US military, animal mutilation cases have also been recorded since the late 1940s.

However, it was not until 1967 that a case became widely publicised and the sinister problem of the mutilations began to mushroom out of control. The case is a classic and has many of the features associated with these bizarre attacks. Furthermore, apart from kick-starting the notorious problem in the USA it also introduces us to one of the most influential people involved in the animal mutilation problem – John Altshuler, M.D., pathologist and haematologist.

Nuclear physicist, UFO investigator and author Stanton Friedman met Dr Altshuler at a UFO conference. Dr Altshuler attended out of personal curiosity and told Stan Friedman that he was the Denver doctor who anonymously investigated the famous horse mutilation near Alamosa, Colorado, in September 1967. Stanton called Linda Moulton Howe to relate Dr Altshuler's account and Linda followed up in Denver where she and Dr Altshuler both lived. That began a period of forensic investigation in which Linda went into dozens of fields with scalpel, formalin solution and plastic containers to gather mutilator's excisions from animal mutilations. Then Linda either hand-delivered or FedExed tissue samples to Dr Altshuler's Denver laboratory for analysis. In Linda's book, *Glimpses of Other Realities, Vol. I: Facts & Eyewitnesses*, the first photomicrographs ever published of mutilated animal tissues that confirmed the pathology of cooked collagen and cooked haemoglobin were published in case studies that Linda and Dr Altshuler investigated.

Doctor Altshuler had studied medicine at McGill University and had an impressive career in which he received several awards for his contribution to medical research into blood coagulation. He also held seven patents for medical inventions. Dr Altshuler also had an interest in UFOs, an interest that he preferred to keep to himself, fearing it might damage his career.

Altshuler became a doctor of pathology and haematology and was working as a pathologist at Rose Medical Center in Denver, Colorado in 1967 when, quite by chance, he became involved in an animal mutilation case.

In September 1967 Dr Altshuler decided to take his family away for a weekend and booked into a motel in Alamosa. That night he went, alone, to the Great Sand Dunes National Monument Park, to carry out a sky watch. Altshuler had heard a great deal about unexplained lights in the San Luis Valley and confessed that the reports of these UFOs *'provoked my intellectual curiosity'*. The park was subject to a curfew after 2200 hours, but Altshuler, his interest fuelled by the possibility of witnessing the enigmatic lights, took the risk and stayed.

At about 0200 hours Altshuler was rewarded for his daring, when he saw three very bright lights, moving slowly below the Sangre De Cristo Mountains. At one point the lights got brighter, suggesting that they were approaching him. Suddenly, the lights shot upwards and disappeared from sight. Altshuler was elated by the experience and fell asleep until sun rise. Unfortunately, he was apprehended by the park police and interrogated as to why he was in the park after hours. Fearing his fledgling career would be over, he begged the police not to release his name and said that his job as haematologist at Denver would be jeopardised. When the police heard that he was a medical haematologist they mentioned to him the curious death of a horse at a nearby ranch and offered to take him there to inspect the animal.

The police took Dr Altshuler to the Harry King ranch, where he met Nellie Lewis, a relative of the ranch owner, who said that Harry King had heard nothing on the night of the attack and that the horse, named Lady, had been in good health before the horrific attack. Doctor Altshuler's own account of what he witnessed was published in Linda Moulton Howe's *An Alien Harvest* © 1989 and with her kind permission I reproduce it here.

> *When I got close to the horse, I could see that it was also cut from the neck down to the base of the chest in a vertical, clean incision.*
>
> *At the edge of the cut, there was a darkened color as if the flesh had been opened and cauterized with a surgical cauterizing blade. The outer edges of the cut skin were firm, almost as if they had been cauterized with a modern day laser. But there*

was no surgical laser technology like that in 1967. Today when we use cauterizing to control bleeding, the flesh still has a soft pliable feeling. But the edges of that horse cut were stiff, leathery and a bit hardened. I cut tissue samples from the hard, darker edge. Later I viewed the tissue under a microscope. At the cell level, there was discoloration and destruction consistent with changes caused by burning.

Most amazing was the lack of blood. I have done hundreds of autopsies. You can't cut into a body without getting some blood. But there was no blood on the skin or on the ground. No blood anywhere. That impressed me the most.

Then inside the horse's chest, I remember the lack of organs. Whoever did the cutting took the horse's heart, lungs and thyroid. The mediasternum was completely empty – and dry. How do you get the heart out without blood? It was an incredible dissection of organs without any evidence of blood.

This experience had a profound effect on Dr Altshuler, who went on to examine countless tissue samples from other mutilations that indicated high heat in excess of 350 degrees centigrade had been used in the mutilation process. It should be noted that laser technology did not come into use until twelve years after the attack on Lady.

Doctor Altshuler's credentials were impeccable and after his spell at Rose Medical Center, his career blossomed as he went on to become Clinical Professor of Medicine (Haematology) and Pathology at the University of Colorado Health Sciences Center in Denver, as well as running his own practice.

Dr Altshuler became more outspoken on the mutilation issue before his death in 2004. He accumulated hundreds of tissue samples and repeatedly emphasised that no known technology on Earth could have been responsible for the mutilations.

Dr Altshuler was not alone in his theory that alien intelligences might be responsible. A number of researchers and law enforcement officers, shared his viewpoint and some published their own books on the problem. One such researcher was the late Frederick W. Smith, who wrote *Cattle Mutilation – The Unthinkable Truth.* This superbly informative book, written in 1976, details the author's investigation into the unusual cattle deaths occurring in Colorado during the 1970s. The book raised several points about animal mutilations and the possible motives for the attacks.

One of the most important theories advanced by Smith was that the attacks and the way the bodies were left at the crime scene (they are rarely hidden), suggested that the perpetrators were making a statement. What kind of statement, you may ask? *We did this! You couldn't stop us! You try and figure out why we've done this!* Smith's assertion that this might be the case is made by two extraordinary animal mutilation cases on Cheyenne Mountain, home of the headquarters of NORAD (North American Air Defence Command), the very nerve centre of the United States defensive capability.

The NORAD base is situated deep within Cheyenne Mountain and the Combat Operations Center is accommodated in solid steel buildings, some of which are three stories high and free-standing on giant metal springs. This huge complex monitors everything that enters the air space of the United States. Security, as you would imagine, is extremely tight and the road to the Operations Center is unmarked and not shown on most road maps. Signs, warning people not to trespass in the area, are located all along this road. The whole area is a military reservation, protected by hundreds of planes and thousands of troops.

On 6th July 1975, next to the electronic gate at the entrance to the huge tunnel, leading into the NORAD Operations Center, a cow was found mutilated. The animal had been due to calf in two months and had died during a 'standard' mutilation, which involved the removal of its genitals. Deputy Sheriff Sergeant Robert Stone, speaking to *The Gazette Telegraph* of Colorado, made the following statement: *'The animal did not struggle when it went down, but was possibly induced with a tranquilizer.'*

Of all the places to attack and mutilate a cow, this was done at the very door of the bastion of US military might. How could they have done it?

'They' came again to the area on Tuesday 21st October 1975, this time to attack and mutilate a fifteen-hundred-pound buffalo at the Cheyenne Mountain Zoo. The zoo was situated within an area where there were a number of expensive properties nearby and it was a mystery as to how the predators had got in and carried out the attack, apparently leaving no tracks in the process.

The attackers had removed the udder, an ear and a section of hide approximately twenty-four inches square and also cut the vagina. The zoo veterinarian, Dr R.C. Walker, performed an initial post mortem and Dr R.W. Urich, the El Paso County Coroner, also examined the carcass. Dr Urich commented *'The cutting was done neatly, cleanly, obviously with a very sharp instrument. The disection was of the type that would eliminate any type of predator.'* He added, *'It was better than I could do if I were trying. It was really an expert job.'*

According to Dr Walker, *'It was a very, very strange incident and there was an excessive amount of sero-sanguineous (blood tinged) fluid in the abdominal and thoracic cavities and the fluid had seeped into the body tissue and even into the eyeballs.'* We shall hear of dead sheep on Dartmoor exhibiting similar symptoms in Part III.

A report from the *Brush Banner* newspaper dated 10th September 1975, commenting on the mutilations, is typical of the attacks being carried on farms across Colorado at that time: *'A Benson, Minnesota farmer fed his cow and later returned to his barn to turn out the lights. He discovered the cow mutilated inside the barn. A mutilation in South Dakota left a steer with the lower jaw removed and some tissue cuttings so delicate that veterinarians maintained it would have taken them two weeks to perform the same type of surgery. The animal was found two hundred feet behind the owner's barn.'*

The American incidents corresponded to a consistent list of mutilations, or should I say surgical excisions: removal of an eye, ear, genitals, areas of the skin, tongue, rectal coring and the apparent removal of blood. Often the exposed bone that had been stripped of tissue had a 'bleached' appearance, as in the case of Lady, the Appaloosa mare mentioned earlier. In the 1976 book *Mystery Stalks the Prairie* by Robert Donovan and Keith Wolverton, there is another strange clue left by the mutilators.

On 9th October 1975 the authors attended the site of a calf mutilation. At the scene of the crime several stones, weighing between six and seven pounds (three or four kilos) had been moved from a nearby mound of rocks and turned over and moved around. Ten days later the calf had a filmy white substance that stretched from the carcass to the surrounding ground, like a cobweb. Laboratory tests identified the substance as petroleum distillate. What was this substance doing there? And why were the stones moved around?

Although cattle and horses have borne the brunt of the mutilation attacks in the United States, other animals have also suffered: sheep, pigs, goats, cats and dogs and a number of wild animals too.

The Canadian researcher Gene Duplantier wrote an excellent booklet about the animal mutilation problem called *The Mutilators.* This book contains a horrific account by five backpackers, camping out in a remote area by the Yukon River near Eagle, Alaska. It begins with an incredible sighting of craft of unknown origin.

One of the backpackers rose, before dawn, left his tent and went to a nearby stream to wash. He was astounded to see approximately twenty saucer-shaped craft hovering nearby but, by the time he had returned to the camp and roused his friends, the craft had disappeared. However, the five men found some unusual ground marking in the area by the stream. There was a large burnt circle, where the grass was brushed out clockwise from the centre, not dissimilar to a crop circle. They also found four triangular indentations that were two to three inches deep in the ground just at the edge of the circle. Nothing could prepare them for what they found next. Near to the assumed 'landing' marks they found hundreds of dead animals.

The legs and antlers of a moose had been removed and put in separate piles. The organs of an elk had been removed, and there were a number of dead grisly bears that were missing their claws and eyes. In the case of the caribou, the skeletons had been removed. The most astonishing discovery, given that Eagle was rather far inland, was the body of a fifteen-foot whale, which had been gutted. Circumstantial evidence points to the occupants of the saucer-shaped craft being responsible for the slaughter. If this is so then how did 'they' get a whale so far inland?

Our next case dates from mid-September 1980 and involves a pig mutilation on a farm outside San Antonio. Mr W.B. Snell was an attorney who also ran a small farm. One day he noticed vultures circling over one of his fields and went to investigate. He found one of his pigs lying dead on its side. There were no tracks around it. On closer inspection he spread the legs apart and was shocked to discover a twenty-four-inch incision that began at the throat and continued down around the left front leg to a hole through which the heart had been taken. The body looked as though it had been cleaned, as if for an operation. Snell gave an interview to a local newspaper and, referring to the incisions, made the following statement: '*The odd thing is that there was no blood around the wound. The hole was smooth and you couldn't see any bones or vital organs through the opening where the heart was removed.*'

The United States has suffered tens of thousands of animal mutilation attacks and still the authorities deny there is a problem other than satanic cultists, whom they consistently blame for the sinister and precise mutilation attacks. We should end this chapter on mutilations in the USA with a quote from Frederick W. Smith that encapsulates the enigma:

> *The mutilators haven't made one misstep. They leave their calling cards, but no one has ever surprised them at their work. They leave too much evidence for any rational person to deny they exist, but never enough to be identified. No one even claims to have taken a picture of them. Afterward, of course, thousands are taken. They're obviously playing with us like a cat plays with a mouse. And it's driving folks, including the authorities, right up the wall.*

16

Animal Mutilations Worldwide

Animal mutilations are by no means restricted to North America and Britain, and I would suggest that almost every country in the world has had a case at some time or other – it's just that they are not always reported. The next account of animal mutilation was reported in *The Times* in 1998.

France

During February 1998, twenty-two striped dolphins were found dead on the beaches of Languedoc-Rousillon between Agde and the Spanish border. The scale of deaths was unprecedented and this slaughter of a protected species baffled environmentalists who regarded the deaths as inexplicable.

The majority of the victims had a gaping, circular wound, about six inches in diameter, in the area of the throat or lower jaw. Guy Olivet, president of the Mediterranean Dolphin Study Group said, *'All the wounds are located in almost exactly the same place. The extreme precision suggests that we can rule out accidental causes.'*

At the maritime laboratory in Banyuls-sur-Mer, post mortem examinations were carried out. Interestingly, no conclusions were reached from these examinations and the dolphin carcasses were sent to Barcelona for further analysis. Monica Mueller, an expert in dolphin behaviour based at Banyuls-sur-Mer, stated that experts had ruled out the possibility that the deaths were the result of a virus called *Moribilis,* an infection that killed sixty-five Mediterranean dolphins in 1995. Accidental death by fishing trawlers was also ruled out. Researchers at the laboratory were of the opinion that the circular wounds found on seventy percent of the dead dolphins were unlikely to be man-made as the wounds were on the underside of the body, which is less accessible to man.

Leo Sheridan, a British dolphin expert, put forward a disturbing theory for the deaths by claiming that the dolphins were used by the United States Navy at one of their Mediterranean bases. He suggested that the dolphins had outgrown their usefulness and that their American handlers had used a radio-detonated charge on their signal collars so that no one could discover their missions. Monica Mueller disputed Sheridan's theory on the basis that striped dolphins are likely to die of stress if an attempt is made to catch them.

Were the killers of the dolphins at Languedoc-Rousillon also responsible for another attack, just over a year previously, this time in Portugal? There are similarities between the two cases as we shall see.

Portugal

On Wednesday morning, 2nd October 1996, a shepherd called Fernando Soares was checking his sheep in a field just north of Idanha-a-Novu in Portugal. He was shocked to discover that nine of his sheep had been killed during the night and that twenty-eight of his sheep had been attacked. Every sheep that had been attacked had an identical wound – a deep circular hole on the right side of the neck. The bodies of the nine dead sheep had been drained of blood.

The Canary Islands

During late April and early May 1979 there was a series of attacks on the island of Tenerife, near a small town called Taco. Six ferocious German shepherd guard dogs were enclosed within the grounds of a local factory, and on consecutive mornings one dog was found dead outside the enclosure. Each victim had a hole in its chest, through which the heart and lungs had been removed. There was no blood and no signs of a struggle.

Shortly after the dog killings and in the same area of Taco, two goats were found beheaded and exsanguinated. The next victim was a hog, which suffered similar injuries to the guard dogs and whose liver was apparently in a very bad state. Once again the deterioration of the liver is mentioned in an animal mutilation attack.

Not long after this attack further victims, including rabbits and goats, were found beheaded. Later that year the mutilators turned their attention to sheep and after a series of attacks the police suggested that the culprits were rats! Local reporters, however, were sure that humans were responsible. It may be only coincidence that a few days before the killings began there was a major UFO sighting right across the Canary Islands. Thousands of people had witnessed a brilliant ascending light, variously described as cup-shaped, cylindrical and pyramid-shaped,

Australia

The vast Australian outback has had many animal mutilation attacks that have been reported by bushmen, such as Larry Dulhunty. The legendary Dulhunty claimed to have come across his first mutilation case in the 1980s. He was on the western side of the Blue Mountains in New South Wales, travelling along a bush track, when he came upon a dead wombat. Dulhunty made the following statement: *'I looked at the body and found its organs had been removed with the same neatness as a surgeon would use during an operation. But the thing that stood out was that there were no flies within a metre of the wombat and no blood.'* Had the wombat been sprayed with some repellent to keep away the inevitable blow flies? As we shall see in Part III there are occasions when the mutilators like to keep flies away from the corpse and for any blow fly going near the body it can mean certain death. Why should the attackers want to stop natural predation of the body? Is it so the body is found as they left it? If this is so – are they giving us a message?

Dulhunty claimed that station workers at Camooweal, near the Queensland and Northern Territory border, at Boulia, Dajarra, Chillagoe and Birdsville had reported dead cattle and kangaroos with organs surgically removed and that the animal mutilation problem was rampant in these remote areas. In 2007 there was a wave of kangaroo mutilations on one of Australia's national park areas, and the killings shocked local officials.

Argentina

South America has also been plagued by the animal mutilation attacks and Argentina, a major beef-producing country, has suffered more than most. There are numerous reports to call on but I have selected this one, as it concerns an attack on a sheep.

On 25th June 2002, in Coronel Pringles, southern Buenos Aires, Argentina, a pregnant ewe was found 'hollowed out' on the property of Juan Carlos Ibarguren, a local farmer. The animal was examined by a local veterinary surgeon, Alberto Sensi who made the following comment: *'The animal was found with cuts in the jawbone and missing its tongue and one eye. We found no tracks or footprints, and the rest of the flock were very far away from the hill on which we found the dead animal.'*

It should be noted that by this date there had been more than one hundred and seventy recorded animal mutilation attacks across Argentina – the vast majority involving cattle. The problem spread to nearby Uruguay and the next two reports happened on the same day and the day before the sheep attack in Argentina.

Uruguay

On Monday 24th June 2002 in the State of Durazno, one hundred and eighty miles from Montivideo, a dead cow was discovered with its tongue, eyes and genitals extracted with surgical precision. The Uruguayan Ministry of Livestock and Agriculture looked into the case, but appear to have made no comment.

The day after the Durazno attack another cow was found dead in mysterious circumstances, this time in Cardona, in the State of Soriano. The cow had its tongue and salivary glands removed, along with its teats, rectum, part of the large intestine and genitalia. The victim also had perfectly cauterised incisions on its head and sides.

Brazil

There have been many animal mutilation attacks in Brazil and I have decided to include the following extraordinary account, which allegedly took place in October 1970.

Pedro Trajano Machado and his twenty-three-year-old son Euripides de Jesus Trindade were on their farm situated approximately fifteen miles from Palma, in the state of Rio Grande do Sul. On the day of the incident, the two men were moving cattle into a corral and had just separated a Jersey cow from her three-month-old calf that was allowed to run loose in the corral. The two men became aware that the cattle were becoming nervous and upset, in particular the mother Jersey cow, which was bellowing and trying to turn her head in the direction of the calf. Pedro Machado looked at the young calf to see what the problem was. To his amazement, the calf was also bellowing and suspended some three feet in the air! Pedro called his son and both men watched transfixed as the calf, still in an upright position and three feet in the air, moved towards a nearby field. Panic broke out among the other animals, as the calf began to rise, vertically. The calf stopped bellowing as it rose gradually to a great height (it appeared a quarter of its size), the animal then vanished. The whole incident had taken less than five minutes.

As you can see the animal mutilation problem is a worldwide one and, in my opinion, it probably needs a worldwide effort to try and understand the motives behind the attacks. In the next chapters we shall look at animal mutilations in the United Kingdom and the efforts by the UK government to suppress knowledge of the problem.

17

Animal Mutilations in Britain

There have been a number of unexplained animal mutilation attacks in the United Kingdom and a wide variety of animals and birds have been victims. Very rarely has an attack or series of attacks made the national press, and when they have done so, they are invariably attributed to occultists.

I have selected some cases that illustrate different aspects of the problem in Britain. You will see that areas right across the UK have been affected and the perpetrators have a preference for remote areas. First, I will give brief details of some cases that illustrate the wide range of attacks.

In May 1995, a group of local hikers were crossing some fields in the north-east of England when they came upon a scene of carnage. In one of the fields they found the bodies of seventeen sheep and, curiously, five badgers. They notified the farmer immediately and when he inspected the bodies, each victim had a precise hole in its head, the rectum had been cored out and there was no blood. In some cases, square patches of skin had been removed.

In February 1997, in a small clearing in the Dalby Forest, North Yorkshire, the bodies of seven rabbits, one fox, one badger, one deer and one sheep were found. Each victim had a precise hole in the head and the rectum cored out. Again, there were square patches of skin neatly removed from the bodies and there was no blood. Note the similarity of the injuries in these two reports, which also indicate a degree of 'sampling' as several disparate species are involved.

In 1997 at the village of Snainton, situated on the main A170 road between Pickering and Scarborough, nine sheep were found with their stomachs removed.

These three reports are all from north-east England and it should be noted that there were numerous reports of animal mutilation attacks in this area over a three-year period between 1994 and 1997. The attacks briefly reached the national press on 10th August 1997, when the *Sunday People* carried a small article about the animal mutilation problem under the headline 'Butchers from another world'.

The next case comes from the book *Abducted* by Ann Andrews and Jean Ritchie. The Andrews family had a smallholding near the small village of Crouch, in Kent, and in 1995 the family cat went missing and was eventually found dead in the barn. The body was stretched out on a straw bale and there was a neat round hole in its head, there was no sign of any blood and the body was stiff, indicating it had been there for at least twenty-four hours. Rats are a constant problem on farms, yet the cat's body had not been touched by any rodent or other natural predator. A few months after the death of the cat, a fox was found in a nearby field, with a similar injury to the head.

On 26th August 1996, four dead mice were found by a gateway to a nearby field. The mice were laid out unnaturally, in a straight line formation and each victim had a tiny hole in the forehead. The left eye of each victim had been removed and the rectums appeared to have been removed. One victim had part of its stomach removed and another had its jawbone stripped. One victim had its front left paw removed.

Once again, in this series of attacks we have similar injuries on different kinds of animals. The hole in the head injury figures prominently in the next case, which involves a number of sheep, this time near Chepstow in south Wales. This case was the subject of an excellent short video, shot during the investigation by David Cayton and Robert Hulse of the APFU (Animal Pathology Field Unit), I have withheld the names of the farmer and the veterinary surgeons involved in this case.

At 0930 hours on Monday 13th October 2002, a farmer, whose property was located at Woolaston on the edge of the Severn estuary, found almost two dozen of his sheep either dead or severely injured. The field the sheep were in was a narrow strip of land set between the Severn estuary and an embankment carrying the main railway line from England into south Wales. On the opposite bank of the estuary lies the Oldbury on Severn nuclear power station. The weather during the night of the attack had been particularly bad with heavy rain, which made the surrounding area very boggy.

The police and the RSPCA were called and it was assumed, because many of the sheep had head injuries, that they had been shot. However, the police were unable to locate a single cartridge case in the field. The police further speculated that there were at least two or more persons with dogs, who had made their way down the railway track in order to access the field. I have to ask why any individuals, however depraved, would risk their lives walking or even just crossing this main railway line in heavy rain in order to slaughter sheep with no apparent motive.

A local veterinary surgeon carried out an inspection of the bodies at the farm and removed five sheep heads for further analysis. At the surgery the vet x-rayed the heads and found that there was no evidence of *'dense metal inclusions'*. In other words, no lead shot or bullets of any kind. This was all the more surprising as there were no exit wounds that could have accounted for the lack of projectile material in the heads. The vet postulated that two holes found in some of the heads could have been caused by some sort of grappling instrument. There was also bruising to the neck and around the vertebrae, the cause of which was unknown.

This is a puzzling case that raises several questions. Why were the sheep in that particular field targeted? I can not believe that human killers were responsible, given the remote location and the danger and difficulty in accessing the field. How were the animals killed? The vet proved that they were not killed by guns or any conventional method. How were the sheep caught? It was a night of heavy rain and the field was boggy. What was the motive? There appears to be no reason for the attack although the close proximity of the Oldbury on Severn nuclear power station may provide a clue. There is a curious footnote to this incident. The APFU were told by an RSPCA officer who investigated the case that one of the mutilated bodies went mysteriously missing. The carcass was in the field and the farmer assumed that a fox had taken it away. I think it is very unlikely that a fox could have removed a dead animal weighing nearly sixty kilograms from any field. The disappearance of bodies from animal mutilation crime scenes is another puzzling aspect of this enigma.

The 1990s seem to have been particularly active years for the mutilators and this next case, from Cornwall, took place in 1996, although there had been incidents there three years previously.

In April 1996 a family who owned riding stables at Lanescott Mines, Cornwall made a disturbing discovery one morning when they found the door to their riding stables, measuring seven by four feet, completely wrenched off. The family pet, a Vietnamese pot-bellied pig, was missing. The police were called and the pig was found almost half a mile away in a field, with its head cleanly removed and one leg missing, neither the head or leg were ever found There was no blood at the scene and the injuries had been inflicted with apparent precision. There was no evidence of blood at the stables, either and the police concluded that the pig had been mutilated elsewhere before being dumped in the field.

The attack rekindled memories of a horrific attack on a horse in a field at the same place in July 1992. A mare in foal had been killed; the attackers had slit her vagina open and removed the foal. The tail and mane of the mare were missing, as was the foal. Bizarrely, a brown horse in the same field as the mare had turned white overnight. At that particular time there had been a spate of other animals such as chickens, sheep and domestic pets, being killed or going missing in the area.

Mutilation attacks on horses have been widespread and I think it would be beneficial to review two waves of attacks, the first in Hampshire and Surrey between 1995 and 1997. This account, which concerned the movements of a black triangular craft, was written by Hillary Porter for BEAMS (The British Earth & Aerial Mysteries Society) and was reproduced by *Flying Saucer Review* in 2006. FSR were plainly concerned about this wave and their introduction to the article contained the following comment: *'This article carries grave evidence of an active campaign of animal mutilation being inflicted by the unknown occupants of the craft on local horses and far more disturbing is the repeated hovering of this object over local schools.'*

The wave of sightings of a black triangular craft came to the notice of Hillary Porter on 13th July 1995, when the craft was noted making repeated sweeps of an area near to where she lived, on the border of north Hampshire and west Surrey. The sighting was accompanied by a strange pulsing noise and the craft seemed to be projecting a pipe-like device that was illuminated with tiny red lights and a single light at one end. The extended tube was casting a pink and bluish light on the trees and rooftops of nearby houses. There were several witnesses to this nocturnal activity and the sightings went on for many months.

A few months later the same (or similar) craft visited the area again and was seen hovering over a local school at a height of approximately one hundred feet. Rods of light were coming from the central part of the craft and the witness stated that the beam twisted and zigzagged onto the school. After a while the craft began directing the beams of light onto local houses before disappearing.

On 8th May 1996 at 0330 hours, the black triangle made another visit and was seen swooping into a local field where horses were kept. The witness also noted that four golden, glowing orbs descended into a field close to a local main road. This activity coincided with the strange and withdrawn behaviour of horses at an adjacent equine centre. Two of the horses had long, deep cuts to the back of their legs and all the horses were not eating and would not be ridden.

On 2nd September 1996 at 0100 hours, the craft returned again. The horses and local wildlife were making a deafening noise as the craft, with its now customary pulsing sound, had a square light attachment that emanated a beam so powerful it lit up the ground with a blinding light. Suddenly everything went silent until one of the horses in the nearby paddock began to scream in extreme pain. The witness stated that a light breeze, blowing through a window, was accompanied by the sickening smell of burning hair, this in turn was followed by the smell of burning flesh. This suggests a method of high heat used in the mutilation attack.

On the 3rd October 1996 at 0040 hours, the witness was alerted by a much louder pulsing sound, which sent the horses and wildlife hysterical. The craft displayed seven lights that changed colour from red, turquoise, yellow, green, pink, white and orange. After a short while the craft disappeared.

On 16th December 1996 at 7.50 in the evening, the witness was driving her car and saw the black triangle, flying very low over some horses in a nearby field. The craft appeared much lower than it had been before and as she approached the A325 the witness noticed that the traffic was going much slower than usual. The traffic on the nearby A331 Blackwater Valley interchange was also slow moving and as she drove over the A331 going south, she could see a white beam of light being projected from what was described as a 'black mass'. The beam was hitting every vehicle, when the craft suddenly 'de-cloaked' and appeared as a white triangular craft approximately thirty feet long by fifteen feet across. The craft was hovering about one hundred feet up, motionless, with a beam of light coming from a diffused source at the front of the triangle. This craft was seen by many witnesses.

The mysterious triangle continued to visit the area until 1997, carrying out similar activity. The equine centre refused to comment further on the attacks on their horses.

Let us now move north to the Peak district of Derbyshire, for another wave of attacks involving horses. On 1st July 2003 the *Daily Mail* carried a story about horse mutilations in an area around Chatsworth, set in the Derbyshire Peak District National Park. The predictable headline was 'Horses are mutilated in spate of attacks "by satanists"'. The assaults involved physical and sexual abuse on horses and there were seventeen attacks in as many days.

There were three owners involved and they had some curious comments to make about the series of attacks. Kay Walvin, who owned three horses, stated: *'These attacks are planned like a military operation. They have occurred in gales, snow, blizzards and torrential rain. Yet they leave no footprints or vehicle tracks.'* Despite keeping an all-night vigil, the perpetrators were never found and the owners of the horses were convinced that they themselves were being watched by the attackers. One animal had been slashed, allegedly with a carpet fitter's knife, and a swastika-like symbol had been painted in blood on a wall. Mrs Walvin also claimed that several occasions the horses had been sedated with a 'mystery potion'. This comment suggests that the horses' blood had been analysed in a laboratory.

Leisure manager Debbie Bell described finding one of her horses dead in a field, with its stomach cut open. She made the following comment: *'I knew straight away this was no accident. Incredibly, despite the gaping wound there was no blood.'*

The attacks spread to nearby Sheffield and South Yorkshire and the police mounted a three-night surveillance over the summer solstice, codenamed Operation Equine. Unfortunately, the police efforts were to no avail and no arrests were made in respect of these attacks.

It is clear from the eye-witness reports of the horse mutilations on the Surrey/Hampshire border that there is a connection with the black triangular craft. However, the Derbyshire wave of attacks are not so clear cut. Although occultists are again accused of what seem to be mindless attacks, there are some interesting aspects that may suggest otherwise. Despite extreme weather conditions, there are no footprints or vehicle tracks. All-night surveillance had failed to identify the perpetrators, or stop the attacks. Despite a gaping wound in one horse there was no blood. Finally, what was the mystery potion used to sedate the horses?

In July 1993 there was a series of attacks in north Dorset in which calves were horrifically mutilated. The injuries were very similar to those on horses that had been carried out in southern England and nearby Hampshire, in particular. The *Western Gazette* carried the story in which the farmers described what they found.

Mrs Carole Cherrett found two dead calves and she described the injuries to the first one: *'Its back end had been opened up and its tail and an ear cut off. I felt sick,'* she said. The second body was discovered by Mr Brian Cherrett, who gave the following details: *'One ear had been slashed off and its tail area had been completely cut around like you cut out an apple core. There was a cut where its testicles would have been and another on the inside of its leg. The tail and ear were missing. There's no doubt it was deliberate. I would just like to get my hands on whoever did it.'*

Although the animals had had the ear with the identification tag removed, the actual metal tag was left beside each body. Mr Cherrett could not understand how this could have been done without leaving some part of the ear attached to the tag.

The injuries to these calves appear very similar to those inflicted on cattle in the USA and the cut on the inside leg has similarities with a mutilation attack on a sheep on Dartmoor, of which we will hear more in Part III. The curious aftermath of this incident involving the bellowing circle of cows has already been recounted in Chapter 13.

Two other Dorset farmers, Gordon Wing and Charlie Riggs, also found dead calves amongst their herd and Mr Wing gave the following account: *'We found two dead calves. One had had pneumonia but the other had been perfectly fit. It was stretched out on the grass with its neck and ears cut out. We are afraid that what has been happening elsewhere to horses may now be happening to our calves.'*

The police investigated the killings and the Criminal Investigation Department at Blandford arranged for a post mortem examination to be carried out, the conclusions of which are unknown.

Let us now look at some interesting cases of mysterious sheep deaths, first in Northern Ireland. On 12th April 2005, the *Belfast Telegraph and Derry Journal* carried the story of farmer Gerald McLaughlin, who had endured a fourteen-year campaign of sheep mutilations on his farm at Feeney, near Claudy, Londonderry. Since 1991 Mr Mclaughlin claimed to have lost three hundred and thirty nine sheep to the mystery mutilators and commented:

> *Fourteen years ago I was up on the farm one day and there was a sheep with blood running out of her mouth. Her tongue had been cut out. I called in to the police immediately. Two or three days later there were more. Fourteen years later the police are still handling the case. They say they cannot point the finger at whoever did it – they said their hands are tied.*
>
> *The police did a survey of the area where we live and nobody else has had any problems. I suspect it was someone living very locally but the police are doing nothing about it. The tongues were completely and cleanly cut out. A knife would have to have been used and so this could only have been committed by a human. This is brutal and barbaric cruelty to lambs. This should be investigated.*

The police had denied surveillance for Mr McLaughlin's farm and stated that they did not have the resources available for such an operation. Given the problems of paramilitary violence and terrorism that plagued Ulster for so long, it's perhaps not surprising that the police were unable to provide the kind of long-term surveillance that Mr McLaughlin asked for.

A police spokesman made the following statement to the press: *'It is a bit of a mystery. There is no evidence as such as to how the sheep have died. The sheep are found dead with their tongues removed but the amount of blood present is not as much as you would expect had their tongues been removed when alive. So the case remains at a standstill. There is not enough evidence.'*

The police added that they had arranged for post-mortem examinations to be carried out by Department of Agriculture vets, and that *'None of these examinations has been able to establish the cause of death of the sheep – mainly lambs, but also some full grown ewes. The tongues appear to have been removed after death has occurred.'* I find this last statement to be incredible, that government vets were unable to even speculate what killed these animals. As regards the removal of the tongues, I would suggest that the lack of blood in the mouth has led the vets to conclude that the removal was done after death. However, the lack of blood at animal mutilation crime scenes is a recurring aspect of the attacks. The farmer submitted written statements and photographs to prove that some of the victims were still alive when mutilated.

Mr McLaughlin and his wife were refused a meeting with the Chief Constable, Hugh Orde. They made four applications to the Foyle DCU, demanding an investigation into the attacks. Their applications were unsuccessful.

The large number of sheep deaths and the long catalogue of mutilation attacks on Mr McLaughlin's farm are quite extraordinary, and I cannot accept the theory postulated that the killings are in any way ritualistic, which is a common theory for these mutilations.

The next case involves a series of attacks at Tywyn, South Gwynedd in Wales. The attacks took place over a two-year period and were reported in the *Sunday Express* on 12th May 1985.

In 1984 a local farmer, Major Corbett of Tywyn, and his neighbour, Mr Richard Lewis, began finding dead sheep with strange puncture marks approximately two centimetres in size. There were also severe internal injuries. Up to twenty lambs at a time would die in these mysterious circumstances and in 1984 there were around one hundred and twenty deaths, the majority of which were on the farms owned by Major Corbett and Richard Lewis. A major investigation ensued with the police, local vets and farmers involved. Many theories were put forward and, one by one, they were ruled out. There appeared to be no explanation for the mysterious puncture marks, or the deaths. There was one other tantalising clue about the killings, which were directed at the two farms. The victims were almost exclusively one type of lamb, pure-white Welsh ewes. Brown and off-white lambs and male lambs were almost always ignored.

The killings stopped in October 1984, then started again in May 1985. I presume that the attacks may have declined after 1985, as there appears to have been no further interest from the *Sunday Express* or any other national newspapers in this perplexing case. The small area in which the attacks were carried out and their serial nature shows consistency with other UK cases of mutilation attacks on sheep. The exclusive profile of the victims is also interesting.

The cases detailed here are but a small number of the recorded cases. It should be noted that one researcher claims that there are a thousand cases in the UK alone – these are only the ones we know about! The fact is that the attacks on sheep in particular are often reported as ritualistic killings or predation by ABCs (alien big cats), such as pumas. In Part III we shall see how a major case of serial sheep attacks, described as ritualistic occult killings, was exposed as being something far more sinister.

Part III
The Dartmoor Sheep Attacks

18

The First Attack

During early March 2005 I telephoned Nicola Holdgate of the *Western Morning News* Library department. The purpose of the call was to see if they had any records of strange animal deaths on Dartmoor in the last couple of years. It was obvious, speaking to Nicola, that she had a great love of animals and abhorred animal cruelty. She gave me details of two cases that had occurred which involved sheep.

The first case from 9th July 2003 involved some sheep being run down at Yelverton on the edge of Dartmoor by some maniacal driver who, presumably, felt that such mindless killings were a suitable outlet for a night's exuberance. Five sheep died at the scene and another two were put down afterwards. Police found tyre marks at the scene which indicated that the driver had driven at the sheep then reversed over the bodies. Police were seeking the driver of a blue J-registered Rover. The incident had horrified not only the owner of the sheep but also the local inspector for the Royal Society for the Prevention of Cruelty to Animals. This case was only strange for the fact that you had to wonder about the mentality of the perpetrator or perpetrators.

The second case was much more recent and far more intriguing. Seven sheep had been found dead on a remote hillside at Sampford Spiney on Dartmoor. The bodies had been arranged in a seven-pointed star or heptagon and the story was given an occult slant. The BBC news carried the story under the heading 'Dead sheep found in "occult star"'. The *Western Morning News* headline was 'Mystery of sheep killed for ritual' while its evening sister paper the *Evening Herald* carried 'Police hunt for Dartmoor sheep strangler'. The killings, which had taken place on 2nd January 2005, were regarded as occult, satanist sacrifices. A local farmer, Chris Cole, who had lost two sheep in the incident, was quoted as saying, *'It's the first time in my memory anything like this has happened.'* He also said, *'It's not that easy to get the animals to that site. There must have been a well organized group because they managed to kill all the animals and get them to that one place in one night, that's not very easy if you're on your own.'* The police were also baffled and could find no tyre tracks.

PC Steve Saunders said, *'I haven't a clue how the sheep got there.'* The police were treating the incident as a case of criminal damage. This was just the kind of incident I was looking for and there were names of people in the article, so I could contact them and find out more.

I decided to telephone Hazel Macallister who wrote the story for the *Western Morning News*. I was disappointed to hear that she had not been to the crime scene and that her information had come from telephone enquiries to the police and Chris Cole. I needed to get to the primary source. I remembered the advice of researcher Margaret Fry – you have to visit the scene and get information first hand if you want to get near the truth. I decided to make an appointment with Chris Cole and visit the scene of the crime myself. It was to prove a momentous decision.

I rang the Coles' farm and spoke to his wife. We made an appointment for Friday 1st April 2005. As my car sped down the M5 and onto the A30 westbound, little did I realise how familiar this journey would become. Onto the A386 I glanced to my left at the rolling patchwork of green fields lying in the shadows of the majestic Dartmoor tors. I soon arrived at the outskirts of Tavistock, a beautiful market town, rich in history. I took the B3357 and headed for Sampford Spiney. I soon realised that Sampford Spiney was quite a large area in its own right and that the particular location I needed was Whitchurch, which was situated to the northern edge of Sampford Spiney. Despite my problems with the local geography I arrived at Coomhill Farm, tucked away at the end of a dirt track, bordered by tall thick hedges.

I met Mrs Cole and her son Adrian, who had taken pictures at the crime scene with his mobile phone. It was one of these images that was used by the BBC in their press release. I told Mrs Cole that I was researching strange animal deaths on Dartmoor and gave her some information about animal mutilations elsewhere in the UK and USA. We were joined by Chris Cole who kindly offered to take me to the crime scene, suggesting that we go in his four by four. We were accompanied by Adrian.

The weather was beautiful and it was difficult to imagine that in this idyllic setting there could be such sinister goings on as described in the press. I was to find out later that the area changed its mood after dark and that this picturesque locality belied a sinister atmosphere and was quite a dangerous place to be during the night. While we drove across open heathland and dirt tracks, Chris Cole told me that BBC television had interviewed him not at the crime scene, but just outside his farm some two miles away. Had no one from the media visited the crime scene?

We eventually arrived at the scene of the killings and my first impression was how open it was and indeed, nowhere near as inaccessible as I had imagined. Looking due north I faced Barn Hill, while to the right the ground, peppered with gorse bushes and granite boulders, sloped upwards to Pew Tor. On my left there were the stone walls of Moortown Farm and just a few hundred yards further down the entrance to the farm was masked by a group of tall trees inhabited by a vibrant colony of rooks. The bodies had been found in an area roughly 30 metres square. The location was remote in one sense, but not that far from habitation and Tavistock was just three miles away.

Chris began telling me more about the killings which contained factors that just didn't add up. He and his family had farmed in the area for generations and nothing like this had ever happened. He said, *'At first I thought it was a lightning strike which happens now and again, but I soon realised it wasn't.'* Chris told me that a group of people would have been needed and yet there were no tyre marks, despite the fact that the ground was soft. The ground had been 'poached' in two separate areas about five or six metres apart. Chris explained the term 'poaching' as when sheep are standing in one area, particularly as a group, their feet trample the same piece of ground which eventually brings moisture to the surface and this gives the ground a muddy appearance. The sheep seemed to have been grouped in the two holding areas as evidenced by the poaching, but there were no footprints or marks in the ground to indicate temporary fencing of the two areas. How could they have been kept in the two corral areas? Chris also mentioned that if the sheep were being held and systematically killed by the perpetrators why didn't they 'mess' themselves as often happened when they panicked during transportation by lorry for slaughter. The fleeces of some of the victims had bits of leaves and twigs in them that indicated that they might have been dragged along the ground. The method of killing the sheep was also highly unusual, all had their necks broken. Finally, despite the alleged ritual nature of the killings, there was no blood on the bodies and none at the scene. Chris explained how the sheep that grazed in that particular area were roughly split between his own flock and that of two other farmers, Michael Doidge and Mary Alford. He was puzzled as to why the sheep had been killed at this particular location as they had a tendency to graze further up the common at Feather Tor, approximately one third of a mile away, unless there was stormy weather, which brought them further down towards the farm and shelter. In all his years on the moor Chris had never experienced such a bizarre incident.

During the examination of the crime scene Chris told me something that the newspapers had failed to mention. One sheep had survived the attack and had been found about fifty yards away. I found out a few months later that the surviving sheep was found by walkers in a drainage ditch. The animal was so traumatised that when it was lifted from the ditch it bolted into Moortown Farm, across a cattle grid, and into a back area of the farmhouse. Despite being next to a herb garden the sheep did not eat and remained there until found twenty-four hours later. What had terrified the animal to such an extent?

I took some soil samples from the 'poached' areas and took some photos of the surrounding area. I could not accept the alleged occult motive and the more questions I asked the more remote that possibility became. The three of us returned to Coomhill Farm and over a cup of coffee I asked Chris and Adrian to do a rough sketch showing the approximate layout of the bodies. They referred several times to Adrian's mobile phone pictures and eventually came up with a rough diagram. I have to say that it scarcely looked like a seven-pointed star to me.

I thanked the Coles and made my way to Tavistock, and enjoyed a meat pastie as I sat in my car reflecting on what I had learnt during the morning. Following my brief lunch I made my way to Tavistock police station, situated in the main square. I was disappointed to learn that PC Steve Saunders, who was the Wildlife Liaison Officer, was not on duty. I would have to telephone him at a later date.

I was now hoping that I might interview Chris Warren of the Westmoor Veterinary Centre, who had been called to the scene in January and performed an autopsy to establish the cause of death. Unfortunately, Chris Warren was operating that afternoon and was unable to see me. However the receptionist took my mobile phone number and assured me that Mr Warren would call me when he had finished.

I drove out of Tavistock in the early afternoon and headed along the B3357 towards Princetown, eventually picking up the B3212 which would take me to Postbridge, not far from the scene of the ponies massacre in 1977. As I travelled along this road, dominated on both sides by breathtaking scenery and a remoteness not rivalled anywhere else in England, I stopped now and again to take pictures of the landscape. I got to Postbridge which is a small village that boasts a visitors centre and extensive car park to cater for the numerous visitors to the area. I parked my car and browsed through the books on sale before asking the lady at the counter if she knew anything about the Dartmoor ponies incident of 1977. She did not, but anxious to help she rang the local park warden and asked if he knew anything. I took up the phone and spoke to him. *'What happened was this,'* he said and then told me that the ponies had all died in extreme weather and the bodies were covered by snow. When the snow melted the bodies were discovered. How did the bodies become mangled and torn, I asked? He had no answer. I thanked him for his trouble and continued my journey.

Time was getting on and I was concerned about the reception on my mobile phone. Frankly, it's a bit hit and miss on Dartmoor as the national park authorities do not allow mobile phone masts – quite right too! I was parked in a lay-by when a call came through from Chris Warren. He said that when he arrived at the scene the bodies were still warm, indicating that the deaths had occurred within the last eighteen hours. All the victims had their necks broken, and the method used seemed to be identical in each case. The victims had not been strangled as claimed in the press because there was no indication of any ligature marks around the necks. The bodies had some bruising and small puncture marks to the skin, suggesting that they may have been poked or prodded with some sharp instrument or stick. A toxicology report was not carried out because of the prohibitive cost involved.

Mr Warren said that the method of killing was highly unusual as they had apparently been lifted, then the heads twisted, to break the necks. While Mr Warren had seen such rare deaths occur in innocent circumstances, where sheep rear up and accidentally twist their heads, for this to be done deliberately to seven sheep was, in his opinion, quite inexplicable. He commented on the lack of blood at the scene and said that some sheep had lost eyes, presumably because of predators. He also commented on the lack of tracks that he would have expected to be left by the perpetrators, and that the extremely alert dogs at Moortown Farm failed to raise any alarm. He also stated that the sheep in question were a poor choice for the illegal meat trade as there was no market for old ewe meat.

The discovery of the bodies had also raised a strange anomaly. A couple out walking their dogs had discovered the dead sheep at approximately 0900 hours. Strangely, he had heard that another lady who had walked her dog in the same area earlier that morning had seen nothing.

Mr Warren said that much had been made of the alleged ritualistic elements of the case, and told me that near Vixen Tor, a local prominent outcrop of rock, there were the remains of a Neolithic temple. He did not think there was any evidence to substantiate pagan or satanic involvement in the crime and reiterated his belief that the killings were inexplicable.

When I got home my head was full of it all. I was now convinced that this was nothing to do with paganism, satanism or anything else to do with the occult. This it seemed was another cold case and until there was another attack in the area there was a limit to what could be achieved. I maintained a strange belief that what I had stumbled across in Moortown had a lot more mileage to it, and I was right!

Four days later, on Tuesday 5th April, I telephoned PC Steve Saunders of Tavistock police who was kind enough to give me a review of the case as he saw it. He confirmed the dead sheep were found at 0900 hours by a couple from the nearby camping park who were out walking their dog. PC Saunders was unaware that a lady walking her dog earlier that morning had seen nothing. He was perplexed by the fact that none of the dogs at Moortown Farm had been alerted, especially as they had begun barking when he was within two hundred yards of the farm. PC Saunders made the point that as sound carries further at night it is very strange that the dogs did not react to the presence of what must have been several individuals and their 4 × 4 vehicle.

PC Saunders made no comment about the lack of tracks at the killing area and maintained his belief that the deaths were the result of rustlers taking sheep for the 'smokie' trade. ('Smokies' are sheep that are stolen, killed, then have their fleeces burnt off and sold illegally through the meat trade.) PC Saunders said there were rich pickings for such criminal activities and that while the area was remote it was still in close proximity to the B3357 and Plymouth was only ten miles away, He further suggested that the criminals involved had probably brought two vehicles, a van and a 4 × 4 in order to carry out their activities. In addition, he said that the farmers would have difficulty in establishing how many sheep they had lost because of the difficulties in doing a stock take of their animals.

PC Saunders confirmed that the case remained unsolved and that the police were keeping an open mind about it, to the extent that they would consider a ritualistic motive if further evidence came to light that supported it. However, he remained convinced that rustlers were responsible.

I felt that the two suggested motives for the killings did not stand up to scrutiny and had been put forward more in hope that they offered an explanation for something that was truly inexplicable. When I reviewed the facts there were holes everywhere. If these were killings carried out by some fringe occult group, where was the altar? Where was the blood that would inevitably come from a sacrifice? Why break the necks in such a bizarre fashion? Where were the tracks and marks of those attending the 'ceremony'?

If the killings were the result of criminals involved in the illegal meat trade why come to such a remote, yet vulnerable location where the animals are allowed to roam over a wide area? Where did they park the van that PC Saunders reckons they must have brought to remove all the sheep? Why did they leave the seven dead sheep, especially as no one appears to have witnessed anything? Why were the dogs at Moortown Farm not alerted by all the activity? Why did they kill the sheep in such a bizarre fashion? Let's review the main features of this incident:

1. The killings were carried out during the night of a full moon.
2. The sheep all died with broken necks.
3. There were no tracks or marks at the scene.
4. The sheep had been corralled in two small areas for up to thirty minutes before being killed.
5. There were no marks to indicate fencing around the corral areas.
6. The dogs at Moortown Farm were not disturbed by the perpetrators.
7. There was no blood on the bodies or at the scene.
8. Some of the sheep had lost their eyes.
9. There appears to be an anomaly regarding when the killings were carried out, as a witness claimed to have seen nothing at about 0700 hours.
10. The bodies were not left in a star shape or heptagon.
11. Some of the bodies had leaves and twigs in the fleeces indicating that they may have been dragged.
12. There was no altar.

I did not yet know it but some of these features would come back to haunt what would become a huge investigation.

19

Down on the Farm

The issue of the two corral areas still puzzled me and I decided to contact Linda Moulton-Howe through David Cayton and the APFU. My hope was that Linda, who is probably the world's leading authority on animal mutilations, might come up with a similar case from her extensive files. On 7th June 2005 she emailed me. With Linda's permission I quote from the first part of her email:

> *There was a case in the 1970s in Sterling, Colorado, in which a bull was found dead and mutilated (classic ear, eye, jaw flesh, tongue, genitals and rectum excised). But it had dug an 8-inch-deep hole with its head. Yet, there was not a sign that any of the four legs had moved at all in the powder-dry pasture dirt. I have Polaroid pictures of this animal from the Logan County Sheriff's office. As former Sheriff Tex Graves told me 'Whatever did this was able to hold this big animal in place while those excisions were made and left only the head to move. What could do that?'*

Following my trip to Dartmoor it was apparent that I needed to speak to the other two farmers who had lost sheep in the January attack. It was with some difficulty that I managed to obtain Mary Alford's phone number. I rang her in late April and gave her a few brief details about myself. Mary told me to ring back in order that she could 'check me out'. Her reticence to talk was not surprising given the amount of publicity she had been subjected to over her ownership of nearby Vixen Tor.

The Vixen Tor dispute had occurred when Mary had prohibited access to the rock outcrop because of the potential of public liability claims – if someone injured themselves on the Tor then she, the owner, would be liable. The closure of the Tor had angered various institutions, including the British Mountaineering Council. The BMC felt that their members should have free access to climb all over the Vixen Tor rock and an acrimonious dispute had ensued involving both the BMC and local ramblers, who were similarly opposed to the closure.

The Alfords had also locked horns with the Department of the Environment, Food and Rural Affairs (DEFRA) over the cultivation of land close to Vixen Tor. A high-profile legal dispute resulted in victory for Mary Alford over this issue. Plainly, Mary was a quite a force to be reckoned with. It had been mentioned to me that the Vixen Tor dispute provided a possible motive for the sheep attack on 2nd January. This, like the other suggested reasons for attacking the sheep, did not have any logic or sound reasoning, after all why kill other farmers' sheep as well?

I rang Mary Alford again and she kindly discussed the circumstances of the attack with me. She said that she and her partner had invited some guests to supper and that their friends had left the farm house at about 0200 hours on 2nd January. The night was beautifully clear, due to the full moon, and they had seen and heard no one despite having a perfect view across the common. I wrote to Mary the following day enclosing a copy of the body map put together by Chris and Adrian Cole. In the reply to my letter Mary included some very good photographs of the crime scene taken on a digital camera. These photographs were far superior in quality to the long-range images taken on Adrian Cole's mobile phone. The lie of the bodies looked quite unnatural and in no way did the layout of the corpses resemble a seven-pointed star. Mary concluded the letter with the comment, *'Keep in touch I am very interested.'*

During May my wife and I decided we needed a short break and we booked a cottage in the country for a few days. My wife chose the small village of Milton Combe, set in a small valley a couple of miles from Yelverton which in turn was only a few miles from Tavistock. I sensed she knew I was keen to visit the Dartmoor area again and probably thought we might as well combine the break with an opportunity for me to do a little more research. I made arrangements to visit Mary Alford at Moortown Farm during the July week we were on holiday. I was pleased to find that Mary had requested PC Saunders and Chris Warren to attend the meeting that was obviously designed as a fact-finding conference into the killings.

On Wednesday 13th July 2005 I made my way to Moortown Farm and just after seven o'clock on an idyllic evening I parked outside the splendid farmhouse. I was greeted by Mary Alford and her partner Frank Yeo and it was suggested we sit at a granite table in the front garden. I was told that PC Saunders was unable to attend and that Chris Warren had also sent his apologies because of a meeting he had to attend elsewhere. This was a blow, as I was keen to meet both of them and felt that they were likely to be more forthcoming in a face to face meeting than during a telephone discussion.

I began by telling them about myself and my background, before leading on to the details of my involvement in the case and how my original research into the Dartmoor ponies incident had led to an investigation encompassing a number of strange animal deaths.

I showed Mary Alford some of the APFU photographs from mutilation cases on the Shropshire/Welsh border and stated my view that there was an advanced technology at work in these killings. I did my best to avoid the U (UFO) word.

We reviewed the body map and Mary made a couple of alterations. She also told me that the sheep were grazing on the lower part of the common and not up at Feather Tor as suggested by Chris Cole.

I asked about the eighth sheep, the one that had survived. It had been found in a drainage ditch by the same people who had discovered the bodies. They managed to lift the animal out of the ditch, whereupon it had bolted across a cattle grid up to the farmhouse, where it hid by Mr Yeo's office. The sheep remained by the office, which was adjacent to a herb garden, until it was discovered twenty-four hours later. During this time the sheep, which was evidently traumatised, did not eat at all despite being next to a huge supply of food. When the animal was examined, scratch marks identical to those on the dead sheep were found. Mr Yeo said these marks were not pin pricks as stated by the vet, but scratches.

Mary and Frank told me that they had entertained guests for supper on 2nd January and when they left nothing untoward was noticed. They had three lively dogs at the farm and the rookery in the trees that screened the front of the house provided a fairly sensitive alarm system.

I gave them my opinion that the killings were nothing to do with the occult. My reasoning being that there was no sacrificial altar, no blood and the bodies had been scattered randomly, not in a clearly defined 'star' shape as had been suggested. Frank Yeo then said that the day after the killings they were contacted by a friend who had claimed, without prior knowledge of the circumstances, that seven sheep had been involved and that it was an occult sacrifice to the god Janus. Furthermore, the lady gave details of how the bodies were laid out. Frank felt that the body map could be interpreted as confirming this claim.

I decided to come clean and discuss the possibility of extraterrestrial involvement in these killings and showed some more photos from the APFU file. This, I suggested, was the most likely cause, especially when the high technology and bizarre nature of the attacks in Shropshire and Wales were considered. To emphasise my argument I said that there were similarities to all these cases, because similar scratches had been found on the APFU victims as well.

Frank claimed an intimate knowledge of the Asian and Muslim meat trade and was not convinced by the argument I had put forward. He claimed that the removal of certain organs from the victims could be done to satisfy the demand from the Far East.

Mary had to leave the meeting at this point and Frank continued his argument that humans were responsible. He stated that the manpower required for catching the sheep on the moor (no easy task I assure you) was ten to fifteen men experienced with sheep, and four or five individuals as back up with specialist nets for containing the sheep. Dart guns might have been used and several vehicles would be needed to transport this army of sheep killers. Frank seemed to defeat his own argument, although it was understandably difficult to work out how the killings had been done in human terms and the motive for carrying them out. I ask you, it has to be a bit weird when UFOs and extraterrestrials are regarded as the most logical explanation!

Frank gave me some details of the dispute over Vixen Tor and told me that Mary had been violently assaulted during the dispute and had to be taken to hospital by air ambulance. I was stunned and disgusted that the arguments over Vixen Tor had spiralled into such violence. The individual responsible for the attack, the son of a police sergeant, had escaped with a fine and no custodial sentence. I assumed that the Alfords' confidence in the police would be jaundiced by this incident.

The meeting concluded at ten past eight and I agreed to carry out further research into the occult and the festival of Janus in particular. I warned them both that there could be another attack and that the full moon phase (three days before, three days after) might be the time of an attack.

The remainder of our holiday went all too quickly and when we returned home I felt obliged to do my best to check out the occult angle, although I felt that the crime scene had not yielded a single clue to suggest pagan or satanic involvement.

I decided to contact a friend of mine called Steve Jones. Steve was a lay preacher who had studied and had a deep interest in paganism. We had worked at the same company for several years and shared a similar sense of humour and a hero worship of the legendary Jimi Hendrix. My untimely, 'blood on the carpet', removal from the company in 1999 had not diminished our friendship and we would meet up from time to time, usually in a backstreet pub where the beer was good, and discuss literature, films and music. Steve was different and preferred to discuss intellectual subjects. Money was of secondary importance to him.

On Thursday 18th August Steve collected me from my house and we drove the short distance to the Walsall Arms an interesting pub hidden in a narrow street surrounded by factories on the south side of Walsall. We ordered two pints of beer, sat down and discussed the recent goings on at my former employers. Our discussions usually followed this format and after I had made a disparaging comment about one of my former colleagues I took the opportunity to ask Steve about paganism.

Steve began by telling me there was a popular misconception about pagans. Because the pagans weren't Christians it was assumed that they were satanists or anti Christ. The pagans had a deep philosophy about the sanctity of all life and to demonstrate this point Steve told me a story about a new pagan initiate who was at a pagan weekend camp. The new recruit had been given the task of collecting wood for the camp fire and duly went out into the forest and collected a bundle of what he supposed would be suitable material for the fire. On reporting to the camp elders, he was gently admonished for bringing old branches that were covered in lichen. Lichen is, of course, a living organism and because of this the pagans' philosophy on the sanctity of life determined that the branches could not be burned. He was sent out again and told to bring the 'right kind of wood'.

Steve stated the pagan motto *'Do what thou wilt so long as it affects no other'*. It was obvious that the pagans were unlikely suspects in the Dartmoor sheep killings.

Over the next few weeks I looked into the so-called Festival of Janus. The festival was pagan in origin and had been taken into Roman mythology and worship. The Romans had sacrificed a single animal during this festival, not seven. It appeared that the number seven referred to the Seven Hills of Rome not the number of animals to be sacrificed.

I felt that the research I had carried out reinforced my argument that the sheep killings were nothing to do with the pagans or the occult. During September 2005 I began to read as much as I could about the animal mutilation problem through a steady stream of papers and articles. The seven sheep deaths seemed to be slipping into unexplained history when I received a dramatic phone call that was to change the whole direction of my investigations.

20

The Second and Third Attacks

It was a bright Monday morning in October 2005 and I was driving through the backstreets of Wolverhampton city centre searching for an elusive parking space when the call came through on my mobile. I pulled into a vacant parking spot and took the call. It was my wife and she relayed a call that had been taken on our answerphone from Mary Alford. Another attack! I shoved some coins into the parking meter and rang Mary on my mobile. She sounded distressed and gave me details of the two attacks.

The attacks had taken place on Friday 14th and Saturday 15th October, three days before the full moon and involved six sheep. This was later amended to eight sheep, although both the police and the media reported six victims. The first attack was carried out in a field belonging to Mary and the four victims appeared to be laid out in a rough square. The Saturday night killings were done on Barn Hill which was only a few hundred yards from the field. There was no apparent order to the lie of the bodies. Mary said that some of the eyes were missing and not pecked out by natural predators, which appeared to be keeping their distance from the corpses. I asked her if the bodies were still in situ. They were, she said. I asked her to check to see if the tongues had been removed. If the tongues had been excised it would provide a clear link to other mutilations in the United Kingdom and the USA.

It seemed ages before Mary rang me back. The call was devastating. Yes, all the tongues had been removed by a clear cut to the back of the mouth, and no blood!

I was shamefully elated by this news, as I had rightly predicted both the timing of the attacks and some of the mutilations. The Alfords had lost eight more sheep and suffered the trauma of an attack from perpetrators whose motives and methods were unknown. I had to reassure Mary that the attacks were not personal against her despite the fact that she had lost more sheep than anyone else. Whatever it was, the area from Pork Hill down to the track that separated the farms from the moor seemed an important factor in the killings.

Mary Alford's lack of faith in the police was not repaired by the somewhat unusual police presence. The local police sent scene of crime officers (SOCO) and apparently took many photos of the bodies in the field. This activity by the police would become an important issue in the series of killings, as we shall see later.

On Wednesday 19th October the BBC carried the sheep killings story. The following day the *Western Morning News* and its sister paper the *Herald* also ran the story. I received a cutting from the *Sun* newspaper and although the article was quite brief it was an indication that the killings were creeping towards national news. The media reported the killings as further occult crimes with suitably lurid headlines.

Despite the headlines blaming the killings on occultists and satanists I realised that we had now established a definite link to animal mutilations in Shropshire as well as the United States of America and elsewhere. The removal of the tongues by deep excision to the back of the mouth and the removal of one eye were classic attack symptoms.

I decided to contact Nicola Holdgate at the *Western Morning News* library. I told her there was now an established link to killings elsewhere in the UK and USA and that I was prepared to give information to the *Western Morning News* editorial team. I have to say that this was a very risky gamble.

I was contacted by Linda Moulton-Howe on 26th October asking if I would do an interview for Dreamland Radio. I was only too willing. And when a reporter from the *Western Morning News* interviewed me by phone, I thought I was becoming a media personality. On the evening of 27th October I took a call from the editor of the *Western Morning News.* We talked for nearly an hour and I was sure a full-page spread might follow. My reason for going public was to bring the issue of animal mutilations into the public domain. This in turn would bring other cases to light, so I thought.

The Dreamland Radio interview went ahead and I gave Linda what details I could regarding the three attacks. I also told her about the ponies incident and was surprised to hear that she was very familiar with the case. The interview appeared on Linda's Earthfiles website and I hoped for some feedback. Unfortunately, none ever came.

I waited and waited for the *Western Morning News* to carry my interview. To this day, nothing has appeared. I emailed the newspaper on 3rd November saying that I was coming to Tavistock on 14th November and would be happy to give them a further interview. They never replied. When I think of it, this is not surprising. The *Western Morning News* is not going to cause mass panic by saying that livestock in the south-west are being attacked by aliens! I realised how stupid I was to think that they could have printed such an article.

In late October Mary Alford sent me some photos she had taken of the bodies and general crime scene. I was grateful for the pictures, but very frustrated that I was unable to get to the scene of the crime myself and take my own photos and details of the killings. I felt that vital information was being lost and I just knew there would be another attack. The point was, it was a four hundred and twenty mile round trip, getting quickly to the scene of the crime was going to be difficult. I made a momentous decision that would change the investigation and my life as well.

I had what appeared to be a completely stupid and risky plan. It meant going on the offensive and it required back up. Myself and some volunteers would mount an all-night surveillance on key nights during the full moon phase and monitor any activity going on. Where were the volunteers going to come from? What idiotic individual would consider such an undertaking? Well, me for one! I couldn't do it alone and so I set out to find like minded people. It goes without saying that the sensible people did not want to know. My wife had extreme doubts that anyone would be prepared to join me. However, cometh the hour, cometh the man. I rang Dave Gillham of the Cornwall UFO group and asked him what he thought of my plan and did he know anyone daft enough to get involved? Incredibly, Dave quietly mumbled, *'Yeah, all right. I'll come along. I go with the flow.'*

I thanked Dave profusely and wondered whether he would have second thoughts – who could blame him if he did. A night on Dartmoor in the freezing cold looking for sheep killers, lets face it, you'd think it was a scenario from one of those excruciating television programmes where the contestant has to endure the unendurable in order to get the prize.

I made plans straight away.

21

Night 1 – Beam Me Up!

I made arrangements to stop at a pleasant little hotel just outside Tavistock for two nights, between 14th and 16th November 2005. Although I intended to do a complete night of surveillance I planned to 'crash out' in the early morning and sleep until lunchtime, leaving the afternoon free for researching.

I arrived at Pork Hill car park at about 1400 hours and spent five minutes surveying the stunning view across Tavistock and beyond. I had made arrangements to see Mary Alford at about three o'clock so I had time to drive around the area and acquaint myself more fully with the lie of the land. I discovered a patch of ground accessed by well-worn parallel tyre tracks that was just off the track that ran around and through Moortown. I decided that this would make a good place to park overnight and its close proximity to Pew Tor was an added advantage. Dave and I would call this LUP 1 (laying-up point one). I shamefully took this expression from a book I had read about the SAS. Well, let's be honest, there was more than a hint of 'Who dares, wins' about this whole operation!

I met Mary Alford late in the afternoon and she kindly agreed to take me to the area where the latest killings had occurred. I have to say that I doubted we could get to the upper reaches of Barn Hill, but the red Land Rover showed what real off-road driving was!

Mary showed me the killing area, which was near the top of Barn Hill. It was so remote. I had to ask myself why anyone would come to such a place in the middle of the night and carry out these killings. Mary also pointed out what she described as a makeshift altar with a group of three rocks forming a fleur-de-lys pattern at the foot. This was where they carried out the killings, she stated authoritatively. I was not so sure, although there did appear to have been some activity that had taken place by the 'altar'. The vegetation appeared to have been trampled and the yellow discolouration was something I should have paid more heed to. I was to find out later that the mutilators have been known to change the structure of vegetation during their attacks.

I took some pictures of the killing area and gazed in wonder at just how beautiful this place could be on a bright sunny day. Mary took us back to the farm and as I prepared to leave I assured her that if there were any developments I would let her know in the morning.

I booked into the hotel and checked all the equipment that had been provided. I decided to drive into Tavistock, which was about four miles away, and visit the police station in the hope that I might speak to PC Steve Saunders, who had dealt with the January attack. I drove to Bedford Square, situated in the centre of Tavistock. The baronial façade of the police station was fronted by several police vehicles. I was surprised to find that the police station kept strict office hours, nine to five, and that the door to the station was firmly shut. Disappointed by this example of eroding public services, I decided to head off towards the A30 and journey down to Cornwall and pick Dave up.

It was about twenty past seven and I took what I thought was the road to Launceston. I drove through several small villages and hamlets and the thing that struck me was the darkness. There was a virtual blackout! It was some time before I saw another car and gradually it dawned on me that I was lost. I stopped at a crossroads in a village that appeared to be observing a curfew and took my bearings from a fingerpost that only revealed the name it was pointing to when I got within three feet of it. Where was everybody? I managed to establish that I was drifting in a north-easterly direction into a remote part of north Dartmoor. I would learn from this and never trust my hitherto strong sense of direction again. The relief I felt when the A30 slip road came into view was tangible. I stopped momentarily and telephoned Dave Gillham to tell him I was forty minutes behind schedule.

I eventually got to Dave's daughter's house near Indian Queens, just off the A30. I was greeted by Dave, struggling with a huge flashlight that he'd been charging up for the best part of twenty-four hours. *'They'll know where we are when I flash this at them!'* he proclaimed. Who 'they' were he did not say. We jumped into the car and set off towards Tavistock.

Although this was my first meeting with Dave – we had spoken at length on the phone – I soon realised that he was good company and that the night would not be boring. Dave spoke non stop about anything and everything and the journey to Tavistock passed quickly. We turned onto the B3357 and headed out of Tavistock, towards Pork Hill.

There were three other cars in the car park when we arrived at about 10.30. There was regular traffic on the B3357, then, at eleven o'clock, the other cars disappeared and the intermittent passing headlights of the local traffic ceased. We decided to change location and I suggested we moved to LUP 1, the parking area I had identified earlier in the day.

The time was getting on for midnight and a thick mist had descended on that part of the moor. We took the decision to mount a patrol which would take us towards Moortown Farm and up past the scene of the January killings. Progress was difficult and the visibility was deteriorating fast. My concern was that we would get lost and could be wandering around for ages. The conditions for walking were, to say the least, treacherous. During the day the area could be idyllic – but at night you needed a good torch and night vision to avoid the numerous holes, rocks and culverts that are a feature of that part of Dartmoor. The time was nearly half past midnight and I told Dave that we would have to abandon the patrol and return to the car. I didn't like quitting, but to proceed any further when visibility was so poor seemed the only option.

The time was approaching one o'clock in the morning as we sat in the car, with Dave talking non stop. Only the occasional bite into a Mars Bar caused him to pause as I sat attentively, listening to the story of his life. All of a sudden I became aware of what initially appeared to be the headlights of a vehicle. The beam of light, however, was going across the track and seemed to be coming from the field on the opposite side of the road. The beam seemed to be pulsing and was yellowish in colour. Approximately one metre across, the beam penetrated the thick mist, which turned brilliant white as the beam cut through it. I was stunned and terrified! Dave was unaware of what I was seeing as he sat in the passenger seat. My jaw must have sagged as the beam was in my sight for some eight to ten seconds. I could not get the words out and, to be frank, I was too scared to get out of the car. (It would be almost a year later before I confessed my lack of courage to Dave.) The beam stopped suddenly, as if terminated by a switch. I told Dave what I had just seen and we both leapt out of the car. We could see nothing and Dave's torch, more reminiscent of a World War Two anti-aircraft searchlight, proved ineffective. This was an unnerving experience for me and was the last thing I expected to see on our 'stake out'. To this day, I have no idea what it was that I saw that night – it would not be the last bizarre experience I would have on this dark part of Dartmoor.

We decided to make our way back to Pork Hill and drove carefully through the mist that enveloped the landscape like a huge eerie cobweb. The approach to Pork Hill was shrouded in an ever-thickening dense mist. The visibility was down to three or four feet in places. The car crawled uncomfortably towards the summit. We could barely see across the road and on two occasions made abortive attempts to drive into Pork Hill car park, pulling back at the last second when we realised there was a low wall of earth in our way. We finally found the entrance and drove in. It was like parking the car wearing a blindfold. The weather had got the upper hand and we retreated to the parking point along the track by Moortown, where we spent the remainder of our watch.

My notes state that we terminated our surveillance at 5.30 in the morning. I drove Dave back to Indian Queens as he slept contentedly. We arrived about quarter to seven and at Dave's suggestion we went to the local McDonalds. Dave tucked in to a bacon roll while I enjoyed an outsize cup of very strong coffee. Dave told me about a number of UFO sightings he had investigated, in fact only my desire to get back to my hotel prevented him from overloading me with information. We gave each other a comradely hug and I knew I had made a good friend. I got back to the hotel and ate breakfast before retiring to my room and a welcome deep sleep.

That evening, after a meal at the hotel, I decided to take the short drive to Pork Hill and Moortown. The weather was completely different. Why couldn't it have been like this last night, I thought. It was about 10.30 and I summoned up the courage to visit the scene of the light beam again. I parked the car in the same position and got out. It was very, very creepy! I was quite unnerved by the experience and quickly jumped back in the car and drove back to the hotel.

The following morning I was surprised to receive a call from Chris Warren, the vet who had attended the January killings. He suggested that any future post mortems would best be carried out by VLA Starcross, the government-run veterinary laboratory at Exeter. He also stated his belief that the Alfords could be the victims of revenge attacks on their sheep because of the Vixen Tor dispute. I have to say that I regard this theory as a non-starter. Mr Warren said that a powerful man could lift a ram by its horns and twist the head, thus killing it. However, this method of killing is not easy with ewes. An interesting fact that came out of the conversation was that the older Dartmoor farmers preferred to ride horses over the moor rather than drive quad bikes, because horses are very sure-footed and can see in the dark. Mr Warren concluded our conversation with the promise to notify me of any further strange sheep attacks that he became aware of.

Although the first night of surveillance had yielded nothing apart from the strange light beam I was sufficiently encouraged to think in terms of further exploits. I felt there was more mileage in this case and decided to give the sheep deaths a priority over my investigation into the Dartmoor ponies incident.

I decided on another visit to Dartmoor to coincide with the next full moon. I wrote to the local farmers warning them of the possibility of another attack around 15th and 16th December 2005. Knowing the importance of getting to a crime scene early I decided to visit Dartmoor on Friday December 16th. I planned an early start (0400 hours) with a return journey at midday.

I arrived at Pork Hill car park at about seven in the morning. The weather was poor to say the least with razor-edged rain that cut through my weatherproof clothing. Thankfully the rain abated sufficiently for me to walk along the fields that bordered the common, checking for any signs of an attack. There was nothing to report.

I decided it would be a good idea to visit the scene of the light beam incident and take some reference photos. I parked the car in pretty well the same position as 14th November then took four shots, two inside the car and two views of the car looking across the track. The inside shots would show how my view was restricted and the exterior shots would show where the car was. Perhaps it's just as well I did not look too closely at the images as they were later to reveal something quite disturbing. As we shall learn later, these images would challenge my views on several issues. I rang a couple of the farmers and confirmed that all was well and as the weather got worse, I made the long journey home.

22

Night 2 – The Eyes Have It!

It was 12th January 2006 and I was nearing the end of a tortuous week at work. I wanted to do another surveillance night and somehow everything fell into place for it to happen. The date was suitable for Dave and my son in law Darren Rudge was also available and willing to join us. The visit was set for Sunday 15th January and I booked Darren and myself into the same hotel I had used in November.

The trip would be much easier for me as I had always travelled alone. I now had someone to talk to and the journey passed very quickly as Darren and I discussed many topics. I have to say that Darren remained unconvinced about UFOs and as far as he was concerned the sheep attacks required more evidence before he could lay the blame on non-human perpetrators.

We arrived at Pork Hill car park just after one o'clock in the morning and in time to see Dave Gillham scouring the clouded sky with his huge torch. After brief introductions we discussed a plan of action. We agreed to move position to LUP 1 and minutes later we were crawling along the track until we eventually found the spot. We sorted out the various bits of kit and it appeared I had drawn the short straw as I was lumbered with the 'body bag', a rucksack full of everything needed to investigate a crime scene. Dave and I carried small hand torches while Darren had the infrared night sight. Our plan was to follow the route that Dave and I had tried back in November. The British army would call this 'yomping' – for us, at times, it was purgatory. We crossed the area of the first attack and went up the steep slope of Barn Hill. The sky remained dark with no stars visible. We were unsure of just where we were, but plodded on in determined fashion. As the ground levelled into a plateau we could see what appeared to be a large pool of water. We continued straight for it. Only when we reached it did we realise that it was not a pool of water at all, but Pork Hill car park! Once again the darkness had played tricks on us.

Going back was always going to be easier and we changed the route so that we followed the line of fields, which we knew would lead us back towards Moortown and the track. Each field we passed was scanned with our torches for any signs of unusual activity. The sheep were conspicuous by their absence, as this was the time of year that they are brought in off the moor for breeding.

The return patrol had been uneventful until we reached a field that lay in the shadows of Barn Hill. The field, which we later learnt was called the North Field, was about one hundred and twenty metres across. The first thing that caught our eyes was the curious sight of a dozen ponies grouped together by some nearby gorse bushes. Ponies are common on the moor, but we had not seen a group all together like this.

I turned away from the ponies and took a position by the granite and earth wall that bordered the field. I shone my torch across the seemingly empty field. I suddenly had the shock of my life when the beam of my torch caught the sinister image of two eyes. No body, just two eyes! I would describe the eyes as being similar to a crocodile. They were motionless, and approximately five or six feet off the ground. I thought that it must be an animal of some kind and that it was probably resting on top of a small shed. But where was the shed? Why could I not see any head or body to it? Within seconds of my torch beam locking on to the 'eyes' Dave Gillham's torch also picked up the strange apparition and we had the thing in the cross beams of our torches. *'Flippin' 'ell, it's got eyes like gobstoppers!'* exclaimed Dave. Regrettably, Dave's huge searchlight torch had not been charged up and he had only a small hand torch. We watched, transfixed, for a few seconds, then it vanished. It did not run or slink away it simply vanished before our eyes.

Darren, who had possession of the infrared night sight, was lagging behind us. Unfortunately he did not see this weird sight in the field. The three of us scanned the field immediately, hoping to catch sight of this strange phantom, but to no avail. The field was completely empty.

Dave and myself were a little shaken by this experience. I for one could not equate the sighting with any known animal or bird. It could not have been an owl, even an eagle owl (*Bubo bubo*) which is a sizeable creature. How would it have remained in mid air? And wouldn't we have seen it take off? How did it just vanish from the centre of such a large field? Dave made an interesting point: Wasn't it strange that we had seen the large group of ponies so close to the field with the 'eyes'?

The incident was debated all the way back to the car. By now the time was 4.40 and our patrol had lasted about two and three quarter hours. We got in the car and, experiencing a weary unanimity, fell into a deep sleep for the next couple of hours. At about six in the morning I decided to take some fresh air and stood by the car for a couple of minutes. As I looked towards the east, a strong wind howled across the granite stones that littered Pew Tor. Inexplicably, I heard the mournful wail of dogs and the thunderous roar of horses. My legs turned to jelly, as I thumped the roof of the car and called Dave and Darren out to listen. The apocalyptic stampede was pure Conan Doyle, conjuring an image straight from *The Hound of the Baskervilles*, but it was just the wind, raging across local kennels and the desolate moor. The arrival of rain put paid to any further surveillance so, after a rest, we departed for Tavistock and huge fry-up breakfast.

Dave returned to Cornwall and Darren and I had some spare time before booking in to our hotel. We decided to visit Michael Doidge, who had lost two sheep in the January attack, and see if he had any comments to make about the killings. Not knowing which farm he lived in meant that we had to take pot luck and visit a few farms in the locality until we found him. The second farm we visited was owned by Peter Hearn, who kindly invited us in for coffee. We told Peter and his wife that we were investigating the sheep killings. Although he had not lost any sheep himself, Peter was most interested to hear about the details of the 2005 killings. I asked about military activity in the area but was told there was none. I avoided any reference to aliens as he probed for my opinion on the attacks. Without any prompting or suggestion that a non-human explanation was being considered by us, Peter came right out and said *'Cards on the table, is this to do with the corn circles?'*

'You could be right,' I conceded. Peter went on to tell us about two UFO sightings he had had on that part of the moor. While one sighting could have been put down to a laser show in Plymouth on the same night, the other could not. Basically, he had been out in the field one night and had seen a star-like object that had split into two. The two parts went around another star-like object then rejoined before flying off out of sight. I found this sighting to be very interesting, but it did not help the investigation into the sheep attacks. We thanked Peter and his wife and made our way to Michael Doidge's house. He did not have too much to say about the attacks other than that they were very strange indeed and he had not encountered anything similar in his long years of farming in the area.

We concluded our investigations for the day, went to the hotel and caught up on our sleep. The following day we drove back to the West Midlands, still debating the strange apparition that Dave and I saw.

An interesting postscript to this trip occurred in September 2006, when I met a member of the Stourbridge UFO group, UFORM. I had given a talk on the Dartmoor attacks to UFORM members and I had mentioned the strange 'eyes' we had seen on the second surveillance night. The gentleman concerned told me that he had purchased some land in Worcestershire and that since the acquisition of the land, he had experienced a number of highly strange incidents. On one occasion, he had seen a pair of eyes, nothing else, just a pair of eyes, in some woodland on his land. He was armed with a shotgun and stalked the 'eyes' in the woods. As he moved forward, the 'eyes' retreated, until they simply disappeared. His description of events was very similar to the North Field sighting.

23

Nights 3 and 4

I was anxious to build on the previous surveillance nights in November 2005 and January 2006. I felt a larger operation in March might bring results. I contacted likely candidates for the team. Dave Gillham, whose name was the first one on the team sheet, expressed grave doubts as whether I could get anybody other than himself to participate in the operation. It is an unfortunate fact that he was quite right. One by one, various friends and acquaintances gave me excuses. It looked like it would be just the two of us when, at the eleventh hour, my son in law Darren Rudge, decided to join us again.

I had selected a cottage via the Internet and its location at Peter Tavy, a small village just a couple of miles out of Tavistock, was ideal for our purpose. I had booked the cottage for two days and we had the benefit of being able to come and go as we pleased. The plan was to drive down to Dartmoor on the evening of Monday 13th March. We would do an all-night surveillance then book into the cottage in the morning. We planned a second night of surveillance on Tuesday 14th March, returning to Walsall on the Wednesday.

I was now becoming very familiar with the two hundred and ten mile journey down to Dartmoor. It was certainly a lot easier with Darren as company and the journey was not arduous. We arrived at Pork Hill car park to find that Dave was already there, scanning the sky with his searchlight. The weather was again poor and the full moon was hidden by a dark blanket of cloud. Could you never see the stars from this place? Dave was particularly frustrated by this continuing cloud, but as I pointed out, we were more interested in what happened on the ground.

We took the decision to cross the B3357 and climb up Cox Tor, which in the darkness did not seem so great a trek. We were amazed how high up we were when we reached the upper layers of granite rock on top of Cox Tor. The car park was hardly visible and the common and Barn Hill seemed very far away. A brief discussion took place as to whether we should carry out the watch from the Cox Tor summit. We elected instead to return to the car park. The descent was far easier and on returning to the car park we decided to move to Moortown and the track.

In the pitch darkness we pulled our equipment from the cars and trudged up the lower slopes of Pew Tor. We made our base camp next to a pile of granite boulders near a disused quarry and set up our cameras for any possible action. We made occasional forays down towards the common and tried our best to get near to the sheep, but that was impossible. It proved to me that whoever or whatever was killing the sheep had to have considerable expertise and knowledge of these animals.

Unfortunately there was nothing to note and the night slipped by as we discussed a whole range of topics, guzzled Lucozade and chomped on Mars Bars – what was good enough for the commandos was good enough for us! I was very disappointed that we had seen nothing, but there was always tomorrow night.

We spent the early morning in Tavistock and again treated ourselves to a fry-up breakfast from the Pannier market café. The market was adjacent to the police station, so I decided to go in and ask if I could see the crime files for the October attacks. The policeman at the desk listened to my request for the files and then went out to consult with the sergeant. His response quite surprised me. *'Yes, we don't see why you can't have these files. However, you must go through the proper channels.'* The proper channels were through the Freedom of Information Act and I had to apply, under this Act, to the Devon and Cornwall Constabulary headquarters in Exeter. That seems very straightforward, I thought. How wrong I was! As we shall see later, getting any information from the police about these cases was virtually impossible.

The cottage, with its log fire, suited us completely and being pretty well exhausted we went to sleep. That evening we agreed to visit a pub I knew of and have a meal. The place I had selected was the 'Who'd have thought it' at Milton Combe, some ten miles away. We arrived at about 7.30 and sampled the real ale before perusing the menu. The three of us ordered the same meal, ironically lamb with red wine sauce. The meals duly arrived and disaster struck Dave. As he sprinkled his lamb with salt, the bottom of the cruet dropped out and the salt rapidly created a large white cone in the centre of his plate. Hmm, I thought, Dave certainly likes his salt! Dave's meal was quickly replaced by the apologetic staff, but it didn't stop the ribbing that Dave received from Darren and me.

We got back to the cottage at about eleven o'clock and got the equipment together for our surveillance. The night was illuminated by a brilliant moon which lit up the landscape. We spent about an hour at Pork Hill before moving to the track. Although it was the first night of clear sky the temperature was extremely cold. I took the decision to send Darren back to the cottage so that he could rest and be better prepared to drive us home the following day. I thought Darren was going to fall at my feet in gratitude! Dave and I remained at our post and endured the most excruciating cold we had ever experienced. Even with our layers of warm clothing, the cold cut into us. What am I doing here, I thought. It wouldn't have been so bad had there been any activity to record, but nothing stirred on that freezing moor. By five o'clock we could stand no more and deserted the camp and headed back to the cottage. Dave piled some logs on the fire and I fell into a deep sleep, unable to move from the settee I had settled on.

The following day I reflected on the events of the two nights' surveillance, desperately searching for anything positive. I had miscalculated the difficulties involved in these operations and the camaraderie generated during our brief stay at the cottage was the only plus point I could think of. However, a chance conversation with Chris Boswell, who owned the cottage with his wife Ruth, gave us an interesting piece of information. On 27th May 2005 Chris Boswell was riding his bike up Pork Hill (no mean feat, I assure you!), the time was about five o'clock in the afternoon and the weather was bright and sunny. A bright, incandescent object shot over Chris's shoulder and over a hedge. Chris had actually flinched when the object passed over him and he was so shocked by this bizarre event that he began to doubt whether he had seen it at all!

At the top of Pork Hill he found that he had a puncture caused by a thorn in his tyre. He set about repairing the tyre but could not re-inflate it because his pump was not working. He sat down and reflected on the situation for a while before deciding to return home on foot. As Chris began walking towards Pork Hill, a gentleman in a van stopped and offered him a lift. Grateful for the man's assistance, Chris put his bike into the back of the van, which he noticed was full of various electronic instruments and equipment. The man was from the Norwich area and claimed to be an aerial photographer. Then, without any prompting, he asked Chris if he had seen the meteorite. Chris was stunned and amazed by this revelation and told the man what he had seen while cycling up the hill. The man dropped Chris back to his home in Peter Tavy, leaving him with the conviction that what he had witnessed was indeed a meteorite.

Chris actually showed me his diary entry for Friday 27th May 2005 with all the details written down. My interest in this incident concerned the locality of the event – by Pork Hill and the common. I was glad to note this event, as some months later Dave Gillham located a witness to another strange event that could have been connected.

Dave was contacted by a radio ham who claimed to have taken some pictures of UFOs in the Horrabridge area, which is only a few miles from Moortown. Although the pictures were found to be a fault on his camera, this witness had an interesting story to tell. On Sunday 29th May, two days after Chris Boswell's 'meteorite' sighting, the radio ham was scanning various radio channels when he picked up radio communications from two RAF pilots using an unusual frequency. They appeared to be pursuing something across Dartmoor. Unable to record the transmission, the witness recalled one intriguing message *'Target going at speed 02 LFT level.'*

'They were chasing something very fast over the moor,' said the witness, who also stated that it was unheard of for RAF jets to practise manoeuvres over the moor during a Bank Holiday.

It seemed more than a coincidence to me that these two incidents occurred on the same weekend. Who knows? Perhaps another witness may yet come forward.

24

Hitch Hiker From the Galaxy

When I returned from Dartmoor I found myself under immediate pressure, as I had promised to do a talk about the sheep attacks for the Stourbridge-based UFORM group. I had spoken to Steve Poole, the chairman of group, and offered to be a stand-in speaker, in the event that the booked speaker would be unable to attend, an unfortunate occurrence from time to time. I had to get a PowerPoint presentation together as well as a script. I called the talk *Killers on the Moor* and awaited the call from Steve.

Steve was apologetic when he rang me. First it was on, then not on, and then, at eight o'clock on Monday evening, it was on. I relished the challenge and the opportunity to tell people about the investigation on Dartmoor and the animal mutilation problem. My wife Jill agreed to accompany me and provide moral and critical support. She was going to take notes of my performance.

We drove into the rear car park of the Mitre public house, situated in the high street, Stourbridge and carried a large plastic box, which contained my computer, up the dimly lit stairs to the small meeting room. The Mitre, with its sombre, weary décor and gallery of sixties' icons adorning its walls, enjoyed a small clientele of pool players and rockers during the middle of the week. The atmosphere in the meeting room was of sedition and forbidden knowledge. The eclectic nature of the attendees was suggestive of the proscribed, and reminiscent of an altruistic resistance group. Unfortunately, there weren't very many of them.

Steve Poole introduced me and with an audience of less than two dozen, I began my talk. I opened with a brief summary of my own UFO sightings in 1970, before describing that seminal moment when I heard about the ponies case on the radio. I spent too much time on the hardships of the Dartmoor stakeouts, but I rattled along despite my lack of a proper script. When I showed the reference photos, taken in December, it provoked an immediate reaction from the members. *'There's orbs on those pictures!'* they said. The pictures had not been enlarged, but several members pointed out a number of white blotches on the image. These, I had assumed, were nothing more than some fault caused by the weather conditions when I had taken the photo. The image of my car parked by the old track at Moortown had plainly caused some excitement. I was personally sceptical of the orb phenomenon and did not attach much importance to the interest shown by the UFORM audience. How wrong I was, as we shall soon see.

After an hour or so we had a welcome break. I was approached by some of the younger members of the audience, who had obviously warmed to the daring antics of the 'team' on Dartmoor. I asked Jill for a progress report on my talk and was disappointed by a lengthy list of too many umms and too many errs.

The UFORM raffle was completed and I was on stage again to finish off the talk. The members were too generous to me and their polite applause was followed by many questions. Had I any comment to make about human mutilations, I was asked. That was a difficult one. There had been rumours and I had been given some unsubstantiated information about attacks on humans, but as far as I was concerned there was definitely no evidence to support this terrifying scenario. I was again approached by some of the younger members, anxious to join me on an all-night surveillance. The trouble was, could they 'hack it', especially if we had a night when absolutely nothing happened and the tedious boredom set in?

Jill continued her list of criticisms during the drive back to Walsall, and I had to admit that I needed to plan the talk and script it better. However, I was still upbeat about everything and as a result of my talk a major development in the investigation was about to add a whole new dimension to the Dartmoor case.

The image of my car showing the orbs had been scanned onto the PowerPoint presentation from a small print that Darren had done. My computer had been under repair and Darren had downloaded many of my original images onto his computer. I asked him for the photo of the car and eventually forwarded it to Rob Tudge and Steve Poole at UFORM.

A week later I received an email from Rob, the contents of which totally shocked me. Rob asked me to put the original image on my screen and look very carefully at it. I was totally stunned by what I saw. Towering over the car was an entity that appeared part giant, part bird. I began to wonder if this frightening daytime spectre was the infamous 'Owlman of Mawnan' referred to by the cryptozooligist and writer, Johnathan Downes. The creature was straight out of the *Mothman Prophecies*, a Keelian nightmare that appeared to have left West Virginia and landed on Dartmoor. I rang Dave and emailed the image to him. I was in a state of shock, but worse was to follow.

I had not looked hard enough at the image, despite Rob's detailed instructions. The sight of the 'Owlman' had blinded me to the detail elsewhere in this mind-blowing picture. Dave rang me and suggested I have a closer look. *'You've got a little passenger!'* he said. I looked again at the picture, this time concentrating on the window in the back of the car. Oh my god! I could scarcely believe it. There was the image of a diminutive 'being' that appeared to be standing on the back seat of the Jaguar, looking out of the rear window. I felt sick! If I had realised these 'beings' were there when I took the picture I would have run back to Walsall and left the bloody car!

I showed the image to several people, all of whom agreed that this was a very creepy picture. Darren, who is a photographer by profession, was perplexed by the white smudges of the orbs. They couldn't be put down to rain, as they appeared to be moving sideways.

I now had to cope with an additional dimension to the investigation. The pictures represented something that was invisible to the human eye and was it a one off? I knew that we would have to take further pictures in the area and see if anything similar showed up. Anyway, I had to ask myself, if these 'beings' were real, were they relevant to the sheep deaths? I was keeping an open mind.

25

The Dead Sheep Scrolls

The day I got back from Dartmoor I made an application to the Devon and Cornwall Constabulary for access to the crime files for the October 2005 attacks. I was naively optimistic about this first letter to the Exeter headquarters at Middlemore. I had been assured, by a solicitor friend, that applications to the police for information under the Freedom of Information Act were relatively routine.

A week later I received a reply from Louise Fenwick, the Assistant Freedom of Information Officer at Exeter. The second paragraph of her letter was the first indication I would get that this seemingly straightforward application was going to have a difficult passage. Officer Fenwick wrote as follows:

> *Unfortunately I am unable to progress with your request at this time. To enable us to meet your request please could you provide this office with clarification on the information that is required surrounding the sheep deaths on Moortown.*

How big was this file, I thought.

I replied on 29th March 2006, stating that I wanted all the information relating to the visit of the scene of crimes officers (SOCO) to Moortown Farm. I requested copies of all veterinary and forensic reports, although I made no mention of any photographs, which were assumed to be part of the reports anyway. It was two weeks later that during a conversation with Mary Alford, I was surprised to hear that they had taken many photos. I immediately wrote to Middlemore, adding further clarification that I needed to see the photographs taken by SOCO.

On 8th May I drafted a letter to the police, stating my concern that with the deadline for a response of 21st May 2006, I had not received any confirmation that my application was progressing. In the event, I did not send the letter and decided instead to telephone the following day. I was put through to the information office at Middlemore and fully expected a delay while my application was sifted from a huge pile of papers. Not so! The lady I spoke to assured me that the application was being dealt with. I found this rather curious: surely they had got more than one application to deal with?

Three days later I received a three-page letter from Officer Fenwick. The letter constituted a Refusal Notice, under the Freedom of Information Act 2000. I was shattered! I could not believe that the request had failed. The letter gave four reasons for the Refusal Notice. I quote directly from the Notice as follows:

> *The exemptions applied are section 31(1)(a) (prejudice the prevention and detection of crime); section 31(1)(b) (prejudice the apprehension and prosecution of offenders); section 41 (information provided in confidence) and section 40(2) (personal information relating to a third party) of the Freedom of Information Act 2000. The exemptions have been applied because the information that you request is held for the purposes of a criminal investigation and includes information provided in confidence by a third party and information about a third party. Disclosure of the information concerning the sheep deaths at Moortown may prejudice the future prevention and detection of crime and prejudice the apprehension and prosecution of offenders concerned with this crime.*

I wrote back on 16th May, expressing my disappointment with the ruling on my request. I also gave notice that I wished to make an amended application for access to the SOCO photographs and forensic reports, concluding that I might be in a position to further police investigations.

A week later I received a letter from John Ellis, Force Information Manager, acknowledging my revised application. I was informed that the amended application was to be treated as a complaint/appeal and as such would be subject to an internal review of the decision. The word internal concerned me, as it appeared that the police conduct their own appeals. I noted that there was a date of 23rd July 2006 by which they would have to inform me of their decision.

After many weeks had passed I was becoming a little anxious about the appeal as I had heard nothing from the police. I decided to telephone Middlemore and get an update. I was told that there was a large backlog of work and that my appeal would be dealt with. The deadline for a response came and went, so I called again. This time I left a message on the voicemail. John Ellis came back to me and left a message on my answer phone, assuring me that the appeal would be processed soon.

On 6th August 2006 I received a letter from John Ellis, advising me that the independent reviewer had upheld the original decision to withhold disclosure of the files. Frankly, I couldn't believe it. How could photographs of the crime scene and dead sheep contain any information about a third party? It was obvious that despite the fact that the police in Tavistock had no objections to me seeing the file, those higher up the chain of command seemed determined I should see nothing. Why was that?

I had one last throw of the dice. Under section 50 of the Freedom of Information Act 2000, I made an appeal against the appeal to the Information Commissioner at Wilmslow in Cheshire. On 15th November 2006 I received a letter acknowledging my appeal and informing me that, because of the large backlog of applications, it might be several months before my appeal could be dealt with. I began to wonder if I would ever get to see those elusive files.

On 30th January 2007 I received an email from Edwina Hunter of the Information Commissioners, advising me that my application had been allocated to Team 2 (Education, Police and Justice) and was further advised that I would be notified when a case officer had been assigned to the case. I was also told that they would inform me of '*the status of my complaint in relation to Team 2's queue*' and they apologised for the long delay. Significantly, the email contained the following comment: '*We appreciate that due to the passage of time your request may no longer be relevant. If you no longer wish to pursue this matter we would be grateful if you could contact us to confirm this at your earliest convenience.*'

I responded quickly, by letter and email, that I was determined to pursue the matter however long it took.

On 23rd March and 6th June 2007 I had two further emails from Carolyn Howes, Senior Complaints Officer for the commissioners, who advised me that there were continuing delays and that my case was still waiting to be assigned to a case officer. In between an apology for the continuing delay, the email stated that I would be advised of my *'status in relation to Team 2's queue'* and notified when a case officer was finally assigned to it. Between 29th March 2007 and 7th May 2008 I received six emails from Carolyn Howes at roughly two-monthly intervals, advising me that my case was awaiting a case officer.

On 7th June 2007 I received a letter from Ben Tomes, Senior Complaints Officer at the Information Commissioner's Office, advising me that he had been allocated to the case. At last! I felt I was getting somewhere.

During June 2007, Ben Tomes and I exchanged letters clarifying my appeal and stating that I was prepared to accept a file with the third party information censored. On 26th July 2007 I wrote to Mr Tomes asking for an update on the appeal, somewhat naively thinking that now the wheels of justice were turning, it would not be too long before I received the police file. However, on 27th July 2008 I received a reply which contained the following paragraph:

> *This case remains ongoing. Unfortunately, it is not possible to give an accurate estimate for when this case will be resolved, but I can advise that this may take several months. Once this case has been resolved, the outcome and the reasoning for this will be explained to you in full.*

On 5th February 2009 I received the Decision Notice from the ICO – the appeal was rejected! I was shattered, and thought of giving up. I decided on one last attempt, which now had to be made through the Information Tribunal, a legal process involving submissions to a panel of three tribunal members. My appeal submission gave seven grounds for appeal, which were as follows

1. The ICO had changed the ruling on section 30, by changing it to section 31, which was deemed more appropriate. I argued that this change had been recommended by the ICO to the police without my knowledge and that my appeal had been based on section 30 of the Act.
2. Section 40 – I was likely to be in possession of the details covered by section 40, therefore it was not applicable.
3. Media coverage – I argued that much detail relating to these killings had been released to the press.
4. A possible miscarriage of justice – I knew that it was highly unlikely that humans were responsible, therefore there was a chance that the police would arrest an innocent person.
5. The police had failed to accept my offer of assistance and this refusal was against the public interest as the police would need all the specialised assistance they could get.
6. The police had closed the file and were unlikely to reopen it.
7. National security – I argued that the killings were part of a series which I had linked to attacks in the USA. Whatever had the capability to strike on two continents was a threat to the United Kingdom.

Although I had hurried my appeal submission I was quietly confident that I might succeed. How wrong I was! The response from the ICO solicitor was professional, clinical and crushing, my grounds for appeal were mercilessly attacked and the submission concluded with an application for the appeal to be dismissed.

I was numbed by this devastating response to my appeal and, realising that my appeal was facing early disaster, decided to 'up my game.' I used the ICO submission as a guide to how it should be done and reviewed the grounds of appeal that I had submitted. I spent all Easter weekend and many nights afterwards on the appeal, checking and rechecking the arguments. I decided that grounds one, two, four and five should be withdrawn, and revamped my presentation and arguments for grounds three, six and seven hoping that my submission would be strong enough to avert dismissal of my appeal.

I could scarcely believe it when I received notification that the Tribunal had ruled in my favour, refusing to strike out the appeal. I was not only rewarded with a further, final hearing, but the Devon and Cornwall Constabulary were now joined in proceedings. This meant that the police not only had to make a submission to the Tribunal, they also had to detail their reasons for withholding the photographs.

I could not have wished for a better result and after all the frustrations I had experienced I now had an opportunity to get the photographs released. Unfortunately, there were some further difficulties to overcome.

The Information Commissioner's solicitor raised a point of law regarding the two newspaper articles that I had referred to in my appeal. The articles had been published in August 2006 and both contained references to the October 2005 attacks. The ICO had argued that as my original appeal had been dated 16th March 2006 the two articles might be inadmissible. The Tribunal asked me if I had any articles that predated the original appeal date. I hurriedly did some checking on the Internet, and to my relief, found an interesting article by Mark Ford called 'Terror on the Tor', which appeared in the *Western Daily Press* on 19th October 2005. This article gave far more details about the attacks and I realised straight away that this would give my appeal fresh impetus.

Over the next few weeks the Devon and Cornwall police missed the deadlines set by the Tribunal for explaining their refusal to let me see the photographs. I became frustrated by this and complained to the Tribunal. Eventually, the police made a submission to the Tribunal that was a rehash of their earlier arguments but still avoided giving any clear reasons why I was not allowed to see the photographs.

As I worked on putting my case together I decided that I would attack the police submission and bring my strongest arguments to bear on them as the 'Terror on the Tor' article had given me plenty of ammunition regarding sensitive details that had been released by the police. Incidentally, in this article the police had accused the pagans of carrying out the attacks!

My final grounds for appeal were put forward as follows: Ground 3, Media Coverage – I argued that the Devon and Cornwall police had released many sensitive details about these attacks to the press and I was able to quote the following comments:

> *'Our understanding is that this place used to be some sort of meeting place for Pagans.'*
> *'Six sheep were found with their necks broken and eyes removed.'*
> *'Police confirmed the animals had their necks quickly broken and there were no indications of a prolonged struggle or suffering.'*

PC Pickles of the Devon and Cornwall police was quoted in the *West Country News*, dated 31st August 2006 as follows: *'One farmer found a rough shelter with what appeared to be a kind of altar – three stones laid in a Fleur de Lys pattern – a wooden stake nearby. There were possibly bloodstains on one stone.'* I made the point to the Tribunal that the police had failed to submit any of the alleged evidence from the 'altar' to forensic scrutiny.

The police released critical details of the attacks to the press which were as follows:

1. The method of death – the necks were quickly broken and there was no evidence of a prolonged struggle or suffering.
2. The lie and arrangement of the bodies.
3. The eyes were removed.
4. At least two people were involved.
5. The dead sheep were worth six hundred pounds.
6. The bodies were still warm – this is important forensic evidence, indicating the time of death to be within eighteen hours of discovery of the bodies.

Ground 6, Operational Matters – My argument was that the release of the photographs could not prejudice a case that the police had closed and were apparently disinclined to reopen. As evidence of this I made reference to the police meeting with the Dartmoor Commoners' Association held on 25th September 2007 (this meeting is dealt with in more detail in a subsequent chapter).

Ground 7, National Security – The use of high technology and the link with attacks in the United States, where the perpetrators appeared to act with impunity, suggested to me that the security of the United Kingdom was indeed compromised.

The police submitted a rather poor response to the Tribunal and among the points they made in their final submission were that the photographs contained 'sensitive information' and that release of the pictures would disclose the investigating techniques of the Devon and Cornwall Constabulary. Furthermore, they had suggested that the graphic nature of the images might have an adverse affect on the community as a whole!

My final submission mercilessly attacked these arguments and I felt that I had 'shredded' the police case. My response to the Information Commissioner's Office was more conciliatory as I suggested that the ICO had been misled by the arguments put forward by the police.

During the preparation of the final submissions I received a copy of the Bundle, a legal term for a folder that contains all the documents relating to the case. It was with some surprise that I noted within this file of papers notes of telephone conversations between the Information Commissioner's Office and the police.

The ICO had offered the police an opportunity to disclose the contentious photographs to me outside of the Freedom of Information Act 2000. This offer would have negated all the tribulations we all had to endure from October 2008 onwards. The police stated that they would have to refer the matter to ACPO, the Association of Chief Police Officers, as well as the Force Legal Department. After some weeks the police declined this proposed resolution.

In October 2009 I received the news I had dreamt of for three and half years. The Information Tribunal had, under appeal number EA/2009/0012, unanimously ruled that the Devon and Cornwall Constabulary must disclose the photographs to me and the appeal was upheld.

There was still a possibility that the police could appeal to the Law Lords at the High Court in London, but as the time edged towards the twenty-eight-day deadline it became apparent that no such action would be taken. On reflection the police, having lost the appeal so emphatically, perhaps did not wish to pursue their weak arguments in the higher court, or risk the publicity such an action would bring.

I was euphoric with this victory – a victory for persistence, and against considerable odds. The prize was the photographs! These images were better than I could have expected and showed in great detail the mutilators' bizarre use of high technology, precise cuts, no blood and identical in one image to a mutilation attack in the United States in 1993.

The photographs now form part of an ever-growing body of evidence that proves the case for alien involvement in these sinister attacks.

26

Night 5 – Dazed and Confused

It was just after eight o'clock in the evening of 10th May 2006 when I took the call from Dave Gillham. Did I know it was a full moon that coming weekend, and was I going to Dartmoor? Yes, I did know it was a full moon and no, I wasn't going to Dartmoor. In fact, wild horses would not drag me down there. The truth was that I couldn't see any benefit in taking another long shot at catching the perpetrators in the act. And the thought of another blank stake out was too much to contemplate. I told Dave this and he quietly accepted my argument. I reinforced my decision by giving Dave a long list of family commitments that took precedence over another night of discomfort on Dartmoor.

I had carried on the programme of surveillance through the summer months, despite the fact that statistically, the mutilators' activities were much reduced during the summer months, but convinced myself that we should wait and see if there were further attacks before making further plans.

Why was it, then, that on the following night, 11th May, I felt that I had to go to Dartmoor? In fact, nothing was going to stop me going to Dartmoor! I cannot explain this illogical and dramatic change of mind. I rang Dave and told him the news, which was accepted with quiet resignation and Dave's catchphrase, *'I go with the flow.'* I don't know what possessed me to experience such a volte-face, and I had to explain the situation to my wife.

Saturday 13th May was chaotic. I was totally disorganised. It wasn't as if this was the first visit I had made to Dartmoor. The quiet routine had disintegrated. I had promised my wife that I would taxi my younger daughter to and from a birthday party in Walsall, before setting off to Devon. Despite picking my daughter up earlier than expected, poor preparation meant that I did not leave home until eleven o'clock. I was soon on the M5, cursing my lack of organisation and wondering whether I should really be making this trip. I was battling against the clock throughout the whole journey although, as I drove down the A386 towards the outskirts of Tavistock, the adrenalin kicked in.

Dave, who had arrived late himself, didn't waste any time pointing out my lack of punctuality as my car swept into Pork Hill car park at five past two in the morning, I was greeted with the words, *'Where the hell 'ave you been then? Late, as usual!'* We briefly shook hands and I asked Dave whether he had seen anything. No, was the reply. The sky was overcast, with the full moon completely obscured. We were both aware that time was getting on and our late start had cost us an hour or more already. We decided to sit in the Jaguar for a few minutes and catch up any news. Neither Dave nor myself can explain what happened next. I was aware of feeling a little drowsy, as if awakening from a deep sleep, though it was only a minute or two since we had got into the car. I turned on the car ignition, to illuminate the digital clock. The time was 0320 hours! What the hell had happened to the last hour and a quarter? *'Dave, look at the time, we'd better get over to Pew Tor, time is getting on.'* I said. Dave robotically got out of the Jaguar and walked towards his car. He was very quiet.

Still unsettled at 'losing' an hour and a quarter of precious time, we drove round to Moortown, along the track and parked up at LUP 1. Dave and I remained subdued as we trudged up the slope towards the disused quarry and our base camp. The sky remained dark and uncompromising, as we approached the light grey pile of granite. What a waste of an evening, I thought. It was now getting on for four o'clock in the morning and we barely had more than an hour and a half of darkness left.

We quickly unloaded our rucksacks and I set up the tripod and analogue camcorder. This was done in an air of forced optimism, as the time edged past four o'clock. A couple of minutes later, Dave and I had an extra-ordinary sighting. What looked like a vehicle of some kind was on the moor. This was quite astonishing, as we had not seen anything even remotely human, in any of the previous nights of surveillance. The vehicle, which appeared to have two dull headlights and a large red light on top, came right to the edge of the plateau, next to Feather Tor. Within a minute it appeared to reverse, turn round and drive off. The rear of this vehicle had two large lights, one red and one white. Curiously, there was no sound from the vehicle. I should point out that even small sounds can carry some distance across the moor. Neither Dave nor I appeared to grasp how astonishing this sighting was at the time. However, it did galvanise us into some action and I decided to start the camcorder. I reckoned there was approximately an hour and a half of battery life, so we had enough to film during the remaining hour or so of darkness. I struggled to find the right buttons in the darkness but eventually, the soft whirring of the camera began.

Dave was the first to catch sight of a flash of intense white light from Cox Tor. He was still trying to evaluate it when he stated in a matter of fact manner, *'I think it was a star.'* A skylark began singing as I surveyed the area with the night sight telescope. We heard the whinny of a horse or pony that was disturbed. Another light soon followed, it was as if there was a lighthouse on Cox Tor. We both saw it this time. Dave exclaimed, *'That's no star!'* He was dead right! However, we were both disorientated and confused because, at different times, we mistook Great Staple Tor for Cox Tor and Cox Tor for Barn Hill! I have stated before how the darkness can play tricks and distort distances. There were further flashes of light and the tension and excitement rose dramatically. We had never seen anything like this before on Dartmoor, or anywhere else for that matter! One of the flashes came from the second attack zone, on Barn Hill. The excitement was at fever pitch. What was going on?

We scanned the hills for further activity then, at 4.16, they were back. The lights differed in intensity, but what the hell were they? Dave asked what the quickest route to Barn Hill was. I told him that the best way would be to go back to where the cars were and drive round to Pork Hill, then cut across the common. To avoid any confusion about the lights I pointed out where the BBC transmission masts were situated. As I described the surrounding terrain to Dave, there was another flash. A minute or so later, a thick mist descended, obscuring Barn Hill and Cox Tor. That was it, so we thought.

Dave took the opportunity to mention the camcorder and asked if it was running and was the night shot mode on. *'I hope so,'* I replied, unconvincingly. As the time edged towards half past four, I began telling Dave about my personal experiences with UFOs. Strangely, I had never told Dave about the large number of sightings I had in the 1970s. Our short discussion was prompted, not by UFOs, but by UGOs, unidentified ground objects – for nothing we had seen so far appeared to be airborne.

Dave suddenly realised that he had a digital camcorder and, after some frenetic pressing of buttons and guesswork on its operation, succeeded in starting the second camera. The introduction of Dave's camera was propitious, as the mist lifted and we were witness to some increase in activity. The light flashes had moved down to Barn Hill and at 4.34 we saw a red flash. This was followed by numerous white flashes. Dawn was breaking and we didn't need binoculars to see where the flashes were coming from. It was now about 4.40 in the morning and we watched, astounded, as the intermittent flashes of light moved down Barn Hill and across Whitchurch common. They were coming in our direction!

The light flashes seemed to be intelligently controlled and there were none in open ground. They appeared to come out of the numerous gorse bushes that were spread unevenly across the hill and the common. As further flashes came from Barn Hill, I noted that the sequence had lasted about half an hour. I asked Dave if he could see anything human. I knew he could not. I was clinging to the hope that it could all be explained, in bizarre fashion, that these flashes of light would be some sort of practical joke, carried out by camping pranksters. It was however obvious that Dave and I were the only humans on that part of Dartmoor. We were quite alone, and vulnerable.

The lights were definitely moving towards our position. There appeared to be a single red light and several white lights. Dave wanted contact with them. *'Come over 'ere!'* he shouted. There was a flash of light from a bush about three hundred metres or so away. Dave decided to flash his giant 'searchlight' torch at the bush. At the time, Dave thought that he had flashed the powerful beam a half a dozen times, and he confirmed this by email to me a couple of weeks later. However, when the footage from the analogue camcorder was studied, I counted twenty-three flashes from Dave's torch!

It was now nearly 4.50 and after another huge flash of light from Barn Hill, Dave and I debated how to confront these intelligences. I suggested that we should go back to the cars, drive swiftly round to Pork Hill, then race across the plateau to Barn Hill, thereby outflanking 'them'. Barn Hill seemed to be the main place of activity and I was sure that this was the best idea. Dave had a different view, and advocated a trek towards Barn Hill from our position on Pew Tor. Dave was swayed by my argument and, as the half dark began to disappear, we switched off the cameras, threw our equipment into the rucksacks and scampered down Pew Tor to the parked cars.

We decided to take my car and hurriedly threw our equipment onto the back seat. The car hurtled down the narrow track, across a small bridge, up to the crossroads and the B3357. There was no traffic, as we screeched away from the crossroads, running up the gears till we reached fifth, we were flying! I have never driven so fast up Pork Hill. We passed the summit and I swung the car into the car park, where we slid to a halt in a style reminiscent of a police chase from a movie. The doors were flung open and, grabbing what we could from the back seat, we began to run and jog across the grassy plateau towards Barn Hill.

We arrived, breathless, on the top of Barn Hill. We had covered the distance from Pew Tor to this point in less than fifteen minutes. The view was unexpectedly serene as we surveyed the area, trying to get our bearings and find the source of the lights. We walked among the gorse bushes below the brow of the hill, occasionally taking photographs. Dave scanned his camcorder across to Pew Tor on the opposite side of the valley. There were no lights, there were no humans other than us and there were no signs of anything that might have been responsible for the lights. There was an air of disappointment, as we realised that the party was over – if party is the right word! Dave had some trouble with his camcorder, which appeared to have developed a will of its own. The focusing went haywire and filming was eventually abandoned. We would later ponder as to whether the focusing on the camcorder was being interfered with in some way. It was that kind of night.

Having found no trace of the mysterious lights, we returned to the track at Moortown and trudged wearily back up to our camp on Pew Tor. On a morning of breathtaking beauty and early rays of golden sunshine, we sat and quietly discussed the events of the night. We saw Mary Alford's red Land Rover driving into North Field, it was like a tiny red ant from our lofty position. Dave frustratingly pushed the buttons on his camcorder until he let out a yelp of triumph and excitement. The camera did record and had picked up some of the light flashes! Not only had we witnessed some fantastic phenomena, but we had evidence as well.

'You're very quiet,' said Dave, over our now customary breakfast. I was still stunned by the events, in fact I was utterly dazed and rather confused. After all, why had I changed my mind about being there in the first place? And what happened to that hour and a quarter of 'lost time' in Pork Hill car park? What was that vehicle doing on the moor? And most of all, what the hell were those lights!?

I drove back to Walsall without stopping, despite my lack of sleep. I had not telephoned Mary to check if all was well before we left, so I made a mental note to contact her the following day. When I did call Mary I was to find out that other things had happened during this night of drama.

27

The Lights – Further Developments

Incredibly, it was not until Wednesday 17th May that I contacted Mary Alford. It was my presumption that nothing had occurred elsewhere during 'the night of lights'. I was soon to realise that I was well wide of the mark.

I began our conversation by telling her briefly about the events of 14th May. In passing, I mentioned the whinnying horse, heard quite distinctly by us, at about four o'clock in the morning. Mary corrected me by saying that a pony makes the same sort of sound and that curiously a pony stallion was missing from the North Field that night. Furthermore, she said that the gate to the North Field had been left open by someone during the night, someone who she alleged may have taken the pony. I could not believe that such a thing could have occurred, right under our very noses.

The missing pony was not the only strange occurrence that night. Another farmer in Moortown (I have been requested not to name him) found that a small herd of cattle and a similar number of sheep were missing from his farm overnight. The curious thing was that the cattle turned up at another farm, which was near Princetown, some five miles away. The sheep were found at another local farm. What the hell was going on? The farmer who had lost the animals, was accused of making mischief and the inference was that he had moved the animals during the night to cause trouble. This explanation defied belief.

This bizarre occurrence of moving animals from one place to another, without logic or apparent motive, had precedents elsewhere. I was immediately reminded of a strange incident investigated by the APFU and myself, back in September 2005. A BBC news bulletin reported that twenty-three Texel sheep had disappeared from a field near the Malvern Hills, in Worcestershire. The news report, under the headline of 'Sheep flock disappears from farm', stated:

> *The animals, valued at more than £1600, disappeared from a 72-strong Texel flock in a field in Parkhill, Brockhill Road, Malvern.*

> *Owner Meriel Picton said she was at a loss to explain how the sheep, ideal for breeding, had been removed as there were no signs of tracks and added, 'It's almost as if they used a helicopter to remove them from the field,' she said.*
>
> *She said she thought the thieves had targeted the best breeding animals from her flock.*
>
> *'We are at a loss to know how the sheep were taken as there are no sign of fences being cut, tracks of where they might have been herded or vehicle tracks,' she said.*
>
> *Some of the stolen animals, including two with grey fleeces, have a tuft of wool on their heads and they all have silver ear tags.*

The police were notified and the incident was serious enough to make the BBC news report. There were some interesting factors in this alleged theft: the best breeding animals were selected and there were no visible signs of how they had removed the sheep. In fact, it was if they had used a helicopter.

We managed to ring the Pictons a week after the theft and were surprised to learn that the sheep had been returned. Thinking that the culprits had been arrested and charged with theft, we were astonished to learn that the missing sheep had turned up in another field, a few miles away. The field had a padlocked gate and there were no signs of forced entry to the field. When we visited Malvern to speak to Meriel Picton, she was unwilling to discuss the matter any further.

There was another unaccountable movement of livestock, or teleportation as it is often referred to in a book by the crop circle researcher Pat Delgado called *Crop Circles – Conclusive Evidence?* which contains the following, interesting account.

On 19th July 1991 a ten-metre crop circle was reported at Lapworth in the West Midlands. The morning following the creation of this crop circle, twenty-five sheep were found wandering about together, in a different field from the one they had been in the night before. The sheep appeared frightened and nervous, as though something had disturbed them.

A further incident occurred at the same time as the movement of sheep. One hundred baby pheasants, owned by the farmer, disappeared. Their pens had been flung open. One of the researchers who discovered the crop circle also mentioned that the leaves of a large oak tree that was facing the circle had turned yellowy green very much earlier than the rest of the tree. When I read about this, I immediately thought of the alleged effects on the chlorophyll of vegetation around animal mutilation sites.

A further major development came in the week after the lights. I discovered that despite my failure to put the camcorder on night plus, the camera had picked up many lights and furthermore provided a full soundtrack of the last fifty minutes of our surveillance. I was overjoyed! Until now we had only fourteen minutes of Dave's footage, now we had a lot more, which could also be cross checked with Dave's film of the events. I rang Dave and told him the news.

One of the negative points about both pieces of footage was the lack of any coherent commentary that explained just what we were seeing. This was extremely annoying as the cameras were not always pointing in the same direction as we were looking. The night generally was a bit of a shambles, and Dave and I realised that it did not show us in a particularly professional light. We felt guilty enough to send each other a list of guidelines that we should both adhere to in future. A list of recommendations was as follows: (1) MAF not putting the video on night shot, (2) too much effing and blinding, (3) no accurate commentary, (4) no audio recording of events, (5) no photos taken from Pew Tor, (6) no compass taken to lights area to see if there was any magnetic disturbance, (7) lamp beam used indiscriminately, (8) inadequate preparation and knowledge of surveillance area, (9) not using zoom on the camcorder, (10) not using ordnance survey map to locate area of lights, (11) definitely too much effing and blinding, (12) not noting weather conditions – where mist was coming from etc. and was it connected to the lights, (13) not having time and date on camcorder, (14) not going up Cox Tor, (15) should have used night vision more and taken detailed notes, and finally, (16) absolutely too much effing and blinding! Despite the long list of self-criticism Dave and I had made a remarkable achievement recording what we had and over the next few months we would unravel some mind-blowing information from our footage.

I spent the next couple of days writing up a timeline of the events, using my footage. The film was very dark, with the occasional intense white flashes. The quality was not as good as Dave Gillham's footage, nonetheless there was a great deal of information on the analogue film. I used the camera clock, which was an hour behind, to mark the times of any significant events and after a couple of nights I completed this first step of analysis. Using the 'script' I had compiled I now spent many hours analysing some of the key events on a frame by frame basis. Examining each frame was both time consuming and an arduous and difficult task. I found that there were intense white points of light that were visible for only a couple of frames. Sometimes, there was a point of light that seemed to jump a hundred metres or so in two frames! There were things going on that were outside the field of human vision. I should point out that there were two different light forms that were witnessed by Dave and myself. The larger flashes came from Cox Tor, Middle Staple Tor and the top of Barn Hill. The smaller flashes, which appeared to rise upwards out of the bushes, were mainly white, but also red in colour. As the dawn came the quality of the images increased, although I could not see as many of the flashes that I remembered from the night. The camera did not pick up the red flashes. In addition to all this, there appeared to be things going on in the sky, over Barn Hill. Lights seemed to be moving around one part of the hill. What on earth was going on?

I viewed the section showing Dave flashing his torch at a gorse bush from which we had seen a bright flash of light. The massive 'searchlight' torch flashed twenty-three times, not six, as Dave had thought. On the eleventh flash there was what appeared to be a light form that exited the bush. There was some extraordinary activity on the film, but I felt I was missing some of it and that further analysis was required. I contacted Steve Poole at UFORM and asked if there was anyone he knew who could help. Steve put me in touch with a guy who had some pretty sophisticated software and I handed the tape over to see what he could come up with.

Following a series of furtive meetings outside a pub in Stourbridge, more reminiscent of cold war espionage activity, I handed over the original tape for analysis. It took some weeks before I was given a DVD with digital analysis of some of the key points from the analogue tape. The wait was worth it, because the analysed footage revealed two mind-blowing incidents. In the first, there was a series of flashes and immediately after one of the flashes, a bolt of light shot diagonally across the screen. This bolt of light was visible for a split second and appeared to be directed to where Dave Gillham and I were standing! The second incident showed additional detail from the light form that exited the bush. Whatever it was appeared to rise from the ground and shoot off to the right of the bush. The sequence, which was again in a split second, showed how incredibly fast these light forms were.

However, the most revealing images from the analysed footage were the intense flashes of light from Cox Tor and Middle Staple Tor. A frame by frame analysis showed that the lights appeared to emanate from a dark structured craft that was flat and rounded in shape. I deduced that the light was caused by the front of the craft opening and revealing a very intense light. What we had on the film was a craft, or crafts, of unknown origin. The lights were not beams of light as we thought at first, but the interior light from a craft that had the capability of appearing and disappearing in a split second! Who or what was getting out of that craft of unknown origin when the front opened up for that split second? And what was their purpose for visiting this remote part of Dartmoor?

Near to the end of May I called Mary Alford and was told that the missing pony had been found up on the moor. I have to say that I did not expect her to see that pony again.

Dave Gillham had also been busy in the days after the lights. A press release saying that there were some unidentified lights seen on Cox Tor was given to the *Western Morning News* by Dave. Unfortunately, there was no response to Dave's request for other witnesses to come forward. The lack of other witnesses was disappointing, especially as an event known as 'The Ten Tors Walk' was taking place during that weekend. The Ten Tors Walk attracted many walkers, and Dave and myself had seen two RAF helicopters flying over nearby Vixen Tor on the morning of 14th May, which were probably providing support to those involved.

Dave told me that many of the flashes, picked up by his camcorder, were square or rectangular. He had also managed to get his footage copied onto a DVD and sent me a copy. A square flash of light, what was all that about?

We had captured some remarkable and possibly unique images of something – but what? Both pieces of footage needed further investigation, although they were intriguing enough as they were.

In addition to the film, I had taken a number of photographs with my trusty Olympus digital camera, and these needed examination as well. So I began to peruse the images I had taken on that eventful night. The majority of the shots were from the top of Barn Hill and were taken between 5.10 and 5.20 in the morning. The pictures had a remote beauty about them, with dramatic clouds fronted by the awesome wilderness of Dartmoor. Only one picture contained a clue to the mayhem of that early May morning. An image taken from Barn Hill, looking across to Pew Tor, revealed the faint outline of a sphere, or orb. I asked Darren Rudge for his opinion on the picture. He put the image onto a digital photo programme and played around with it. His fingers danced across the keyboard and he soon produced an image full of orbs. *'That's lens flare,'* he stated authoritatively, before reversing the process back to the original image. *'But I'm not sure what that is,'* he said, looking at the faint sphere hanging over Pew Tor. *'It could be anything – I just can't say,'* he stated in a resigned way.

I had taken some other pictures on the night at the track area near LUP 1 and these had revealed a plethora of orbs. The area where we parked our cars was providing us with some truly puzzling images. For the time being though, I considered the jury was still out on the orbs issue and a correlation between the 'lights' and some of the strange phenomena we were photographing, near the track, would come later. The digital images were worthy of an investigation on their own.

However, it was the evidence of our own eyes that left an indelible memory of the night's events. Dave and I have never seen anything like it before and neither of us will ever forget the silent, flashing visitors we witnessed on that amazing morning in May.

Jim Thorrington's outstanding photograph from 1977, showing a dead pony lying across rocks with its head lying on the bank. Note the 'bleached' appearance of the skull and compare the picture to the horse mutilation in plate 5. The rocky outcrop in the far background is Bellever Tor, 3½ miles away. *(Tavistock Times – Thorrington Archive)*

Another dead pony showing signs of advanced decomposition.
Again the skull area has a bleached appearance.
(Tavistock Times – Thorrington Archive)

A dead pony reduced to bones. The lower jaw remains, but the rest of the skull is missing perhaps showing the violence of its death.
(Tavistock Times – Thorrington Archive)

Above:
View from the top of Hollocombe Bottom in 2008. Postbridge is 2½ miles distant to the left.

Below:
Appaloosa mare named Lady, owned by Berle and Nellie Lewis, about three weeks after she was found dead and bloodlessly stripped of flesh from the neck up and all internal chest organs removed near Alamosa, Colorado, 1967.
(Don Anderson, from An Alien Harvest © *1989 Linda Moulton Howe.*

Above:
2nd January 2005, cellphone image taken by Adrian Cole. This picture was used by the BBC and others when they reported the 'occult' attack. Moortown Farm is situated beyond the trees.

Below:
Digital image taken by Frank Yeo looking up the slope towards Pew Tor, showing victims of 2nd January attack.

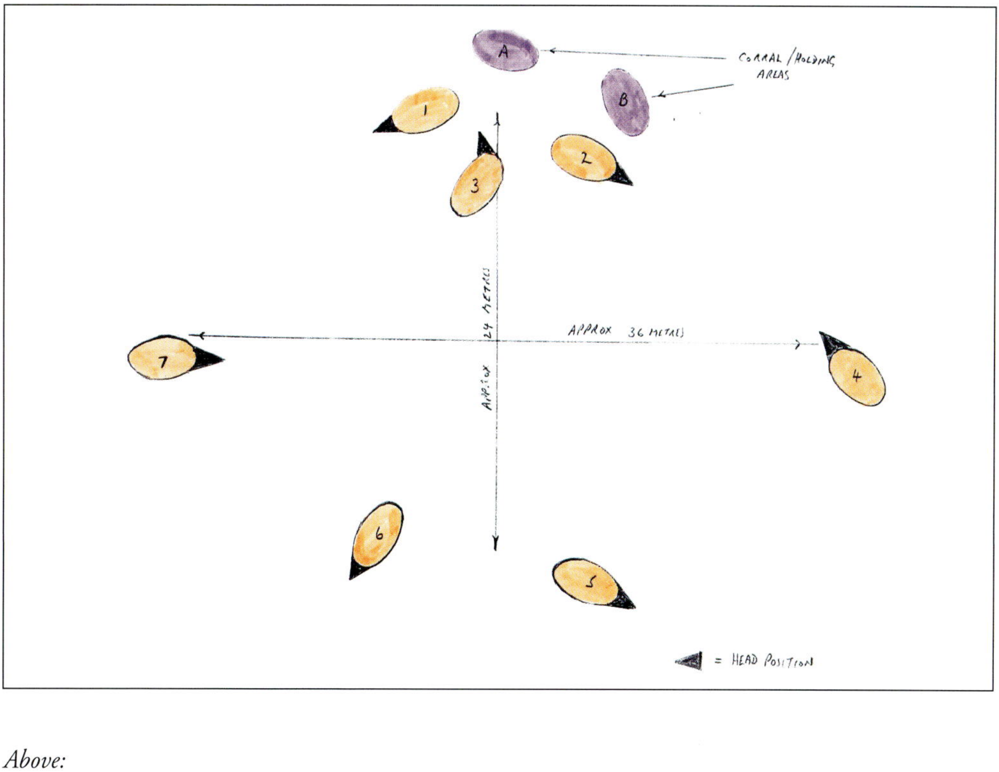

Above:
Digital image taken by Frank Yeo looking down the slope. Note the unnatural lie of two of the bodies nearest the camera.

Below:
Body map compiled from eye witnesses. Where is the occult star?

Left:
Close up of victim in the field. The precise, bloodless removal of tissue from the jaw can be seen. The police photographs clearly expose the clinical nature of this injury to the jaw tissue. *(M Alford)*

Below:
Positioning his car for a reference shot on 16th December 2005, the author was unaware of the white 'smudges' that came out on the image. The white 'orbs' seem to be moving sideways.

Inset:
'The Owlman'! Closer examination of the reference shot revealed this Keelian nightmare, a shadowy entity standing by the boot of the Jaguar. Two pictures were taken from this position only a few minutes apart, both show the 'Owlman'.

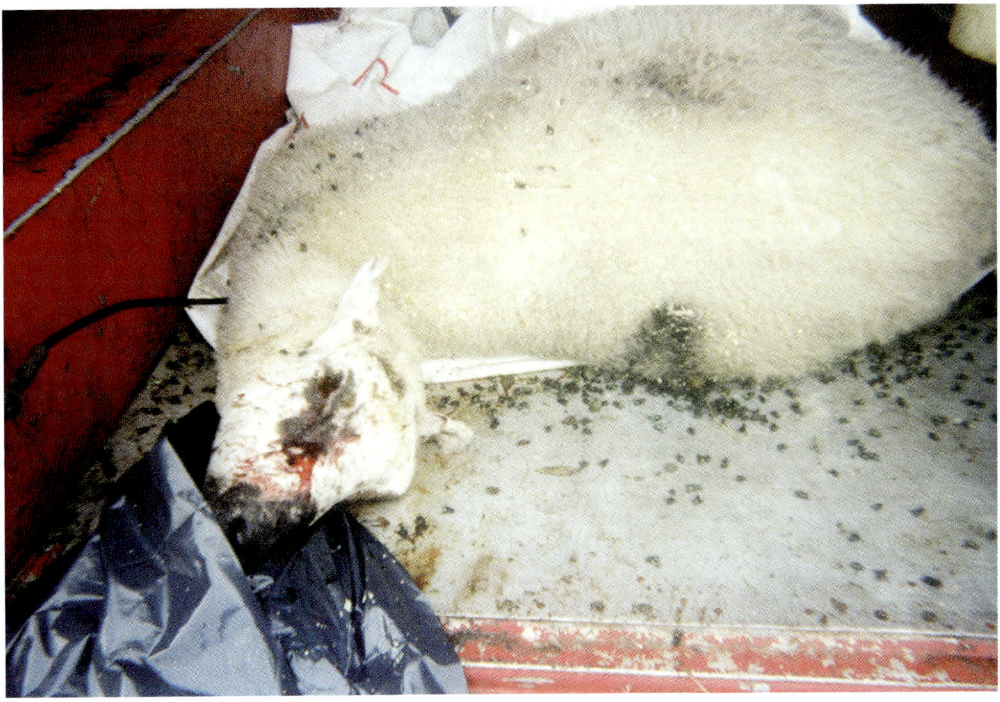

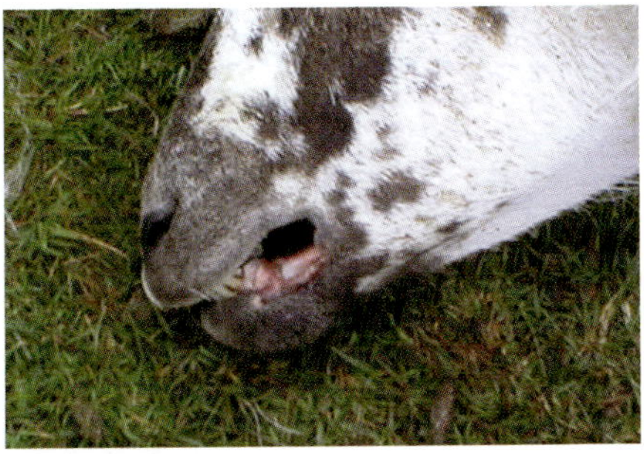

Above:
What did the mutilators do to this dead sheep that killed all the blow flies? *(M Alford)*

Left:
28th June 2006 one of three victims found on the plateau next to Pork Hill car park. This victim has the classic 'cookie cutter' mutilation to the jaw.

Left:
Long shot of 'cookie cutter' victim as natural scavengers have begun their work. Pew Tor is prominent in the background.

Above:
Entrance to Leahurst Campus at the University of Liverpool. *(D Cayton)*

Below:
Long exposure shot showing a silhouetted Dave Gillham at LUP1 as we gathered equipment for another long night.

Above:
Flash image taken near the track showing orbs and rectangular light forms the origin of which are unknown.

Below:
Second flash image showing that the light forms appear to be moving.

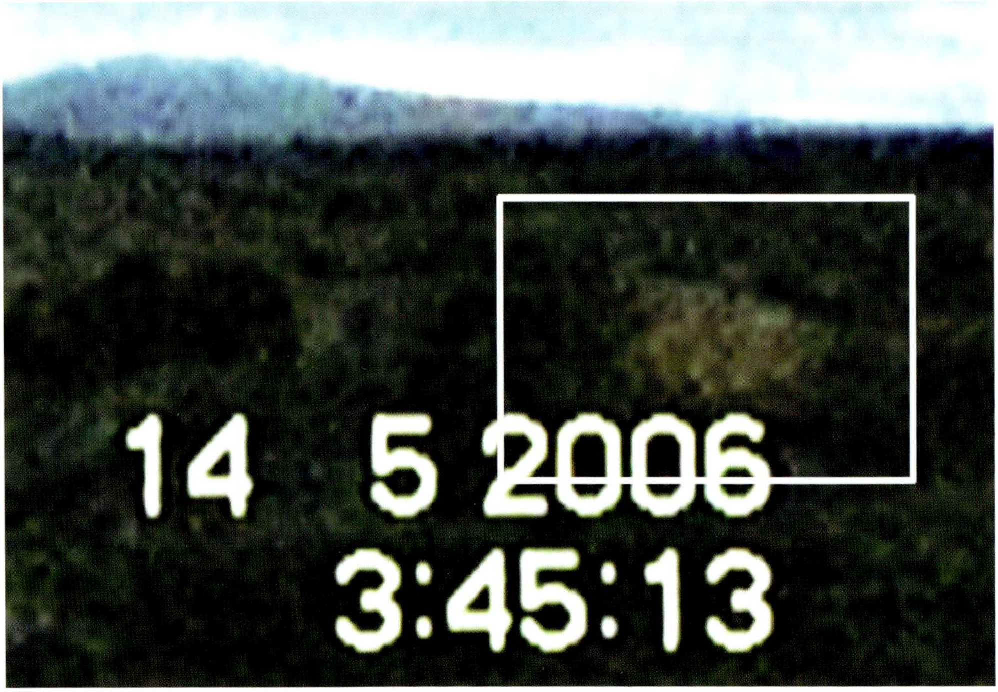

Above:
From a sequence of images taken from footage on 14th May 2006, showing an object of unknown origin that appears and then disappears in a couple of seconds.

Below:
Image from analysed footage of an object rising from the moor floor and exiting to the right. The camera time is incorrect, it is in fact 4:45:13, one hour behind.

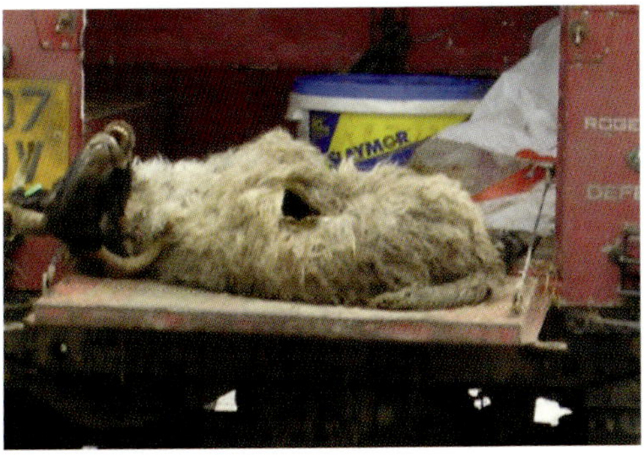

Above:
Dramatic image of Pew Tor from site of 4th November 2007 attack.

Left:
Image taken by Dave Gillham on 16th November 2008 of the last recorded victim lying in the back of Mary Alford's Land Rover.

Left:
Dave Gillham's car parked near to the place where the last recorded victim was found.
(D Gillham)

Above:
One of two victims on Barn Hill, 16th October 2005. The elliptical wound to the lower jaw can be clearly seen. © Devon & Cornwall Constabulary.

Below:
Same victim showing another elliptical wound on the underside of the body.
© Devon & Cornwall Constabulary.

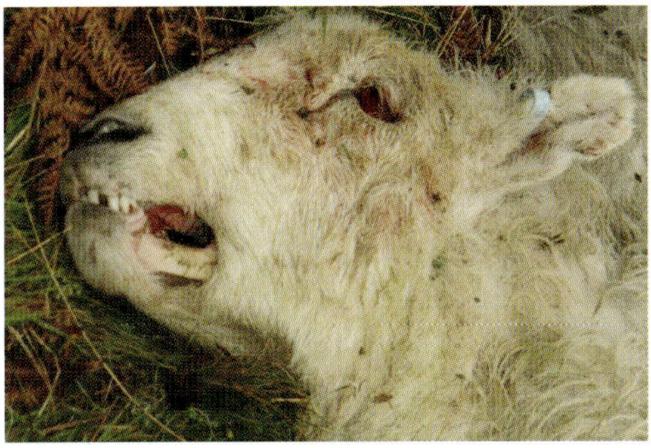

Above:
The same victim showing elliptical wound on the lower jaw and removal of one eye.
© Devon & Cornwall Constabulary.

Left:
Close up of jaw wound – no blood and a 'machined' appearance to the incision.
© Devon & Cornwall Constabulary.

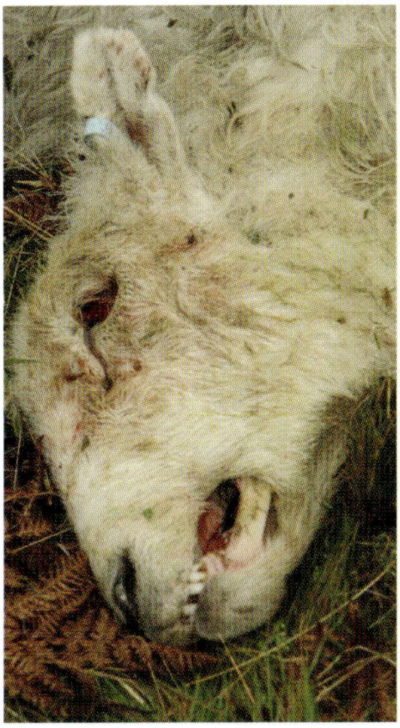

Left:
Another close up, this time from a different angle.
© Devon & Cornwall Constabulary.

Above:
One of the four victims in the Alfords' field displaying almost identical injuries to the victim on Barn Hill. *Inset:* Close up shows the wound more clearly and note the eye has been removed. © Devon & Cornwall Constabulary.

Below:
Why was this victim treated differently? It looks as though the animal has been 'unzipped' and all tissue and organs removed. © Devon & Cornwall Constabulary.

Above:
Another of the victims in the Alfords' field. Note entire lower jaw has been stripped and no blood. *Inset:* A closer view of same the victim. © Devon & Cornwall Constabulary.

Below:
Another victim in the field and it displays identical wounds to the previous victim.
Inset: In this close up of the same victim the remarkable precision and straight edges are plain to see. © Devon & Cornwall Constabulary.

Above:
Sheep circle photographed from the A9 in Scotland by Mrs Pamela Penfold.

Below:
The author (right) and Dave Gillham at Tavistock.

28

Night 6

The fact of the matter was that Dave and I could not get back to Dartmoor quickly enough in the hope of getting a second shot at the lights. The week following 14th May, Dave had threatened to go back to Pew Tor on his own. I had talked him out of such a reckless enterprise, stressing the need for back up on these risky expeditions to Dartmoor. There was also no guarantee that we might see and record something. Despite this, we made our plans for surveillance night six. The date was set for the night of Sunday 11th June, however because of storm warnings Dave suggested bringing it forward twenty-four hours. The adjustment to our plans did not dampen our enthusiasm and we were highly optimistic and raring to go.

The day before we were due to meet on Dartmoor, Dave had an interesting telephone call from a gentleman in Horrabridge, who claimed to have taken some UFO pictures, could we drop in and see him? Dave arranged an appointment and I promised to meet him at Horrabridge as soon as I could.

I set off for Dartmoor at about eight o'clock in the evening. The journey was a piece of cake and the two hundred mile journey slipped by with ease. I was so keyed up for this trip! I was convinced we would make another breakthrough. It was not long before I reached the western outskirts of Tavistock. I was running about half an hour behind my planned schedule, when I drove the last couple of miles into the village of Horrabridge. I had some difficulty finding the house I was looking for and I had to make a couple of calls from my mobile to Dave, in order to reach my destination. It had turned eleven o'clock and I was concerned as to whether my arrival at such a late hour would be welcome. However, as Dave ushered me through the front door, I was greeted with warm hospitality by the man, whose name was Phil, and his invalid wife.

Phil made us a hot drink and we sat down and discussed the interesting images that he had taken in the Horrabridge area. Phil and his wife were most interested to hear of our exploits on Dartmoor. After a while, Phil gave us details of a UFO sighting he had at the nearby Burrator reservoir. Another interesting piece of information he gave concerned the sighting of a puma on Dartmoor, in broad daylight. I knew it was likely that a big cat or two might be roaming the desolate moor, but I discounted them from any involvement in the sheep killings.

The time was getting on, so Dave and I thanked our hosts and set off to the moor. It was nearly ten to one in the morning, as we surveyed the area around Pork Hill car park. There was no activity, so we made our way to Pew Tor to continue our watch. We parked the cars by the track and I took the opportunity to take several photographs of the surrounding gloom. Dave's car, triumphantly displaying an English flag, was a subject I could not resist, so I took a couple of shots of Dave as he lifted his burden of equipment.

The weather conditions were deteriorating fast, as we trudged up the steep hillside towards Pew Tor. We made our camp above the usual site, near the disused quarry and were approximately one to two hundred metres from Pew Tor summit. A thick mist had now descended, which obscured Barn Hill and the common. Just as we were settling into our new position, I experienced the kind of misfortune that is an ever-present booby trap for the unwary on that part of Dartmoor. As I began setting up the camera tripod, my foot suddenly slipped into a hole and I fell helplessly onto a floor of granite rocks. How I didn't break anything is a mystery, but save for some mild bruising I escaped with the valuable lesson that you have to be very careful on Dartmoor during the night.

The surveillance proved to be a night of tantalising promise. Dave and I kept seeing what we thought were flashes of light from the common and Barn Hill. But we had to concede, on each occasion, that our eyes were 'playing tricks'. At 3.20 in the morning Dave saw the summit of Pew Tor momentarily light up with an intense white light. I had been facing the other way and missed this strange event. It prompted Dave to go up to the summit to find the source of the light. Although concerned that Dave was on his own I nonetheless agreed, and remained at the base camp.

Within five minutes of Dave's departure the mist over Barn Hill began to clear and I immediately sighted a large white light that appeared to glide down from Cox Tor. Later investigation led me to believe that it was probably a car descending the track that skirted round Cox Tor.

Dave finally returned to the camp about half an hour later. I was becoming concerned at his absence and it was with some relief that I saw him trudging along, some distance from our established position. The time drifted towards four o'clock and the skylarks struck up an early morning chorus. The remainder of our watch slid into obscurity as the closing mist, followed by a steady rain, brought the night's activities to a premature end.

We sat in my car and dozed, while the rain fell upon the car with increasing ferocity. At 6.30 we agreed to return home, forfeiting the customary big breakfast in exchange for an early return. For both of us, this had been a night of anti-climax that even a glimpse of high strangeness could not assuage.

29

Night 7 and the Fourth Attack

The frustration of our recent surveillance 'adventure' was barely forgotten, when I had a call from Mary Alford – there had been another three killings!

Apparently, three sheep had been killed near the top of Barn Hill and about six hundred metres or so from Pork Hill car park. The victims were a lamb and two ewes and each animal had an excised tongue, one eye removed and a broken neck. This seemed to be a classic animal mutilation attack. It was surmised that they had been killed on Monday evening, 26th June, before nine o'clock in the evening. The weather conditions had been quite poor during that particular evening, but it was very strange that no one saw the perpetrators. The car park was invariably busy during daylight hours and was a regular haunt for people walking their dogs. The police and the RSPCA were notified and inevitably the press reported the incident as further occult killings.

The BBC news also issued a report which included a statement from RSPCA Inspector Rebecca Wadey, who said, *'These sheep must have been rounded up on the open moor by whoever carried out this barbaric attack. That would have required a number of people and potentially been quite a spectacle. The bodies were found on open exposed ground very close to the road, so somebody must have seen something, even if they did not realise at the time that it was suspicious.'*

I rang Dave and announced my intention to visit Dartmoor that very night, and photograph the crime scene in the morning. Dave, as ever, gave me a resigned, *'OK, I'll go with the flow.'* I hurriedly made plans, and gathered all of my equipment. It was a piece of good fortune that the following day was my day off work. Everything seemed to be coming together.

Later that night I was cruising down the M5, full of anticipation, the familiar journey that of a commuter on autopilot. I reached Bristol in customary time, but began to feel an uneasy drowsiness that I had not experienced on any of my previous journeys. I was ten miles south of Bristol when I started to have problems keeping awake. I soon found a motorway service station and pulled thankfully into the car park. Almost immediately I surrendered to a deep sleep. I came to life about an hour and a quarter later, the time was past one o'clock. Now refreshed, I continued my journey warily, anxious that Dave would be wondering where I was as he stood alone in the bleak car park on Pork Hill.

It was 2.30 in the morning when I finally drove up the steep, winding road that took me to the summit of Pork Hill and the car park. Dave was already there and as we shook hands, Dave pointed to his car and said, *'I've got a volunteer with me.'* It was one of his sons, Mark. After a short while we decided to move down to the track, park our cars and make the trek up to Pew Tor. We eventually reached our base camp by the disused quarry. The cloudy sky hid the stars and we began our surveillance, the time was well past three o'clock in the morning.

The night was bereft of incident and the time passed slowly with tedious boredom. Only the sheep and nocturnal birds punctuated the quiet of the moor. The dawn came and we took the decision to move back to Pork Hill car park and look for the site of the latest sheep deaths.

The search for the crime scene began under the pale blue sky of a promising summer morning. We walked in a wide sweep, past the fields that bordered the moor, round to Barn Hill. We continued round to Feather Tor and back to the car park. Time was getting on and we couldn't understand why we had not found the bodies. Dave suggested I rang Mary Alford, this I was unwilling to do. I suggested we should walk out from the car park, three abreast, with about fifty metres between us. We were a little more than six hundred metres from the car park when Dave shouted that he had found something. At last! We had found the crime scene.

Crows and ravens, the vultures of England, wheeled menacingly over the scene. A single body remained in situ its rear legs splayed outwards, its head twisted. Cotton balls of fleece were scattered over the killing zone. I wondered what had happened to the body of the lamb – who or what had removed it overnight? As I started to take photographs, I immediately had a problem operating my new high-definition camera, so I was forced to revert to the trusty Olympus. Dave started his camcorder and I gave a commentary as I examined the crime scene. The dead sheep looked as though it had been stopped in its tracks and I had to wonder how the victims could have been caught at all, on that very open ground. While giving the remaining corpse a cursory examination, I noticed that apart from the missing eye, a small piece of tissue, about five or six centimetres in length, and approximately five millimetres deep had been removed from the left side of the lower jaw. Incredibly, apart from the fact there was no blood, the edge of the remaining tissue had a serrated edge – was this the classic 'cookie cutter' mutilation mentioned in many cases in the USA?

I had left the crime scene bag in the car due to the weight of this particular rucksack. Because of this, I was unable to take a sample of tissue from the dead sheep. We trudged back to the car park, quietly reflecting on the sight of the disturbing corpse we had just witnessed. What could do that? *'The way them back legs was splayed out was a bit strange, don't you think?'* said Dave. The time was now getting on for 9.30 and I rang Mary Alford. She was under the weather with a cold, but asked if we could visit the farm and see her. I told her about the lamb that had disappeared overnight and she suggested it was probably a fox – I was not so sure. Mary confirmed that the remaining body was in the back of her Land Rover, as I had requested. My concern, when Mary had first telephoned me regarding the incident, was that the body might be subject to predatory attack and that valuable evidence could be lost. Removing the body from the crime scene ensured we had a reasonably intact corpse for examination.

We drove up to Moortown Farm and parked near the back of the farmhouse. Mary greeted us and we were invited into the kitchen to discuss the circumstances of the latest attack and any developments we had made in our investigations. Mary told us that the RSPCA had been in touch and that Inspector Rebecca Wadey was investigating the incident. Mary encouraged the involvement of the RSPCA, but I had my doubts as to whether they would provide any information for us. We were joined by Danniel, Mary's son, and we gave an account of our experiences on the night of 14th May. I had brought a disk with the footage of the lights and Mary expressed a wish to see it as soon as possible. We all agreed, and it was decided that we would go to Danniel's house at Horrabridge and view the DVD there. Before we left, however, we took some video footage of the dead ewe in Mary's Land Rover. Again, I had some trouble with my camera. The ewe had been dead for possibly thirty hours and I had to make a decision on what to do with the body. For an effective post mortem to be carried out, the vet needed to get the body within twelve hours. What was I to do?

I wandered away from the back of the farmhouse and called the vet on my mobile. I was anxious to keep the name of the vet to myself, as recommended by others. The reason for doing this was that I had been told that in mutilation cases elsewhere in the UK helpful vets and scientists had been 'warned off' and, as a result, it was difficult for researchers like us to get specialist analysis. I told the veterinary practice manager that I had a sheep that had been dead for possibly thirty hours and would the vet be willing to carry out an examination? She promised to ring me back. Meanwhile, it was agreed that I would travel with Mary and Danniel in the

Land Rover (now thankfully minus one dead sheep!) Dave and Mark would follow in their car.

As Mary's red Land Rover bounced along the narrow lanes towards Horrabridge, I took a call from the vet on my mobile. It was the vet and the conversation was initially, rather bizarre. *'You want to bring in a dead sheep for examination?'*

'Yes,' I replied

'Did you kill the sheep, Mr Freebury?'

'No, I did not.'

'Did you find the sheep, Mr Freebury?'

'No, I did not. The sheep died in mysterious circumstances and I have been given permission by the farmer to take it away for a post mortem examination.'

'Oh, I see!'

I explained that the sheep had been dead for approximately thirty hours. The vet said she was willing to do a cursory examination if I could get the body to the West Midlands, two hundred and ten miles or three and a quarter hours driving away by 2 pm, before surgery started. I said I would try.

We arrived at Danniel's house and crowded into the living room. Danniel began fiddling with the controls of his television, in an attempt to get the DVD working. Eventually, the opening title 'The Lights' appeared on the screen and the drama of the night of 14th May was replayed. Straight away, we were corrected by Mary as to where the majority of lights were coming from. It was Great Staple Tor, which is adjacent to Cox Tor. Mary also made the comment that quad bikes, in fact vehicles of any sort, could not get to the top of Great Staple Tor. So what was emitting these flashes of light? The strong language that Dave and I came out with during the video caused much merriment with the Alfords. When the viewing was over there was agreement all round that we had witnessed something quite inexplicable – but did this solve the sheep deaths mystery? The fact was that it only deepened the mystery in which we had all become embroiled.

The time was nearly 11.30 and I was conscious of the deadline I had with the vet. Dave, Mark and I travelled back to Moortown Farm together. On arrival, we were relieved to have the assistance of a farm hand, who put the dead sheep into two body bags, after which the corpse was placed in the boot of my Jaguar. It was approaching twelve o'clock as I made another call to the vet, begging for an extension of the deadline. *'Get here when you can,'* they said reassuringly. As I pulled out of the tree-shaded entrance to Moortown Farm I realised that a lot was riding on the next few hours. I owed it to the vet, I owed it to Mary, and I owed it to myself to ensure that the animal was delivered on time. At last! We could have an expert opinion that was not confined to just the cause of death, on one of these strange killings.

I drove as fast as circumstances would allow, aware that the decomposing corpse in my car boot was giving off an unpleasant odour. As I reeled off the miles the smell from the boot of the car became more pungent. Luckily there were no traffic jams on the motorway and I was soon negotiating the complex motorway interchanges that have made Birmingham and its conurbation famous. It was not long before I turned up a side street and pulled into the rear car park of the veterinary surgery. The time was ten past three and I knew I could not have done the journey any quicker. I walked into the surgery and told them I had a dead sheep in the car.

I was told to bring the corpse around to the back of the surgery. This was harder than I thought as the dead weight proved rather difficult to lift out of the boot of my car. I managed to drop the dead animal at the back door and retired to the surgery waiting room. I sat for about twenty minutes, hoping that the dead ewe would yield some vital information. Eventually, the vet came out to see me. *'I'm afraid I could only do a cursory examination, as the amount of decomposition has made an internal post mortem impossible,'* she said apologetically. However, the examination had revealed some interesting features.

1. The tongue had been excised by a 'smooth' cut to the back of the mouth.
2. A two centimetre hole had been made through the underside of one leg into the abdominal cavity
3. The anal sphincter had been removed and the vet was able to put her finger through the anus, directly into the vaginal cavity.
4. There was a two and a half centimetre bruise mark on the chest area.
5. One eye had been completely removed.
6. There was a small amount of brown fluid behind the existing eyeball. The vet took a sample of this fluid and promised to send it to Birmingham University for analysis.

The vet promised to put her findings in writing, as soon as she had the results of the tests on the brown fluid. I thanked her for carrying out the gruesome task of examination and paid the fee, agreeing to collect the written report from the surgery, rather than trust it to the post.

I realised just how valuable this expert opinion had been, as Dave and myself had not picked up the hole in the underside of the leg, nor the removal of the anal sphincter, which was the first indication we had of rectal 'coring' in any of the deaths. The cored removal of the rectum was a familiar feature of the animal mutilations in the United States of America. I was also intrigued about the brown fluid at the back of the remaining eye – what could that mean?

I felt 'lifted' by the day's events and the long journey to and from Dartmoor had been really worthwhile. We were starting to get some real evidence together, which I regarded as a reward for the effort and commitment we had shown so far. The optimism I felt, dulled the memory of the discomfort of those arduous nights on Dartmoor.

A couple of days later, I rang Mary Alford and told her that I would let her have a copy of the post mortem report. I also told her that there were some unusual features concerning the injuries that the sheep had suffered, in particular, the hole into the abdominal cavity and the removal of the anal sphincter. We agreed to stay in close touch, should there be any further developments. We did not know it at the time, but there were more major developments about to happen.

30

TV or Not TV?

With all that had been going on, it was perhaps not surprising that on Tuesday 20th June Dave Gillham received an email from Mathew Balaam, Associate Producer for Satellite Park Productions in Plymouth. Satellite Park were producing a series of programmes that dealt with the paranormal for ITV West Country. Mathew asked Dave about being a possible contributor to the planned programme about UFOs and alien abductions.

Dave rang Satellite Park and discussed the proposal. He was asked not only about UFOs and abductions, but also about animal mutilations. Dave told them he could not say very much about the animal mutilation problem, but he knew a man who could, and put my name forward.

It was not long before I had a call from Mathew Balaam who wanted some details on the animal mutilations, in particular any cases from the West Country. I was a little uncomfortable about discussing the Moortown sheep killings, as the case was very much ongoing. Besides, I did not want the TV people knocking on Mary Alford's door – she wouldn't thank me for that! I told Mathew that talking to any of the farmers would be extremely difficult, if not impossible. However, I promised some information about animal mutilations in general and told him that Dave and I were willing to take a film crew along on one of our surveillance nights. Mathew seemed very keen on this idea and he agreed to contact me again to firm up some arrangements.

I spoke to Dave about the proposed visit to Dartmoor with a TV crew. Dave had been involved with the media several times through his association with the Cornwall UFO Group. He advised caution, with the wise and prophetic words, *'They're always chopping and changing things – you never know where you are with them.'*

A week or so later I rang Mathew to tell him that Dave and I were preparing a visit to Dartmoor. I was told that the idea of taking a film crew up to Pew Tor had been abandoned because the Duchy of Cornwall, who owned the land, wanted five hundred pounds for an hour of filming. *'They think we're made of money,'* said Mathew. I was told that an alternative possibility might be to do a short interview, well away from the Duchy of Cornwall's land.

I rang Satellite Park again and spoke to the producer, Mike Geldard, who told me that they were considering doing an interview with Dave and myself at Burrator reservoir, which was only a few miles from Moortown. *'We can shoot the interview on the bridge at Burrator and we can do a couple of things to make it look like night time,'* he said. I was also asked if I could provide photos of any animal mutilations. I assured Mike Geldard that I would do my best and that in the meantime I would send some information on the kind of injuries that the victims of these attacks might suffer. I was asked again if there was any footage available. I replied no, there was no way Dave and I were going to hand over any of our film footage to these people.

When I rang again to get some firm details about the interview I was told that the Burrator interview plan had been scrapped, in favour of an evening shoot at the Norman Lockyer Observatory near Exmouth. I was advised that the cost of getting me down there was prohibitive and I was thanked for my involvement. I was a little peeved to say the least. The whole episode had been frustrating and Dave's warning about our involvement with this capricious medium was proved correct.

I never kept my promise to send any pictures of animal mutilations through to Satellite Park and I have not heard from them since. Dave, on the other hand, spent an evening at the Norman Lockyer Observatory, enjoying the largesse of the TV production team, in between an interminable number of 'takes' under an uncooperative sky.

31

The Watch of the Damned – Night 8 and the Fifth and Sixth Attacks

It was Sunday 9th July and I was with Darren Rudge in the Brasshouse pub in Birmingham. We were listening to the Dave Moore Band who were playing at the Brasshouse as part of the Birmingham blues and jazz festival. They had just finished their first set as Darren and I jostled to the bar to order a bottle of Australian red wine. My mobile phone rang and I pushed my way from the front of the bar to the entrance, so I could take the call and hear myself above the cacophony of clarinet solos and raucous banter.

The call was from Mary Alford, who told me that there had been two more killings. I could scarcely believe it. We had been down there only two weeks previously. What the hell was going on? Mary said that the victims, both lambs, had been killed at two separate locations. One on the familiar killing area of the common, and another on open heath land near Tavistock Golf Club. The latter attack was less than a mile from Moortown Farm, but in an area where there had been no previous attacks. There was no indication as to the precise time of death in either case, and they were both linked by the injuries they received – excised tongues and one eye removed. I promised Mary that I would visit her on the following Friday.

We had been caught off balance again. Had the perpetrators moved up a gear? When I got home I studied the ordnance survey map and picked out the locations. What had made 'them' move that far from their normal killing zone? Why were these two lambs selected? We were losing control of the situation.

The following day, I rang Dave and gave him the details of the recent attacks. I told Dave that I was going to go down to Dartmoor on Friday. I did not expect Dave to meet me during the day on Friday, but hoped he would join me for surveillance night eight. It goes without saying that Dave readily agreed, and a couple of days later asked if he could meet me during the day, so that we could go and see Mary Alford together.

On Monday 10th July I had a call from the vet to inform me that the written post mortem report was ready for collection. The report contained all the information given to me verbally by her, together with a couple of lines about the brown fluid. I quote directly from the post mortem report: *'A dark brown fluid was present within the anterior chamber of the right eye. Cytology of the fluid revealed macrophages containing rod shaped bacteria.'*

The vet suggested that the rod shaped bacteria might have been responsible for the death of the sheep. Having seen the other body, in situ, I had to disagree, the three sheep had met a sudden and violent end.

On the morning of Friday 14th July I made a last-minute check of everything I needed, which included two copies of the post mortem report, one of which had all details of the vet censored. At nine o'clock I set off for Dartmoor, wondering what we might see on surveillance night eight.

On a glorious Devon day I arrived at Pork Hill car park. For once, I was there before Dave. It had turned midday and a stiff breeze swept across the car park. I looked at the majestic sight of Cox Tor, towering behind the B3357, and listened to the sustained warbling of skylarks, thinking how idyllic it all was.

Dave arrived just after one o'clock and after a brief chat we decided to ring Mary, to see if it was convenient for a meeting. Mary asked us to come down to the farm. We were soon driving up the tree lined drive to the farmhouse and were greeted by Mary, who suggested we discuss matters in the kitchen.

I began by giving details of the vet's report, explaining the difficulties of getting a full post mortem done within the recommended twelve hours. The logistics were against us I argued and Mary agreed, suggesting that she, or Frank her partner, could meet me near Bristol. This offer, gladly accepted by me at the time, was to have severe consequences for me in the future. I felt that the offer showed that we were getting somewhere, as the travelling for me was excessive and in any event, the best turnaround I could manage was seven and a half hours. Mary also stated that she wanted to give the next body to the RSPCA, to see what they could come up with. I agreed with the proposal, but secretly I was sceptical of their involvement.

Mary also said that the Dartmoor Livestock Association were willing to put up a substantial reward for information leading to the arrest and conviction of the perpetrators. I told Mary there would be no takers! I had a mental picture of two policemen, frogmarching a diminutive alien into Tavistock police station, saying to their superior, *'We've got him Sarge! The little rascal has coughed to the lot, and we've booked him for parking his space craft in a restricted parking area!'*

I also told Mary that I was prepared to give a presentation about the series of attacks, and our investigations so far, to the Dartmoor Livestock Association. She agreed to sound them out on the offer. The meeting concluded with another moment of major significance, although the repercussions of it could not possibly have been realised at the time. I gave Mary a choice of post mortem report, either a full copy or the censored copy, with the vet's identity expunged. I trusted Mary completely, but felt I should give her the option. I had explained previously how difficult it could be to retain the assistance of experts, because of the nature of the subject we were involved with. Mary hardly hesitated. *'Give me a censored copy, if there is ever a leak, you'll know it couldn't be from this end,'* she said. Mary's decision was a seminal moment and one that would have dramatic implications for the investigation.

Mary took us to the scenes of the two recent killings. The first was situated in open heath land, close to Tavistock Golf Club. The area was a favourite place for people to bring their dogs for exercise and always had people coming and going. I looked across the open heath bordered by gorse bushes, a shallow pool dominating the scene. The mother of the lamb had obviously been distressed by the attack, unable to do anything about the horrific violation – if only they could talk! Two questions sprang to mind concerning this attack. How did they carry out the assault in such an open and popular place, without being discovered in the act? And why was just one lamb selected? I took some photos of the scene, before squeezing with Dave back in to Mary's red Land Rover to head back to the farm.

We took the main B3357, turning right into an unmarked track and a winding circuitous journey to the next crime scene. Once again, Mary gave us a taste of what real off-roading was! The field where the second attack took place was both large and secluded with tall hedges all round it. Apparently a single lamb, the best specimen in a flock of one hundred and twenty sheep, was selected and killed. The body was left in the corner of the field. Again, questions had to be asked. Why did they select one, very fit, lamb from the large flock that was present? And how did they get to this secluded field, which was not that far from the farmhouse, without being detected?

The visit to the two crime scenes finished in hilarious fashion as Mary drove her Land Rover in zigzag fashion across the next field, herding the cattle through a gateway, to a chorus of yelps. All this was achieved as Dave hung out the window of the red Defender, with his camcorder, recording the event for posterity!

We thanked Mary for her time and made our way down the track towards nearby Pew Tor. We decided to climb to the top and reconnoitre the area from the high vantage point. In bright, warm sunshine, we surveyed the area from the summit of Pew Tor. Surprisingly, we were unable to see Pork Hill car park from our lofty position. We decided against using the summit for our surveillance, as we had both good viewing and quicker access to the common from the disused quarry. The time was now getting on for five o'clock and I suggested we drive to Princetown, some five miles east, and get something to eat.

Princetown is the home of Dartmoor prison, built by French prisoners of the Napoleonic war, and used for home-grown criminals ever since. We settled into a pleasant café and planned our next move, as we ate an excellent meal. The hours of darkness were much restricted and we had plenty of time before darkness fell, so we took the opportunity to visit Burrator reservoir, which was only a few miles away. This was the place suggested by the TV people for an interview, so we drove around the reservoir, took some photos and generally killed a bit of time. We were both anxious to get down to the serious business of surveillance work, so we had made our way back to Pork Hill car park and sat in the car as the evening sunlight gave way to the chilly darkness of night, the moor had changed moods again. As the time moved on to eleven o'clock, we made our way round to the track and parked the car. The sky was clear and dominated by the shining moon. We trudged up towards the disused quarry on Pew Tor, complacent about the weather conditions we might face that night.

I have to say that we were both feeling very tired. Whether this was because of an accumulation of stress and mental tiredness, understandable given the amount of things that had happened in the last six months, or maybe we weren't as well prepared as we should have been. I think it was the former.

Apart from the occasional shooting stars there was nothing of note to report and again, any human activity was absent from the moor. The cold wind made our watch quite miserable. As we stood among the granite rocks, mentally pleading for some respite, the ice-cold wind whistled around us like an individual tornado. There was no escape from it and the night developed into a battle against sleep and the cold. It was not surprising therefore, that we abandoned the surveillance as the time crept towards four o'clock in the morning. Disappointed that we could stand no more, we stumbled wearily back to the car and fell into an uncomfortable sleep.

The night had been very difficult for both of us and the long nights on Dartmoor were, I thought, beginning to take their toll. The surveillance nights had become the watch of the damned and we both needed a rest. I began to feel that I could not go on for much longer and I was conscious of drawing Dave into the dangerous spiral of exhaustion and mental tiredness.

There was an air of depressing disappointment as we took the decision to cancel our customary breakfast and head for home. The journey became a trip of endurance, as I fought off desperate tiredness, relieved by regular 'cat naps' in anonymous service stations all the way up the M5. When I got home I had a text message from Dave. I felt mightily relieved that he had made it back to Cornwall safely. I wondered if we could carry on like this and whether we should take a break from it for a while. However, there was to be a new twist in this complex saga and a turn of events that I could not have bargained for.

32

DEFRA From the Very Top

A week after our exhausting trip to Dartmoor I was busy at work, preparing the financial schedules that were my stock in trade. It was Friday and only a couple of hours remained of my working week. My mobile phone rang and initially I did not recognise the number. It was the vet. I thought she might have some more information for the post mortem report, but I was soon to discover otherwise. She asked if she could speak to me for few minutes, her tone of voice was that of a strict schoolmistress about to admonish a wayward pupil. What was coming next, I thought.

The vet informed me that the veterinary surgery had been contacted by the local Environmental Health Officer, who had demanded a copy of the post mortem report that she had carried out on the dead ewe on 28th June 2006. Furthermore, he wanted my details as well! The vet was unwilling, at first, to accede to this request and had taken the advice of a solicitor. Vets, like doctors, take their responsibilities very seriously and this demand for confidential information was unwelcome to say the least. The legal advice was that the veterinary surgery had to comply with the request, which the Environmental Health Officer had now faxed through. The vet seemed to feel some embarrassment about the predicament and asked what my thoughts on the matter were. I said that I had nothing to hide and that I took full responsibility for bringing the dead ewe to her for examination. I assured her that I had no problems with any disclosures she would have to make and that if I did not hear from the EHO, I would ring him myself.

I sat momentarily stunned, barely able to comprehend this sinister development. How on earth had they found out? How could the Environmental Health Officer have known? Who could have told him the identity of the vet? Only I knew, and I had been very careful to keep it that way. The enormity of Mary Alford's decision to have the censored copy of the post mortem report suddenly dawned on me.

On Monday 24th July I called the vet and asked if it was at all possible that someone at the veterinary surgery could have notified the Environmental

Health Department. She was confident that no one connected with the surgery would have mentioned the post mortem, either in passing or in an official capacity.

By Tuesday 25th July I had still not received a letter from the Environmental Health Officer. I decided to try and ring him, unfortunately he was out and I was told to try and ring him the following day. That afternoon I took a call from Mary Alford, who told me that PC Pickles of Tavistock police had visited her on Friday 21st July and asked for the telephone number of the Dartmoor Livestock Association. Mary considered this to be rather odd as the police already had the number on file. Mary also told me that there had been three more sheep deaths, which had been put down to a dog attack.

On Wednesday 26th July I rang the Environmental Health Officer, deciding that attack was the best form of defence. The Environmental Health Officer took the call and asked for brief moment while he adjusted his phone. I was sure I heard a click prior to our conversation and wondered whether the call was being recorded. Not to be outdone, I held my small Dictaphone to the earpiece, and attempted to record the conversation from my end. Unfortunately, this attempt was undone because the recording of the Environmental Health Officer's comments was affected by some unknown interference. I was, nonetheless, able to complete a transcript of the conversation from memory and notes taken at the time.

I began by introducing myself and, after confirming that the post mortem was carried out on my instructions, I asked the Environmental Health Officer how he had come by the identity of the vet. He replied, '*I had a request from the Ministry Regional Vet for information relating to the circumstances surrounding the post mortem carried out on this sheep, especially as it had been transported across several counties, to the borough in order for the post mortem to be carried out.*'

I found myself on the back foot as the Environmental Health Officer said, '*The movement of dead animals is obviously of some concern to us and this is why I have been asked to look into the matter.*

'*The Ministry Regional Vet has powers under the Animal Health Act to ensure that there are strict controls on the movement of dead animals. Moving a dead sheep from Devon to Walsall is plainly an issue that raises some concerns.*'

I asked when the Ministry Regional Vet had made the request for information and was told it was Friday 21st July 2006, the same day that the vet had contacted me. Plainly, the instruction had been acted on immediately. The Environmental Health Officer said that the Ministry Regional Vet had obviously got concerns. I decided to go on the offensive, and said, '*What is quite interesting is that first of all I am quite sure that the Ministry Regional Vet knows precisely what it is that I'm looking into. I'm investigating a series of unexplained killings and beyond that I'm not prepared to say at this stage.'*

'Animals?' the Environmental Health Officer asked.

'Animals? Yes, I am staggered that they could have found out the identity of the vet, which makes me think! And I assure you that what I'm actually doing is basically, carrying out my patriotic duty,' I stated zealously.

The Environmental Health Officer countered, *'We cannot allow the unauthorised movement of dead livestock around the country willy-nilly as there are all kinds of issues involved, such as the spread of foot and mouth and other highly infectious diseases.'*

I had to reassure the Environmental Health Officer that we had taken adequate precautions in the transportation of the carcass. He then asked about the involvement of the police. I told him that they were unable to help at all.

We then got onto the subject of the post mortem report. I gave details of the unusual injuries, highlighted by the vet's report, suffered by the sheep. I also said that there were links from the Dartmoor killings to similar cases in the United States and that they were being put down as occult killings. This, I assured him, was not the case. I was asked how long I had been investigating this series of killings and told him eighteen months. The Environmental Health Officer asked, *'Could this not be down to the occult or satanists?'*

'Absolutely not, no, there is a sampling aspect to this, as if something is sampling the livestock,' I stated authoritatively.

'I see that's very interesting,' commented the Environmental Health Officer, intriguingly.

I said, reassuringly, *'Yes, I certainly don't wish to cause any trouble or transgress any laws or regulations, but I really don't think that there has been any risk in this particular instance.'*

The Environmental Health Officer agreed.

I then asked him if he had written to me. He confirmed that he had and that when I received the letter I should disregard it as we had already discussed the issues involved. He then said that he would let the Ministry Regional Vet know the outcome of our discussions. I said that they could contact me directly, if they wished.

His curiosity remained and he asked if the animal attacks were confined to Devon. I replied that they were widespread and that there was a pattern to the attacks across the country, of which the Ministry Regional Vet was probably aware.

The call ended amicably and had lasted just under eleven and a half minutes. I was surprised that he had simply followed instructions from the Ministry Regional Vet and that the demand for information had been no more than that. I hadn't been sure what to expect when I called him and at the back of my mind I thought that some legal sanction might have been initiated. But the question remained – How did they find out the identity of the vet?

I rang Mary Alford that evening and told her about my conversation with the EHO. Mary was perplexed, as I was, as to how they had obtained the vet's identity. Mary also asked which area the Ministry Regional Vet represented. It was a basic question that I had forgotten to ask, although I assumed it to be the Midlands area. There are eight regions within DEFRA and it was likely to be one of two – the Midlands or South West. Anyway, I had an excuse to ring the Environmental Health Officer again and hopefully elicit more information about the origin of his instruction.

I visited the veterinary surgery on Friday 28th July and spoke to the vet and Charlotte, the practice manager. They were both adamant that no one from the practice would have disclosed knowledge of the post mortem to anyone. What would be the point, anyway?

I had my suspicions as to how DEFRA had obtained the identity of the vet. I had been very careful not to disclose the name to anyone, even my wife and Dave Gillham. I had always used my mobile to speak to the vet, never a land line.

Has the penny dropped yet? The police or the security services, under instruction from DEFRA, no doubt, had obtained my mobile phone records and traced the vet from the calls I made. A time line of events tells the story:

28th June 2006, the vet carried out the post mortem.
10th July 2006, I collected the post mortem report from the veterinary surgery.
14th July 2006, I gave Mary Alford a censored copy of the post mortem report.
21st July 2006, PC Pickles visits Mary Alford.
21st July 2006, the Ministry Regional Vet contacted Walsall Environmental Health Officer.
21st July 2006, the Environmental Health Officer contacted the vet

DEFRA contacted the local Environmental Health Officer three weeks after the post mortem was done, why was this? I believe that someone in the Moortown area, possibly the police, found out that a post mortem had been carried out on one of the dead sheep. They would only have found out about the post mortem when Mary Alford gave a copy to the Dartmoor Livestock Association, but it was a censored copy, so the only way they could have discovered the identity of the vet was to check on the person who had requested the vet to carry out an examination – me! The police or the security services would have found little difficulty in getting the vet's identity. The information they needed was available on my confidential mobile phone records: eight or nine calls and a bit of straightforward deduction and they had what they wanted.

How could they do this? I was seething, after all they were treating me like a criminal. I had no doubts now about the scale of this investigation and the 'dark forces' ranged against us.

On Monday 31st July I received the letter that the Environmental Health Officer had mentioned he had sent. I noticed that the letter was dated 27th July, the day after we had spoken on the phone and it was not posted until 28th July. He was, I thought, ensuring that he complied with the instructions he had been given. He had obviously told the Ministry Regional Vet that he had written to me and sent the letter, despite having discussed matters with me already.

On Thursday 3rd August I telephoned the Environmental Health Officer again and asked him which Ministry Regional Vet had contacted him about the post mortem. After shuffling some papers about, he asked if he could ring me back, as the original email was lost on his desk. I bet I don't hear from him again, I thought, negatively. How wrong I was! He rang back within a couple of minutes and what he said was a bombshell.

'The whole thing was done by email and the instruction came from the Regional Ministry Vet at Stafford (West Midlands Area) and they, in turn, were acting on an email from Leahurst, whatever that is.'

The Environmental Health Officer did not know what Leahurst was, but I did!

Leahurst, or to give it its full title, Leahurst Campus, University of Liverpool, is based at Neston, south of Liverpool and is fully funded by DEFRA. It is the Animal Health and Welfare Disease Surveillance Centre and draws information from across the UK, through a number of veterinary laboratories run under the Veterinary Laboratory Agency. These include VLA Starcross at Exeter and VLA Preston, otherwise known as Barton Hall, which the researcher David Cayton has established, runs an animal mutilation section.

I was staggered! What on earth was going on? I was being investigated by DEFRA from one of their establishments in Liverpool. What did that tell me? The Dartmoor sheep deaths were being monitored at a very high level and they were very interested in our research. Why did they not contact me directly? What had they got to hide?

There was one thing I knew for sure I would never underestimate a government agency again. I also knew that they could not play this particular card again, because I resolved to be as cunning and devious as they were!

33

August and the Seventh and Eighth Attacks

It was Monday 21st August and I arrived for work as usual, contemplating the problems that I would be dealing with that day. After the usual round of good mornings and moans about the heavy traffic, a work colleague asked if I had seen an article in the *Mail on Sunday*, about the Dartmoor sheep deaths. I was taken aback as I had not anticipated a prominent article on the killings appearing in the national press at this time. I decided to get a copy of the article and find out who wrote it.

The article, which had been written by Nick Constable, a freelance journalist, carried the headline 'Occultists slaughter sheep on Charles estate' and was full of references to the occult. The story made much of the fact that the killings occurred on land belonging to Prince Charles as part of the Duchy of Cornwall. Princetown beat officer PC David Pickles made the statement that the attacks were being treated as 'criminal damage with a ritual motive'. We had heard all this sort of stuff before, and not just in relation to the Dartmoor killings. The article and the headline were reminiscent of similar headlines in the United States. Perhaps I should have called PC Pickles and told him that no one has ever been arrested in America for any of the tens of thousands of so-called 'occult' killings.

On Tuesday 22nd August I had a call from Mary Alford, who informed me of another attack, the seventh. Incredibly the attack, which happened the previous day, appeared to have been carried out between two o'clock and five o'clock in the afternoon, in a field close to the farmhouse! The victim was a lamb, its tongue and one eye had been removed and there were signs of possible rectal coring. How did they do it? The farm was very busy, yet no one saw anything.

Mary also told me about some highly unusual military activity during the night of Wednesday and Thursday 16th and 17th August. At around midnight a large plane (possibly an RAF Hercules or similar-sized aircraft) had flown so low over the farmhouse that in Mary's words, *'It nearly took the roof off.'* The plane appeared to manoeuvre over the common and Barn Hill as if photographing the area. It should be noted that this part of Dartmoor is never used for military exercises. I believe this incident was very significant, as we shall see in a later chapter.

I told Mary that I was unable to get down to Moortown and take the body for examination. However, Mary had decided to offer the dead animal to the RSPCA, so that they could get a post mortem done, promising me, fatalistically, that we could have the next body. I agreed to the proposal, although I did not share her confidence in the RSPCA giving any feedback on any post mortem that they carried out.

I spoke to Mary again on 24th August and she told me that RSPCA Inspector Rebecca Wadey did not turn up for the body until two o'clock that afternoon. Unwilling to put the carcass in the boot of her car, Inspector Wadey had sourced a flat trailer to transport the dead animal. She told Mary that the post mortem would be carried out by VLA Starcross at Exeter. It was with some considerable surprise that while Mary was driving near the common, she saw Rebecca Wadey parked by the roadside. The time was 3.30 in the afternoon and the trailer, with the body still on it, was still attached to the back of Rebecca Wadey's car. I have some sympathy for Rebecca, as the transportation of dead sheep over relatively short distances can be quite unpleasant! It was some time later that Mary got a copy of the post mortem report and gave me a copy, asking me for my comments.

The report, carried out by VLA Starcross, highlighted something that would be found in later killings, the abdominal cavity was severely bloated and the left eye socket was empty. In addition, the tongue had been removed (although without the usual precision) and the rectum was missing. You will remember that the ewe examined by the vet in the West Midlands also had this type of injury. The report concluded that natural predators could have been responsible for the removal of the tongue, eye and rectum and that the other injuries to the lamb could have been caused by a vehicle. I should point out that the dead lamb had been found in a field close to the Alford farmhouse. Are we to assume, therefore, that the lamb was run over by Mary Alford herself? I don't think so!

On 15th August I gave a talk to the Stourbridge UFO group, UFORM. I was better prepared this time and the talk went really well. I was able to show Dave's footage, complete with expletives! Seeing it on a large screen was a considerable improvement over a small TV screen and I noticed that there were flashes of light much closer to us than we had thought at the time. I felt that the topical nature of the Dartmoor attacks gave an edge to the talk, which was heightened when I told them about DEFRA and my mobile phone. I was able to throw in the pictures of the orbs and other strange lights that I had photographed and there was much enthusiasm for the wide range of strange elements that were coming together in this case. I overran and I had to curtail my talk towards the end so that there was some time for questions. The talk gave me a morale boost and I felt I had something to say about animal mutilations and UFOs. This injection of confidence could only be beneficial to me on the long, hard road to find an answer to the Dartmoor sheep killings.

At 9.30 on Wednesday 30th August I had a call from Mary Alford, telling me that there had been another attack, this time up on the common. The attack had been on Tuesday 29th August and the victim, a ewe, had one eye missing, possible rectal coring, but no tongue removal. In addition to this there were three sheep killed on another farm, just a quarter of a mile down Pork Hill, the cause of death was unknown. I told Mary I would ring back that evening for more details and to discuss the possibility of making another trip to Dartmoor.

That evening I rang Mary and told her that I would be unable to come down to see her about the latest killings. She gave me some further background to the three sheep deaths. Apparently, it was thought that dogs were responsible, but this was considered unlikely, as the bodies were not torn. The grass around the bodies was flattened as if the sheep were stampeded. The cause of death remained unknown.

On 31st August Mary rang to tell me about a centre spread that had appeared in the *Western Morning News*, under the headline 'Is the Devil's work being done on Dartmoor?'. The large article was peppered with references to the occult, and was written by the same reporter who had also penned the story for the *Mail on Sunday*. The double-page spread contained all the elements of the story in the *Mail* with a number of further embellishments. There were pictures too, one of Chris Cole, one of an apparent pagan ritual with people dancing around a fire, and the iconic image of the dead sheep in the first attack, taken by Adrian Cole on his mobile phone. Interestingly, the article mentioned two post mortems that had been carried out. The first apparently was inconclusive, although the vet had said that the animal was probably alive when the injuries were being inflicted – this was plainly a different post mortem from the one we had carried out. The second referred directly to the October 2005 attacks and said that six sheep (there were eight) had their eyeballs removed and, to quote directly, *'Vets later confirmed that the mutilation was not the work of birds.'* Note the word vets, plural, and as Mary Alford was not aware of any post mortem, then the vets must have been instructed by the police. No wonder they did not want me to see the police file on the killings! The article also mentioned a killing near

Plympton, some miles away, and that a half moon had been carved into the body.

The article was a triumph of tabloid journalism, succeeding as it did in bringing several popular elements together. In a masterful piece of writing, the reporter managed to bring in the notorious Aleister Crowley, once described as 'the wickedest man in the world'. Not content with this he even mentioned the Seventies cult film *The Wicker Man*, before appeasing the modern cult of celebrity by mentioning that Noel Edmonds, Adrian Edmondson, Jennifer Saunders, Lenny Henry, Dawn French and Peter de Savary had homes in Chagford, twelve miles away. They might just as well have been a million miles away! The article concluded with the viewpoint of the Church of England that *'This is a nasty business and the people responsible clearly need spiritual, if not mental, help.'*

Mary also mentioned that she had spoken to Rebecca Wadey's superior at the RSPCA about the lack of feedback and information concerning the post mortem. The superintendent seemed indifferent to Mary's complaint and was unable to offer hope that information would be forthcoming. Interestingly, when Mary told him about the latest attack victim, he immediately inquired as to what had happened to the body.

On Friday 1st September I had a call from Mary saying she was going to Scotland for a few days and would be away during our next visit to Dartmoor. I was given Danniel's mobile number and it was agreed that he would be our point of contact.

Mary concluded the conversation by telling me that she had checked the body of the ewe in the back of her Land Rover and was astonished to find a large pile of dead blow flies, beside the body. There were dead flies all around the corpse and Mary expressed some alarm that she had handled it without gloves. She had taken a photograph of this disturbing sight and promised to send it to me.

When I received the picture some time later, I was completely taken aback, so much so that I sent a copy of the photo to the vet, for her opinion. Further research revealed that this was no isolated phenomenon. In a book by the American researcher Frederick W. Smith, called *Cattle Mutilation – The Unthinkable Truth*, published in 1976, there was the following reference to this disturbing development:

> *What might be much less ridiculous is that mutilated carcasses, and especially the cut areas, are sometimes sprayed or coated with something to repel predators. Why would that be done? To make sure the mutilations are recognized for what they actually are. The repellent would be another form of calling card. Have any labs*

checked for that? We doubt it, and also doubt that labs would know what they had after they found it. Can we conclude from this that the predators are inherently smarter than the scientists?

Oh yes! They're smarter than the scientists all right!

34

Night 9 – More Flashes of Light

I was only too well aware that our previous trip to Dartmoor had pushed us to the edge, physically and mentally. I was determined to avoid such a dangerous situation again. The fact was that after a night of surveillance on that unforgiving moor, we just had to have some proper rest before making the return journey. My solution to this problem was to book us into the campsite that was adjacent to Moortown Farm. We would be able to sleep in the tent for a few hours before our journey home. We planned the trip for Friday 8th September 2006, with a return on Saturday 9th.

On the Friday morning of 8th September I went through the familiar routine of packing my equipment. There was, however, a change to the manifest, as I had purchased a small two-man tent and sleeping bag. I thought we would book in for one night and retain an option for a second night. The cost would be minimal, a factor that was becoming more important, especially as the expense of the investigation so far had been fairly heavy because of the distances involved.

The regular attacks on the sheep, which now appeared to be without logic of timing or date, made me feel optimistic about our chances of seeing something, or at least being first to the scene of the crime. It was with these positive thoughts in my head that I set off on the journey that was now so familiar to me.

As I drove through the western outskirts of Tavistock I felt the relief of a weary commuter, as the end of another journey to Moortown came near. I turned left onto the B3357 and drove under the canopy of trees until the steep climb up Pork Hill. I pulled into the car park and looked around at the numerous cars that were coming and going, each one disgorging its cargo of owner and dog to enjoy the bracing wind and bright sunshine. The lofty concourse was always busy at this time of day. I took a walk across the common, pressing on through a stiff breeze, towards the fields that that skirted the moor down to Moortown. After twenty minutes or so I began to retrace my steps back to the car park. I was within a hundred yards of my car when I saw the familiar figure of Dave. We spent a long time catching up on news and topics of conversation that we felt uncomfortable discussing over the phone (we were suspicious at this time that our phones were being monitored). Late afternoon approached and we thought it wise to organise our accommodation for the night.

We booked into the campsite and found a suitably quiet corner, ringed by tall trees. A bonfire burned a large tree root nearby, which spewed charred fragments of wood and white smoke above us. The tent was erected amid muffled obscenities and tetchy arguing as to the correct sequence of installation. Our amateur performance was viewed, disdainfully, by the 'professional' campers, who looked on from their awnings and luxurious motor homes. When the task was complete we basked in the snug, but basic, comfort of the tent trying to convince ourselves that no hotel on Earth could match the luxury we now found ourselves in. As the gathering gloom made way for the darkness of the night, we left our homely den and made our way to the familiar remoteness of Pork Hill car park

We spent the first few hours at the car park discussing a variety of subjects. You would have thought that we had exhausted every subject known to us, not so! The night sky was again cloudy, but revealed a star or two as the dark clouds occasionally parted. We looked at the dark mass of Cox Tor behind us, nothing stirred and even the road was empty of traffic. The time was approaching midnight and as we were aware of a surreptitious tiredness, we decided to head back to the campsite and the snug comfort of our tent, to get a couple of hours sleep before resuming our vigil.

When we got to the tent, Dave set the alarm on his mobile phone as we clambered awkwardly, into our sleeping bags. Both of us submitted, almost immediately, to a deep sleep that was only interrupted by the mobile phone alarm. The time was about 2.30 in the morning and we extricated ourselves from the sleeping bags with the same difficulty we had had in getting into them. We crept stealthily from the tent and made our way to the car. There is no way of starting a car quietly and my guilt at possibly waking our tented neighbours, in the middle of the night, was lessened by the twisted reasoning that if they had posh tents, then they probably had double glazing in them!

We soon reached the parking place along the track and after I had taken my usual batch of photos, we loaded ourselves with equipment and set off for the disused quarry up Pew Tor. The time was nearly three o'clock in morning as we encamped in a flurry of activity. We both knew the drill now and it was not long before my camcorder was set up in readiness. The first twenty minutes passed without incident and it looked as if we were in for another night without reward. Dave, hoping to make something happen no doubt, decided to go on one of his wandering searches of the upper reaches of Pew Tor. As usual I was not happy about this, but consented on the proviso that he was back within fifteen minutes or so. The dangers of wandering around on Pew Tor, at that time of night, were all too obvious.

Dave had been gone only a few minutes, when I saw a large flash of light from Cox Tor. They're back! I thought, triumphantly. The flash of light was just the same as those that had begun the invasion of the common on May 14th. I immediately set the camcorder running and anchored the tripod direction setting in the direction of Cox Tor. I scanned the area with the night vision telescope, it revealed nothing. I raised my binoculars and swept the area before me. As I dropped the binoculars, so that they hung around my waist, there was another flash – again from Cox Tor. I was quietly elated, as the camcorder was fixed in the right direction to record the image. I watched anxiously, in the hope that there would be another bright flash. Where was Dave?

A few minutes after the second flash of light, Dave returned. I blurted out the good news and chastised him for not being there to witness the return of the 'lights'. We were both optimistic that there would be further flashes of light and this prompted a long period of high alert. Anticipation was high, as the minutes became an hour with the time passing four o'clock, then 4.30. The darkness of the night gradually drained away our upbeat mood and the watch concluded in anticlimax. At daybreak we packed our equipment and wandered down the slope to the car, drove back to the campsite and a welcome sleep in the tent.

We slept well and woke refreshed and ready for a large breakfast. The tent was dismantled with some alacrity and was rammed, somewhat untidily, into the boot of my car. We drove the three miles or so to Tavistock and settled into a small café for our breakfast. It had been another frustrating night, full of promise but finishing in disappointing fashion and it was this that dominated our conversation as we ate bacon and eggs. I left Dave in Tavistock, as he had decided to distribute leaflets giving details of the forthcoming CUFORG tenth annual conference around the town.

I drove out of the eastern suburb of Tavistock, heading along the A386 and remembered that I should ring Danniel Alford and check that nothing was amiss. I pulled into the first available lay by and rang him on my mobile phone. Danniel said that everything was fine and that there had been no incidents that he was aware of. I told him that we had a glimpse of the light flashes that we had seen before, on 14th May, but a glimpse was all we had. I told Danniel to call me if there were any developments and that I would write to Mary in due course.

I did not know it then, but the fleeting lights I had seen during the night might have had a lot more significance than I realised and were the precursor of the most dramatic and sinister events. In fact, I could not have imagined the carnage that was to follow.

35

The September Massacre

The morning of 10th September 2006 was warm and sunny and the time was approaching eleven o'clock as my wife Jill and I sat in the conservatory talking. My mobile phone rang and I immediately thought it might be my daughter Emma or Darren, my son in law, as they had been invited to dinner that afternoon. To my utter surprise it was Mary Alford, ringing from Scotland.

Mary informed me that there had been two attacks and that no fewer than nine sheep had been killed. I could scarcely take in what she was telling me. The bare details were that six sheep, belonging to local farmer Charles Mudge, had been killed near a small barn situated on the north-westerly side of Cox Tor, while two of the Alfords' sheep and one other had been killed on the common. I promised Mary that I would ring Frank Yeo immediately and get further details.

I telephoned Frank and did my best to note all the things he told me about the bodies. There was the usual removal of the eyes and part of the tongue missing from another. There were signs of bruising and a hole half an inch wide under the main body cavity. A teat was half hanging off one body and completely removed on another. The claws on the back of the hooves had been cut off. One of the dead sheep was twenty yards from the two Alford sheep and could not be identified, as its ear had been removed and, curiously, it was of a breed not seen on the moor. Frank said that the crows were pecking at its rib area. Frank concluded our discussion by offering to meet me half way, with one of the carcasses.

My mind was in turmoil, not just because of the scale and detail of the two attacks, but also the offer from Frank to meet me on the M5 with a body! What should I do? The few minutes I spent deliberating on this proposal seemed like an eternity. Forensic information was paramount in this investigation and the more we had, the more we might understand what lay behind these sinister attacks. Furthermore, the sheep had probably been dead less than twelve hours. Time was against me going all the way to Dartmoor and examining the crime scene. I made a decision in my mind, knowing full well the trouble it might cause with my wife. Jill looked disapprovingly at me as if knowing what was coming. *'Frank is willing to meet me half way at Sedgemoor services on the M5, the sheep have been dead less than twelve hours,'* I said half pleading for approval. *'Emma and Darren are coming for dinner you know. Can you get back for five o'clock?'* she asked in a resigned tone. *'Yes,'* I said with determined confidence. Jill was unhappy, but willing to make the sacrifice of our precious time on that Sunday. I did not know it at the time, but my decision to go would push me mentally to the edge and would prove very costly. Basically, my eagerness to move things forward clouded my judgement, and the decision to meet Frank was the wrong one.

I rang Frank and asked him to confirm the likely time of death of the sheep. He again stated that it must have been overnight on Saturday. I told him to bring two bodies, if possible, one from each batch of killings. I lined out the boot of the car and set off in the return direction of the journey I had made just twenty-four hours earlier.

Weather conditions were fine and ideal for driving. As I cruised down the M5 towards Bristol I thought how crazy I was to be doing this. There was the loss of my time, there was the unpleasant task of transporting the bodies, and there was the stress involved. Why was I doing it! Because I wanted answers, that's why!

I got to Sedgemoor slightly ahead of schedule and promptly rang Frank to see if he was close. Unfortunately, Frank was unlikely to make Sedgemoor for another half hour, so I told him that I would drive down to Taunton Deane services and meet him there. I arrived at Taunton Deane and parked the car in isolation, in the middle of a large car park. Frank arrived in the red Land Rover Defender and pulled alongside the Jaguar.

After a brief handshake Frank told me more about the two attacks and said that Charles Mudge had called out a vet from Launceston, who had been astonished at the bizarre killings. Furthermore, she had stated that she had not seen anything like it before. Apparently, two bodies were removed from the Cox Tor killings, for post mortem. I thought that it would be very interesting to see if the separate post mortems picked up on any similar injuries or anomalies. As soon as our brief chat ended, we took the two bodies from the Land Rover and placed them in the boot of my car. I gave Frank another supply of the plastic 'body bags' to replenish the ones he had used for the two carcasses. I promised to keep him and Mary updated on anything that might be learnt from the post mortem. I then jumped into the car and headed north for a race against the clock.

The return trip was without incident and thankfully not too hot, although I was aware of a creeping stench from the bodies. I could not understand this, as I had not experienced the same strong odour with the older corpse that I had transported in June. I arrived home with time to spare and sat down for dinner, having left the macabre contents in the boot of the car.

An hour or so after our guests had gone I took the opportunity to check the dead sheep. The first thing that surprised me was the pungent smell – they were rapidly decomposing! I ran an electromagnetic wave detector over the two bodies and was shocked to note that the reading on the Tesla scale was 0.16. When I checked the reading on myself (and a day later, the empty boot of the car) the reading was 0.02. The dead sheep were giving a reading eight times more than normal! What had caused that? There was a further disturbing development. The bodies appeared bloated, and when I moved one of them the gas erupted from the corpse in a rippling hiss. My god! What was going on? The bodies were plainly decomposing at an alarming rate. For the first time in the investigation I felt true alarm. The night was thankfully cool and I slammed down the lid of the boot, hoping against hope that the problem would not worsen.

I hardly slept that night, as the worry of what I might find in the morning ate at me like a persistent toothache. Early in the morning I checked the contents of the boot. The smell was appalling and I had a real problem. I drove the car to work and told Sallie, my colleague, that I needed to pop out for an hour, sometime that morning. I rang the vet, but was unable to speak to her and was advised to ring later. Every half hour I went out to check the boot of my car. The stress I felt was indescribable. I called the veterinary surgery several times before, at last, I was able to take the bodies in for examination. The time was midday.

It was with a mixture of shame and relief as I quickly put on an old pair of overalls and staggered through to the back door of the surgery to deposit first one, then two dead sheep, by the path to the door. The stench was horrendous and, in between apologies, I told the poor assistant that only a cursory examination might be possible. I paid the fees, which included a disposal cost, then cast off my overalls, throwing them into the boot, before driving back to work. I should never have done it, I thought, thinking back to the moment I made the decision to collect the bodies. I had not bargained for the rapid decomposition, which was to become a feature of the September killings.

I got back to my place of work very quickly and slung just about everything that had been touched or near the two bodies into the rubbish skip conveniently placed in the works yard. At this point I must pay tribute to my work colleague, Sallie, who gave enormous help in the clean up operation that was required to remove the smell of the bodies from my car.

In fact, it was a few weeks, and a programme of regular valeting, before I could claim to have removed the persistent odour from the Jaguar.

I felt utterly drained by the events of the last two days and I even felt like walking away from the whole thing. I had to ask myself if it was really worth it.

On Tuesday 12th September I had a call from the vet to tell me that the bodies she had examined were far too advanced in decomposition to reveal anything significant. However, the livers from both animals looked abnormal and she had sent them for further analysis. There was something else she mentioned: the tongue from one of the sheep had a triangular cut. According to the vet the bodies must have been several days old when she examined them. How could that be? The killings occurred overnight, surely they could not have been that old? The suggestion, by some of the farmers, that the sheep had been killed previously, then kept somewhere before being dumped at the crime scenes seemed utterly preposterous.

The rapid decomposition had been noted before in animal mutilation cases and my memory of the Dartmoor ponies case from 1977 when the rapid decomposition, *within forty eight hours* was one of the most prominent features of that particular incident, came to mind. I appeared to have come full circle, I thought.

On Wednesday 13th September I had another call from Mary Alford. There had been two more attacks and another nine sheep killed. Six of the animals, three owned by Charles Mudge and three belonging to Mary, had been attacked near Barn Hill in the early hours of Wednesday morning. In a separate attack three sheep belonging to Michael Doidge had been killed near Feather Tor. At least six of the victims had tongues and eyes removed and all the bodies exhibited a gaseous, bloated appearance that suggested they had been dead for some time. If they were killed overnight, how could this be?

On Thursday 14th September Mary was on the phone again to inform me that three more sheep had been killed overnight on Barn Hill. Two were from the Mudge flock, while the other belonged to Mary. This was ridiculous! Now it was getting out of control. What was the motive for this acceleration in the killings? I just did not know what to think.

I now come to the conclusion that apart from the total number of victims, which now stood at forty-six, the repeated attacks, within this comparatively small area, put the Moortown killings in a class of their own. It dawned on me that we were now dealing with the biggest case of its kind in the United Kingdom.

The criminal erosion of their livelihood now prompted the local farmers to mount their own surveillance during the weekend of 16th and 17th September. However, it did not stop the killings. On Sunday night at about half past eleven the body of a lamb was found on Barn Hill. There had been no body there half an hour previously, yet someone or something had carried out the attack right under the noses of the farmers! The following morning another body was discovered on the common. The death toll had now risen to forty-eight and the attacks were unstoppable.

There had been seven attacks and twenty-three sheep killed, without apparent logic or motive. There was no pattern to the attacks, other than the fact that they were all carried out in a relatively small area and were done in a covert manner. Was it the area that attracted them and if so, why? If the answer lay in history it was unlikely to be anything to do with ancient burial places or Neolithic sites. Merrivale, which is adjacent to Moortown, is the site of the Merrivale stones, which are of Neolithic origin. But if this ancient site was the key, then why weren't the sheep killed there?

I had to ask myself if the killings were a sign or calling card from some entity of unknown origin. This had been a recurring theme in several books written in the United States about the animal mutilation problem and if it was true, then what was the message they were trying to put across to us? Perhaps it was, *'You'd better recognise what we're doing, and why, before we wipe out your stocks of sheep!'*

On the night of Tuesday 19th September there was a huge army exercise on the northern side of Cox Tor. The operation involved Chinook helicopters and a large number of army personnel. My informant told me it was the first exercise that they had ever seen carried out on that part of Dartmoor, and curiously just two days after the last sheep attack and a month since the unusual air activity on 18th August.

I had to ask myself whether there was some connection between the army's activity on the moor and the sheep killings. Once again, there was a development in this complex case that was to take Dave Gillham and myself by complete surprise.

36

Party Time!

The situation was plainly out of control and I telephoned Mary Alford to advise her that Dave and I would be coming down for a night of surveillance on Friday 22nd September. It seemed to me that we were highly likely to encounter some strange activity, especially given the dramatic events of the last ten days.

Two days before our planned visit I spoke to Mary again, it was a strange discussion because Mary asked if we were definitely coming, said, *'We would love to see you'* and that there was likely to be a party going on. I sensed there was something else she wanted to say but was reticent, because of the possibility of the phone call being monitored. I assured her we would be there and agreed to ring her on arrival to arrange a time for the meeting about the killings.

I had booked a day off work on Friday 22nd September and arranged to meet Dave Gillham at Pork Hill car park at mid afternoon. The drive to Tavistock was eased by the wild electric guitar of Jimi Hendrix that tortured the speakers in my car. I soon reached the familiar outskirts of the ancient stannary town and took the sharp left-hand turn onto the B3357. Once again I found myself strutting impatiently around the car as a stiff breeze blew across the common. Dave arrived at about three o'clock and after pleasantries had been exchanged, I began to relate more details of the recent killings and the near catastrophic collection of the two dead sheep. Usually it was Dave who did the majority of the moaning, now it was my turn. I told him that I had nearly had enough of everything and that my car still reeked of the two bodies. Was it all worth it? And was anyone going to take any notice of anything we said? I admitted to being on a real 'downer'. Now, when I said I had nearly had enough, I only meant *nearly.* I was going to follow this through, whatever, and I believe Dave felt the same.

We decided to book into the campsite and get the tent sorted while the weather was still good. We were advised to pitch our tent in the corner of a small walled field. We had learnt from previous visit about the correct procedure for erecting the tent and the operation went relatively smoothly. I carried on griping about my life, my work, UFO researchers and the sheep deaths. *'What the bleedin' 'ell's the matter with you, you've never been like this,'* said Dave, with some exasperation. I suddenly realised that my diatribe on life was misplaced and that I ought to get on with things, instead of moaning. *'I'm sorry Dave I don't know why I'm talking like this,'* I said in an apologetic tone.

The time was approaching six o'clock and I rang Mary to find out what time the meeting was going to start. She suggested that we come to the farm at about 7.15 and then we could all go in my car to Danniel's house at Horrabridge.

We drove the short distance from the campsite to Moortown Farm, went round to the kitchen and knocked on the door. Mary invited us in and said that Charles Mudge and his son would be at Danniel's house and that it was an opportunity for me to discuss with him my theories as to who, or should I say what, was responsible for the sheep deaths. Mary went out of the kitchen briefly and returned with a hamper-style basket, the sort that was usually filled with Christmas puddings, jam preserves, crackers and various items of Christmas fare. On this occasion though, the basket was filled with cans of lager, beer and bottles of red and white wine. Dave gallantly offered to carry this treasure trove of liquid goodies to the car. I thought to myself, my god its party time! The three of us got into the Jaguar and drove out of the entrance to the farm onto the track that led past Pew Tor. I confess to being a little peeved at this point as it was obvious that I would be doing the driving, and that meant that I would not be able to drink like all the others.

As we drove past Pew Tor, Mary asked what our plans were. We told her that after the meeting we would be going up to Pew Tor and carrying out a night's surveillance. What she said in reply stunned the both of us. *'We would rather you didn't go up there tonight.'* Why on earth not, I thought. The answer soon came. *'A group of young farmers are going up there and they have volunteered to carry out a surveillance operation. You and Dave can have the night off!'* The sudden realisation that we would not be needed to stand on the moor for a possible seven hours of considerable discomfort filled me with momentary euphoria. I think Dave and I were stunned by this revelation, but independently kept our counsel until after the meeting.

We eventually arrived at Danniel's house, after a journey down anonymous country lanes, guided by Mary. We had already met Danniel, so were introduced to Charles Mudge and his son, also named Charles. The meeting began with me explaining to Charles Mudge what my involvement in the sheep deaths saga was, and who, or rather what, I thought was responsible. I told Charles about my research that had begun with the Dartmoor ponies incident and had led to the Moortown sheep attacks. Various other theories were proposed as to the origin of the sheep deaths, although the majority seemed to favour satanists as being the culprits. This left Dave and me, and our theories, on our own.

Charles Mudge reckoned a forensic team was required to descend on any future crime scene in a 'CSI Miami' style investigation. Hang on a minute, I thought, we've already had one of those. What happened to the October 2005 police investigation, involving the scene of crime officers? Charles expected too much. I said that if a human body had been found on the moor, then it would be a different story.

The discussion moved on to the most recent killings, and it was these killings that had brought the farmers together. The bloated appearance of the bodies and the rapid decomposition was discussed and the opinion of some was that the sheep were killed and kept somewhere else, prior to the bodies being dumped at the crime scene. As far I was concerned, this beggared belief. There was another theory about the bodies and the amount of time they had been left. The grass underneath and around the bodies showed a certain amount of yellowing, suggesting that the bodies had lain there for a while. I was not convinced of this, remembering what had been said about the effects on vegetation and the chlorophyll in attacks elsewhere.

There was a suggestion that remote cameras could be installed in likely attack areas, but who was going to foot the bill for that? There was also the question as to where the cameras could be situated, after all it was not as if all the killings were taking place in one particular field.

Mary requested that we should only discuss the sheep killings with her as point of contact and that she would keep us updated on any developments on the moor. I was not entirely happy with the request, as the flow of information could be interrupted by Mary's commitments to the farm and might reduce my independence in the investigation, in certain circumstances. Nonetheless, I went along with Mary's request.

We were joined at about ten o'clock by Frank Yeo and the debate continued in the same theme, although becoming gradually raucous. The Mudges departed at about 11.30 and the evening finished in a crescendo of riotous laughter that gave Dave and me the warm impression that we were among friends. The night seemed to be a culmination of eighteen months of involvement during which we had won the Alfords over, if not to our point of view regarding the killings, then at least as brothers in arms against an unseen enemy.

On the way back from Horrabridge, as we raced to keep up with the Alfords in case we got lost in the inky darkness and towering hedgerows, Dave and I discussed the evening's events. Although the meeting, which was more of a party, had gone reasonably well, in that we appeared to have been 'accepted' by the farmers, we both had misgivings about the dramatic intervention of the young farmers. Dave suggested that we should go on the moor anyway, despite our assurance to Mary that we would give it a miss. I managed to persuade him otherwise, and we elected, instead, to stop off at the parking point that we called LUP 1, and take some photos. There were two pony foals stepping lightly among the bracken and this unusual encounter prompted me to take a couple of pictures of them, despite the dark conditions. I took some more photos of the immediate area, as I had captured some bizarre and mystifying images in the same place on previous visits. As we got back into the car, Dave said in a disgruntled tone, *'I bet they ain't even up on that flipping moor.'*

We arrived back at the campsite and were treated to the magnificent sight of the Milky Way, a river of stars, arching through the sky. We had some difficulty in getting to sleep, as Dave would not let up about the sudden involvement of the young farmers. I preferred to wait till morning and review the situation then. The wind and rain that suddenly sprang up could not penetrate our snug tent and eventually we both fell into a deep sleep.

The following morning was mercifully free of rain and we rapidly dismantled the tent and packed it into the boot of the Jaguar. We drove our cars to Tavistock and went to the small, unpretentious café that we had visited on previous occasions. Over a full English breakfast we discussed, quietly and in coded terms, some of the previous evening's events. I told Dave that while I welcomed more resources in the 'war' against the mutilators, I preferred to have overall control of the surveillance operations. We both agreed that the young farmers' initiative would not last very long as it was highly unlikely that they would sacrifice many Saturday nights out for a grim night of discomfort on the moor.

An hour or so later I shook hands with Dave and began my familiar journey back home, reflecting as I did so that there would be many more developments in this extraordinary saga.

37

Orbs and Things

One of the most puzzling enigmas of the investigation into the Moortown sheep deaths has been the number of strange images captured by my digital camera. The majority of the pictures have been taken within the very small area where we park our cars for the trek up Pew Tor to the surveillance point. The bizarre nature of this part of Dartmoor was, of course, first highlighted by the incredible image of the 'Owlman' and the diminutive 'entity' in the back of my car. However, during our nocturnal visits I have taken numerous reference shots that have revealed some rather strange phenomena.

The most prevalent of these phenomena has been the strange oddity known as orbs. These light forms, which are usually white and sometimes blue in colour, have been the focus of much debate by those interested in the paranormal. I do not wish to court controversy or become embroiled in this debate. However, it is apparent that these light forms usually show up on images taken by flash photography and, of course, give the appearance of being spherical in shape. The camera manufacturers state that dust on the camera sensor is the most likely cause of the puzzling images. Lens flare has also been proposed as a likely cause of many orb images.

While I have seen large numbers of small spheres, momentarily, at the time that the camera flash operates, I thought that these could be moisture droplets, but what of the large, 'beach ball' light forms I have seen? One thing is for sure, I have rarely managed to get anything like the same results elsewhere. There is something very curious about that small area of Dartmoor and orbs are not the only thing that I have photographed there.

If orbs are moisture droplets, or dust particles on the camera sensor, then what can we make of the rectangular light forms I have captured on my camera? These enigmatic photographs look, at first glance, like the rear lights of a car, but I assure you they are not! There were two images taken in quick succession and they appear to show that the light forms were moving. Is there any relationship between these images and the rectangular flashes of light seen and recorded by Dave Gillham and myself on 14th May 2006?

The images taken at LUP 1, the parking place beside the track, suggest that there may be some phenomena at work. The area itself is less than a hundred metres by fifty metres, so why is it that these weird things are being picked up? Why not elsewhere, such as Pork Hill car park or Barn Hill? Is this place by the track some sort of window area? Is it possible that there is some sort of interdimensional gateway and that the traffic through it, which is operating or vibrating outside the field of human vision, can only be glimpsed by the speed of a camera flash?

I have taken a number of other images from different parts of the moor, in particular from the surveillance point on Pew Tor. Despite the many pictures I have taken, there have only been a couple that have revealed anything strange. One of these photographs, taken at about 4.30 in the morning looking across towards Barn Hill, revealed an intense white object that looked very similar to the intense white flashes of light recorded by Dave Gillham and myself on that extraordinary night in May 2006. The picture was taken with a flash and at the time I was not aware of anything strange when I was taking the image.

Another picture that was taken looking across to the common with Cox Tor and Great Staple Tor in the background shows a plethora of orbs. This is curious, because I have not had a similar result from previous photos taken from the same place and in similar conditions. When this picture was shown to Steve Poole of UFORM he pointed out that there was the outline of two entities in this picture!

The enigma of the photographic images taken in the Moortown area does not suggest the identities of the sheep killers and could be a phenomenon that is quite separate from the strange goings on in that part of Dartmoor. However, I feel it is more than a coincidence that in this very small part of the moor we not only have a series of bizarre sheep deaths, whose perpetrators appear untouchable, but we also have strange entities and light forms being picked up on camera.

38

Taking Stock

In late November 2006 I had a call from Dave Gillham telling me that he had been approached by a documentary film maker called Jason Hendriksen. Hendriksen worked for Windfall Films, a highly reputable film company that produced documentaries, principally for Channel 4. Hendriksen wanted to do a film about the Moortown sheep killings and had picked up Dave's name from the CUFORG website. Dave had said very little and had referred Jason to me, as I was conducting the investigation. Dave repeated his usual caution, but advised me to speak to him.

The following day I rang Hendriksen at Windfall Films and introduced myself. Straight away I realised that Jason was a different kettle of fish from the previous TV people we had dealings with. For a start, he seemed a lot more clued up on the sheep killings although it was obvious he had gained much of his information from newspaper articles. He was also familiar with the area, having been brought up in nearby Ivybridge, and he'd done some homework on the animal mutilation problem. He told me that he wanted to catch the perpetrators in the act, if possible and was prepared to bring in some sophisticated equipment such as night vision cameras and former SAS soldiers to carry out surveillance of the area. During our conversation Jason continually tried to put me on the spot to say who, or rather what, I thought was responsible for the killings. I told him that it was not the occult and that we had no 'smoking gun' that could enable us to make a statement on the matter. However, it was plainly obvious that as I was involved with Dave Gillham, and as he had picked up our details from a UFO website, there was a pointer to the direction we were coming from. But I still refused to confirm or deny that aliens might be responsible. I warned Jason about some of the problems he might encounter in the area. However, it seemed that Jason was a lot more determined and not easily deterred from making his proposed documentary. I admired his style and proactive approach. Jason said he was making a fact-finding visit to Dartmoor the following week. I told him that Dave and I were planning a night of surveillance on Saturday 3rd December, and we agreed to speak then.

Both Dave and I were looking forward to the Saturday night surveillance as, apart from anything else, we would have the chance to discuss things that were too sensitive for the telephone. The weather reports were, unfortunately, very bleak and as the day got closer it became apparent that a night on the moor would be impossible. We later learned of one hundred and thirty mile-an-hour winds on the Tamar Bridge at Plymouth, which was only ten or twelve miles away! Not to be outdone by the vagaries of the British climate, we decided to go to Dartmoor on the following Monday night. Unfortunately, the high winds and torrential rain persisted and it was with some reluctance that we abandoned our plans for surveillance night 10.

I had a call from Jason on the Monday evening that was interrupted by the contrary reception on his mobile phone. I called him back and he related how things had progressed on his initial visit to the area. He had met Charles Mudge and been much impressed by him. Mudge had spoken with some candour, although it was plain that Jason had not been given access to Mary Alford. Mudge had told Jason that in addition to the sheep he had lost through the killings there were a further twenty-five missing; this was attributed to rustling. Mudge had also said that Cox Tor was a place of 'bad vibes' – he would not elaborate on this statement. Jason told me that he was hoping to speak to Becky Wadey for the RSPCA take on the killings and that he also planned to meet Chris Cole. Jason again tried to get me to make a clear declaration as to who, or what, was responsible and like an artful politician I avoided making a definitive comment. Jason promised to call me when he had obtained approval from Channel 4, to make the film.

On Sunday I had a call from Mary Alford and we agreed it would be beneficial if we could meet and discuss various matters. Despite the postponement of the stake out, I felt that the meeting was high enough priority to warrant a visit. I decided to journey down to Dartmoor on Tuesday afternoon and return home straight after the meeting.

It was late afternoon when I arrived at Pork Hill car park. A blustery wind swept across the common, shaking the car intermittently. I drank some hot coffee from a flask and pondered my next move. I rang Mary to confirm the meeting time and with an hour to spare, I decided to pay a visit to LUP 1 and take some photographs. I considered this to be an interesting experiment as the time was only about 5.30 in the afternoon and it was quite dark. Would I get the same results as those from the early hours of the morning?

As I drove past Moortown Farm, along the track I came upon a small group of ponies wandering aimlessly across the road. I stopped the car and took a shot of the timid residents. I took some further pictures at LUP 1 before heading back towards Moortown Farm and my meeting with Mary.

The meeting commenced just before six o'clock and as I sat down at the kitchen table. Mary poured me a mug of tea and asked if there were any developments at my end. There were, I assured her. I then gave details of the primary footage analysis. The tape, which had been in analogue format, had now been converted to digital and some further analysis had been possible. I told Mary about the 'light form' that we had recorded, exiting a gorse bush when Dave's 'searchlight' had been flashed at it. At this time I was not aware that further analysis would reveal important new facts about the flashes of light seen on 14th May.

I asked Mary if she was aware of any sheep losses since the animals had been brought in off the moor. She replied that she did not know, although it was possible Danniel might know. In the event, I did not get the opportunity to ask Danniel. However, Mary stated that when the sheep were counted in the summer, fifty were missing! I was astounded by this revelation and asked Mary how this could have happened. The losses were put down to rustling, an ever-present threat in the farming industry. I told Mary that it was my opinion that villains liked the easy life and that they were far more likely to empty a confined field of its stock of animals, rather than go chasing around the moor.

I asked Mary if she was aware of any attacks since September and she replied that there had been no attacks. Having said this, she also stated that there had been no feedback from the young farmers and she was not even sure if any surveillance was being carried out. I made my concerns about their involvement known and said to Mary that the very least they could do was keep her informed one way or the other.

I thanked Mary for the newspaper cutting she sent me from 1983, and pointed out to her that the police had recovered various paraphernalia from the site allegedly used by occultists on the moor, and that no similar items had been recovered from the scenes of the Moortown killings.

We briefly discussed Cox Tor and Mary said she was not aware of 'bad history' or strange happenings relating to the Tor. Mary said that a local historian, Tom Greaves, had stated that Barn Hill was the site of a Bronze Age settlement.

We then reviewed the meeting that the Dartmoor Commoners' Council had with the police. It seemed to me that the police had little to offer the beleaguered farmers and that the RSPCA were the only organisation to offer resources to catch those responsible. Well-meaning though it was, I felt the RSPCA were on a loser.

We discussed the involvement of Jason Hendriksen and Windfall Films, and I assured Mary that Charles Mudge had made a very good impression on Jason and that if Channel 4 gave approval, then it would provide an opportunity to get some sophisticated resources into the area, which would benefit all of us in the frustrating search for the killers. I countenanced caution however, as Jason had admitted to me that his proposed surveillance of key areas was a high-risk strategy. I warned Mary that if the stake out drew a blank then it was likely that Jason would be tempted to film the 'vigilante' patrols he had been told about and that the impression viewers might get of the local farmers would be that of 'Dads army' – an image that would hardly be positive.

The subject of the dead flies around the sheep in Mary's Land Rover was raised and Mary asked if radiation might have been a possible cause, reflecting no doubt on the recent poisoning by Polonium 210 of a Russian dissident. It was a worthy suggestion; unfortunately I had to advise Mary that getting a Geiger counter to monitor radiation was not easy.

Mary asked me about positive and negative energy lines (not for the first time) and then made the revelation that Hamish Miller, the renowned dowser and writer, had visited the area. Apparently he had visited the scene of the first attack and had dowsed the area from negative to positive energy lines. He had also stated that eight people had been involved in the attack. Perhaps he meant there were eight victims? I realised that I had to speak to Miller and clarify this point.

I told Mary that I was writing a book about the Dartmoor killings that would feature both the ponies incident from 1977 and the Moortown sheep attacks. I assured her that I would give her a copy of the manuscript for approval.

As the meeting closed, a low-flying aircraft swooped over the farmhouse. The plane was not going very fast and was extremely low, I could not make out if it was a civilian or military aircraft, but noted two prominent red lights on the undercarriage.

I drove home in rapidly deteriorating weather conditions, feeling much better for having discussed things with Mary face to face, rather than the coded telephone calls and the slow response of cunningly sealed letters. I reflected on the incredible events of the last year and wondered what January 2007 would bring.

39

Night 10 – January 2007

On Friday 26th January I set off for Dartmoor with a car full of equipment for the first surveillance of 2007. The trip had been postponed a couple of times due to the terrible weather and now at last we had a window of opportunity. I told Dave that even if we were unable to carry out a meaningful watch, we should still meet up to discuss various issues that we were reluctant to talk about on the telephone.

I arrived at Pork Hill car park at about 22.45 and was surprised by the fact that Dave had not yet arrived. I must confess that as I stretched my legs in the gloom of the windswept car park, I felt rather edgy and uncomfortable. I couldn't help thinking about the 'bad vibes' of Cox Tor as I gazed through the dark at the towering formation of rock.

Dave eventually arrived about three-quarters of an hour later and we quickly began our discussions, always keeping a watch on the moor stretching out before us, as we thumbed through various reports from the Joan Amos archive that Dave had brought with him. Traffic on the B3357 was almost non-existent and in the couple of hours we spent there only a police car, which flashed a torch inquisitively at us, and a taxi rumbled past.

We decided to move to our usual surveillance point and drove round to LUP 1. We made our way up Pew Tor to the surveillance area and settled in for a night's watch. The sky was cloudy, but thankfully there was little rain and we spent a fruitless night, hoping that we might catch a glimpse of 'them', the mutilators that seemed so much in control and so elusive.

At about 0430 we decided to finish the watch and elected to forego our customary breakfast, to make an early start for home. Dave's car pulled onto the track and headed for Truro as I changed from my walking boots. I started the car and reversed towards the track, listening to the bleeping reversing sensors. Suddenly, the car would not move, I was stuck on a small bank of earth! No amount of revving or attempted manoeuvre could extricate me from this situation.

In some desperation I called Dave on his mobile and was relieved to hear he was only a couple of miles away. When Dave returned, we tried every method we could to move the car – to no avail. I called a twenty-four hour repair garage and spoke to a nice lady who told me her husband was out attending a stranded motorist at the bottom of Pork Hill, less than a mile or so from us. I took his mobile number and called him.

Within half an hour we had met up with the repair man who duly winched the Jaguar from its stranded position. Luckily I had enough cash to pay the repair man's modest charge for his services. We shook hands and I thanked him for his help.

At 0745 I bid Dave a safe journey, for the second time, before heading back to the West Midlands. I had time on the journey to reflect on how easy it was to fall foul of the moor, even in such a seemingly innocuous place close to the track way.

40

Night 11 and a Walk on the Wild Side

During April 2007 I had my plans to visit Hollocombe Bottom, scene of the notorious ponies massacre, constantly interrupted by the extreme weather conditions. I had hoped to visit the place on 10th or 11th April and take a few photographs, thirty years on. It was not until Friday 8th June that I was able to make the trip.

As usual I met Dave at Pork Hill car park about midday. The weather was glorious and we made straight for the camping site to book in and get the tent erected in case the weather changed. An hour later we were on the way to Postbridge, the nearest village to Hollocombe Bottom. Upon arrival I decided to get advice from the park warden at the visitors centre and was disturbed to hear that I was the first person in twelve years to ask for directions to Hollocombe Bottom. The warden was most helpful, but when you see a map things look far more straightforward than they really are – and so it proved to be.

The first part of our trek was done in the company of two German ladies, who appeared to be relying on us for directions. The walk, or mountaineering expedition as it seemed to me, was becoming harder and harder. We had been advised to follow a stone wall, which we did, but it seemed neverending. All the time the sun blazed down on us and I kept taking short breaks, secretly hoping that Dave would say that he could stand no more and that we would turn round and go back. Dave, I have to say, was made of sterner stuff and the thought in my mind that I would never live it down if I quit, drove us on.

After more than a mile of uphill struggle, we eventually came to a t-junction where we took a left turn and followed the adjoining wall as instructed by the warden. This second part of the hike was as arduous as the first as the granite wall snaked before us well into the distance. After two and a half hours of purgatory, we finally reached the top of the valley, looking down onto Hollocombe Bottom.

The place was so remote, even by Dartmoor standards, as the sound of skylarks mingled with the gentle trickling of the stream which flowed down the gently layered valley. It was difficult to imagine the carnage of 1977, as I sat on the grassy moor and gazed towards Bellever Tor, some two and a half miles in the distance.

After we had taken some photographs and video footage, Dave and I discussed the plan to get back to civilisation. The warden had advised against a more direct route as it entailed walking through marshland that could be treacherous. It goes without saying that Dave and I chose this way because it looked a lot shorter than the way we came. Our reasoning was that the heat of the last few days would have kept much of the area dry. We were proved right by and large, although we had a couple of hairy moments, and we got back to Postbridge in much less time than the outgoing journey.

We drove to Tavistock and ate an evening meal of fish and chips, before returning to the campsite. I rang Mary Alford to arrange a meeting which was set for 0900 hours the following day, before we crashed out in the tent for a couple of hours sleep.

The alarm went at 2330 hours and I woke Dave while I struggled to get my boots on. Half an hour later we slipped out of the campsite and drove round to Pew Tor. Visibility was excellent and despite the cold there was no wind. We took up our position and gazed in wonder at the canopy of stars above us.

At 0110 hours we witnessed some unusual aerial activity. Dave and I independently saw flashes of light in the sky behind Great Staple Tor and Middle Staple Tor. On one occasion I saw what I thought was a huge shooting star, except that it changed direction and shot upwards before becoming a brilliant ball of yellow light. I was stunned by the huge 'J' shape that seemed imprinted, momentarily, in the sky. Dave had missed it because he was adjusting some equipment and had his back to the sighting.

During the next twenty minutes we saw some flashes of light from Middle Staple Tor. These pinpoint flashes of intense white light were very similar to those we had seen in May 2006. The activity stopped at about 0135 hours and we saw nothing of note until 0318 hours when another flash of intense white light was seen coming from Middle Staple Tor. This appeared to be the last of the 'action' for the night.

At 0400 hours I took a couple of flash shots with my Olympus, looking across to Middle Staple Tor. I did not check the images until I got home. When I looked at the first photograph I had an atmospheric shot of Middle Staple Tor. When I looked at the second shot, taken five to ten seconds later, there was a strange light form in the bottom left-hand corner. I had no idea what the image was and we had not recorded anything similar on the moor previously. Our surveillance ended with the arrival of dawn, as we walked down the slope of Pew Tor and returned to the campsite for a few hours sleep.

My meeting with Mary went on longer than expected and we discussed many issues about the investigation, especially the ongoing saga with my Freedom of Information request. I showed Mary some of the enhanced pictures from the May 2006 footage, as well as photographs from the USA attacks. I was shocked to learn that in three months the Alfords had had twenty sheep go missing. Mary had no clear answer for the losses, which had been attributed to rustling. Mary seemed intrigued by the events that I related from the previous night and told me that she hoped Dave and I would continue our nights of surveillance. Despite the lull in killings, there had been none that we were aware of since September, Mary was not going to let her guard down.

I drove back up the M5 and reflected on the events of the last two days. I thought, not for the first time, that there were still things going on in that part of Dartmoor, and I felt that I would soon be drawn back to this wild and wonderful place.

41

The Attacks Continue

It was just after 5.15 on Tuesday 17th July and I was driving home when my mobile phone rang. I pulled into a lay by and took the call, it was Mary Alford. *'Mary, how are you?'* I asked.

'Not good,' was the stern reply. *'We've had another seven sheep killed. We let our guard down.'* I hardly knew what to say and it was clear that Mary was very upset at this latest outrage. However, I assured her that nothing could have prevented the mutilators from striking again. Furthermore, I stated that it was now inevitable that further attacks would follow. The brief details were that seven sheep were killed during the night of 16/17th July and all had broken necks and their tongues excised. Other injuries included the removal of an eye and there was evidence of rectal coring. The bodies were found on the brow of Barn Hill and seemed to be decomposing very rapidly, just like the September 2006 victims. A vet was called out to inspect the bodies and claimed the injuries were probably caused by natural predation. The Alfords were having none of that! The National Park Ranger suggested it was a lightning strike – so where were the burns? The vet found no such evidence.

The *Tavistock Times* carried the story on 26th July 2007 and claimed that a post mortem had revealed that dogs were responsible. I would like to know the identity of the veterinary pathologist who could explain how dogs can remove the tongue of a sheep by a smooth and precise cut. The police, it was stated, were keeping an open mind on the latest attack.

The weather forecast for the forthcoming weekend was rather dismal but I felt compelled to go to Dartmoor as soon as possible. I rang Dave and told him the news.

On Saturday 21st July I met Dave Gillham at Pork Hill car park as we began our now familiar preparations for another all-night surveillance. At around 1100 hours, we trudged up the lower slope of Pew Tor, struggling with our weighty equipment. We reached the disused quarry and set up the video camera in readiness. Despite the warm daytime temperature, it was very cold indeed during the night.

The main topic of conversation was Dave's forthcoming annual conference and the now regular tribulations he had in setting the event up. All the time we maintained our vigil across the bleak moorland that lead up to Barn Hill. It was one of those nights when there was little to report and the capricious Dartmoor climate seemed to be turning against us as drops of moisture spat down from the sky, warning us of impending rain. It was such a night when we 'thought' we had seen a flash of light here and a flash of light there, but we couldn't be sure. The clouds darkened and the rain became more persistent and the surveillance came to a premature end at 0300 hours, when we reluctantly packed our equipment and made our way back to the car.

The rain was in for the rest of the night as our small tent took a battering from the downpour. Fortunately the rainfall abated by morning and Dave and I hurriedly packed the tent and left Dartmoor earlier than usual for the long drive home.

I reflected on the frustration of our inability not only to catch 'them' in the act of attacking the sheep, but also to be first at the aftermath of an attack. Not for the first time I rued the loss of potential forensic clues that such an opportunity might bring.

In early September 2007 I received an invitation from Cherry Seage, Secretary to the Dartmoor Commoner's Council, to attend a meeting that the Commoner's Council had arranged with the police. The meeting was to discuss a range of important issues, including the series of sheep killings. It was an opportunity for me to discuss my investigations so far with the Council members and the police, and I duly accepted. The meeting was set for the afternoon of Tuesday 25th September and Mary Alford kindly made arrangements for me to attend an informal lunch at Moortown Farm beforehand that would be attended by some of the Council members.

I arrived at Moortown Farm just past 11.30 and was introduced to the Council members as they arrived. Most of the attendees were farmers, except for Cherry Seage, the Secretary, and Marion Saunders, Secretary for the Dartmoor Livestock Protection Society. The conversation at the table was of foot and mouth and blue tongue disease, which was an imminent threat to every farmer in the land. I listened, intently, occasionally mentioning various aspects of the sheep killings and at one point circulated the ley line map, which fascinated several of the guests.

One of the Council members, Brian Lavis, told me about a very unusual incident that had occurred on Stourton Common in June. Apparently, a member of the public had been walking across the common when he came upon a dead roedeer that had been decapitated. A few hundred yards further on there was another body, this time of a cow that had also been decapitated. In each instance the head was nowhere to be found. Brian said that removing the cow's head could not have been easy and why had the head been taken? A further intriguing fact was that roedeer are not known to frequent that part of Dartmoor.

The time drifted on towards one o'clock and the lunch would soon draw to a close as the meeting with the police was set for two o'clock. It was at this point that Mary Alford asked the assembled delegates if they would like to hear my theory as to who or what was responsible for the sheep attacks. The room went deferentially quiet and all eyes were directed at me. I decided to be forthright and gauge the reaction. I remember the words I used very clearly:

> *It is my opinion, based on information from both these attacks and attacks elsewhere that the high level of technology involved suggests that the perpetrators of these attacks are not of this Earth and that I believe that an alien intelligence, whose motives are unclear, is responsible.*

There was a stunned silence. I half expected some sniggers, but there were none. The majority appeared to accept my viewpoint without contradiction. *'What can we do?'* I was asked. *'We can only monitor their activities, we cannot stop them,'* I said.

The gathering dispersed as we made our way to Princetown for the meeting with the police. In the car I told Mary that I was shocked at the reaction, or lack of it, to my statement about the attackers. I was used to people being very sceptical of my claims. However, the evidence, as far as I was concerned, was mounting up.

As we filed into the meeting room at the High Moorland Business Centre, I was introduced to Rebecca Wadey, who was representing the RSPCA, and Sergeant Hughes of Tavistock police, who was attending the meeting with an inspector whose name I shall withhold for reasons that will become apparent.

A range of issues were discussed. It was a frustrating meeting for the Commoner's Council as the police appeared unable to offer the level of support demanded by the Commoners on almost every topic that was raised. One such issue was the beheaded animals mentioned by Mr Lavis. The police were unable to do anything about the matter as the cause of death had not been established. However, an interesting comment was made by the Commoners' veterinary adviser who was attending the meeting. He claimed that in 1968 there had been similar beheading of a number of animals in Lydford, only a short distance down the A386. Furthermore, the victims had been from 'a number of different species' and he also mentioned the Newquay Zoo killings.

We finally got onto the sheep attacks and I had my opportunity to speak to the police inspector directly. I began by giving a brief resumé of my difficulties in getting hold of the sheep attacks file from October 2005, mentioning that Tavistock police had no objections at the time to me seeing the file. So what had happened since? What was so secret about this file that I was being denied access, when all I wished to do was assist the police? I was hoping that I might enlist his assistance to extricate my Freedom of Information Act request from the sea of bureaucracy into which it had now foundered. However, nothing could have prepared me for the tirade that was the inspector's response.

In a turbulent rant lasting for about one and a half minutes, he stated that the incident on 14th and 15th October 2005 was 'ancient history', that there was probably a mundane reason for the file being withheld, he was not an expert on the Freedom of Information Act, and he hadn't the time, or inclination to get involved with this particular issue. Finally, he stated that there were no secrets!

Oh dear, I thought, my question appears to have touched a nerve. The stunned silence that followed the inspector's outburst was broken by Sergeant Hughes, who calmly suggested that the farmers themselves should make an application for the file.

The meeting moved on to other topics and finally closed about 1600 hours. It was at this point that I took the opportunity to speak to Becky Wadey of the RSPCA. Becky seemed quite responsive to having a meeting with a view to sharing information about the attacks, saying that she would discuss the possibility with her superior. Unfortunately, the hoped-for meeting did not materialise.

Mary and I travelled back to Moortown Farm with Arnold Cole, a likeable farmer and Council member. The three of us discussed the topics that had been raised at the meeting, which had brought home to me the difficulties faced by farmers in the Dartmoor area and the restrictions of resources that prevented more effective cooperation from the police.

I left Moortown just after six, my journey home preoccupied by my thoughts regarding the astonishing response from the police inspector about my application for the police file. What was in this file that could elicit such a testy response?

On Sunday 4th November 2007 there was another attack. This time a young ram had been removed from a closed field owned by Mary Alford, taken to Barn Hill (half a mile from the field), killed and mutilated. Mary had recovered the body and instructed a local vet to attend.

Remembering that I had given Mary an ultra-violet torch, I asked her to scan the carcass with it for any markings. The scan revealed an astonishing fact, not noted on the previous attacks, that the horns had been marked with a substance only visible under the ultra-violet light. Even more dramatic was the discovery of a v-like symbol underneath the foreleg and near to a hole into the upper body cavity. To my knowledge this was the first symbol discovered on a mutilated animal anywhere in the world. Once again the Dartmoor sheep attacks had posed another enigma.

What was the purpose behind removing this sheep from a field, carrying it half a mile to Barn Hill, then killing and mutilating it? Why was it marked in such a way that the markings were invisible other than under ultra-violet light? Were these markings put on the animal before its abduction and slaughter, or afterwards? Were the markings made at the selection stage (the animal was in a field with other sheep)? Were 'they' trying some bizarre method of communication? Is it a case that if we can solve the puzzle 'they' will consider us worthy of direct communication?

My last visit to Dartmoor in 2007 was on 16th November, for a meeting with Mary Alford. We discussed the recent attack and the vet's findings, which were, unfortunately, inconclusive. We then went to Barn Hill and Mary showed me the spot where the dead ram had been found. It was just below the brow of the hill, and coincidently, near to where the October 2005 victims had been discovered.

We returned to the farm and completed our discussions. Then, as the darkening skies closed in, I made the long journey home knowing that I would soon return and that another attack was inevitable.

My worst fears were confirmed when I received a call from Mary on 15th November 2008 to inform me that another sheep had fallen victim to the mutilators. Mary told me that a neighbour had found the dead animal in a gorse bush near the track way that runs along the lower slopes of Pew Tor. The victim had been removed from a field at the back of Moortown Farm and deposited where it was found.

The attack was a classic mutilation, with the tongue excised by a smooth cut to the back of the throat and a large circular hole in the side of the body. There were scratches underneath the forelegs and there appeared to have been some 'interference' with the anal area.

Dave Gillham attended the scene on my behalf and he had considerable trouble in focusing his digital camera in close proximity to the body. Dave also noted that the circular wound, that was very precise, appeared to be 'layered' as in a 'cookie cutter'. He also found that when he took a compass near the body, there was a constant deviation from north. In addition to this curious effect on the compass, electromagnetic wave readings taken close to the body the previous day fluctuated wildly before settling down to a normal reading of 0.02 tesla.

The questions we have to ask here are, was the victim dropped into the gorse bush? And why was the body left in the very area that Dave and I used on our surveillance nights? I began to wonder if this latest attack was some sort of communication from the mutilators to the two of us.

Part IV
Further Investigations

42

The Beast of Bodmin and ABCs

The inexplicable killing of farm livestock always has a ready suspect – ABCs or alien big cats, alien meaning not native to the United Kingdom. There is a long history of ABCs in Britain, but it was in the early 1970s that the phenomenon began to attract widespread interest. In 1976 the Dangerous Wild Animals Act, which introduced strict and expensive licensing for those who wished to own such exotic pets, resulted in many people turning their animals loose into the wild. Across the UK a whole range of big cats were cast into the wilderness and the moors of south-western England were an ideal habitat for such animals.

Places like Dartmoor, Exmoor and Bodmin Moor provided large areas for the big cats to roam and a steady diet of wild animals, such as deer and rabbits. There is also the livestock of moorland farmers.

ABCs were seen across the UK but it was on Exmoor that the first of many tabloid legends began. In 1983 Eric Ley, a farmer in South Molton, near Exmoor, claimed to have lost over a hundred sheep (some estimates say eighty) within three months. The animals had all died with violent throat injuries and the blame was put on a big cat, or family of big cats, living on Exmoor. Mr Ley claimed that no one in the village had ever known anything like the series of sheep killings. The legend of the Beast of Exmoor had begun.

Theories as to the identity of the big cat varied, but it was widely assumed to be a puma or a panther. An alternative view suggested it wasn't a cat at all, and that the beast was a cross-bred dog, with Labrador, mastiff and lurcher blood. It is alleged that the South Molton sheep killings exhibited similar injuries. I have to say that I find this surprising, as all big cats are secretive in nature and in that part of Exmoor, surrounded by an abundant food supply. So why kill so many sheep? Big cat appetites may vary, however pumas will eat up to ten pounds of meat from a victim and from the couple of photographs that I've seen of a big cat kill they eat through the shoulder of the victim and prefer to eat near a stream or edge of a field. A big cat will devour a whole carcass, especially if there are cubs to support, and if a leg is removed it's probably for the female. Big cats also like to drink the blood of their victims and this could explain the exsanguination of some victims.

The huge number of sheep lost by Mr Ley does not suggest a big cat seeking to improve its diet and I would point out that an average sheep would weigh in the region of sixty kilograms – that's a lot of food for a big cat!

I do not accept the suggestion that all these killings were carried out by a big cat and I find it difficult to accept that such a secretive creature would go on a rampage and then suddenly stop. Despite the unsuccessful attempts to find the big cat allegedly responsible there has been no repeated surge in sheep killings in this area since that time.

Big cats can be very elusive and are known to lie up in secluded places for long periods during the daytime. However, there are very few photographs and little video footage exists of the alleged family of cats.

As the controversy grew, the British Army, at the request of the Ministry of Agriculture, sent sharpshooters from the Royal Marines onto Exmoor in an effort to rid the area of the ABC killing machine. Although there were occasional sightings of an ABC, the marines did not fire a shot and had to abandon the mission when a national newspaper offered a large reward for a photograph of the creature, an offer that drew hundreds of amateur photographers onto Exmoor in the hope of securing the bounty.

The farmers of South Molton were unaware of two incidents that had occurred on Exmoor many years previously. On the night of 10th November 1950 a number of sheep were found dead, with deep wounds to the neck. Beside the bodies a block of ice weighing fourteen pounds was found. The weather in the area had been calm and mild and the origin of the ice could not be explained. Incredibly, this mirrored an almost identical incident in 1910, when sheep with similar injuries were found with ice scattered around them. These incidents are mentioned in the book *Flying Saucers on the Moon* by Harold T. Wilkins who noted another strange incident on Exmoor that took place shortly before the mysterious sheep deaths in 1950. On the night of 31st October 1950, ten days before the sheep deaths, several Exmoor farmers saw a number of strange discs spurting blue-white flames that flew in from the direction of the Atlantic Ocean and Irish Sea.

Its not just sheep that have died mysteriously on Exmoor. An estate that reared pheasants for shooting had eighty birds secured in pens to protect them from natural predators. One morning the estate gamekeeper checked the pens and was horrified to find all the pens forced open and all eighty pheasants dead. Strangely, all the birds had been decapitated and the heads were all missing. The gamekeeper blamed the killings on owls.

At the time of writing the identity of the Beast of Exmoor remains unknown and sporadic killings of sheep are still blamed on the mysterious creature. The Beast of Exmoor was soon to have a rival in the south-west, when farmers around Bodmin Moor reported sheep losses that were put down to the elusive ABCs. We now had the Beast of Bodmin to contend with.

Bodmin Moor with its combination of desolate open moorland and dense woodland provides an ideal habitat for an elusive ABC and there is a history of mystery cats in the area long pre-dating the 1990s, when the legend took off. In 1992 and 1993 there were several sightings of an unidentified large cat that was thought to be a puma or panther. The sightings coincided with a number of unexplained livestock deaths and the farmers put two and two together and laid the blame on the large cat.

Local farmer John Goodenough told the *Farmers Weekly* in 1994 that he had lost fourteen sheep and three calves to the mystery predator over the previous two years. Another local farmer, Rosemary Rhodes, was so angry at the systematic depredation of her sheep that she sold her remaining flock. Rosemary was furious that the Ministry of Agriculture Fisheries and Food (MAFF) refused to acknowledge the problem, let alone do anything about it.

In an interview with the *Sunday Independent* on 4th September 1994 under the headline 'Beast visits me at night!' Rosemary Rhodes gave the following account of the mystery beasts.

There are several big cats roaming around here, they come to my farmhouse at night. Everyone here sees them.

We've seen pumas and lynx, but the most famous Beast is the big black one we've caught it on video. I saw it with its cub last month – and there've been sightings of a bigger one, probably a male.

I think they are melanistic leopards, commonly called black panthers.

There are acres of dense woodland here packed with rabbits, rats and deer – there's an ample food supply for several large cats.

And when food gets short the animals come onto farmland and attack sheep.

I've had a terrible time getting the ministry to believe me, although I've sent them carcasses and they still say there's no evidence – what do they want, the creature to pose for a photo?

I've seen the black one, lots of times – it's a beautiful creature. But I don't want people trying to kill it. I'm happy with them living here as long as the ministry accept it and warn people of the dangers.

We can ascertain a few things from this interesting interview, the first being that there is plenty of evidence to support the fact that there are several ABCs on Bodmin Moor. Second, the farmer herself has considerable admiration for them, despite the havoc they have allegedly inflicted on her sheep. Finally, the indifference shown by the ministry (MAFF). This attitude would be the undoing of MAFF when the devastating foot and mouth outbreak in 2001 hit the UK. Their slow reaction and poor planning made the crisis worse and the ministry was subsequently reorganised and merged into the Department for the Environment, Food and Rural Affairs (DEFRA).

The next incident took place in July 1996, and involved two campers on Bodmin Moor. One of the witnesses called 'James' wrote to Joan Amos and *Flying Saucer Review* about this horrific event and I am including it here as there are some elements that are similar to ABC reports. Two young men were camping on Bodmin Moor, near the Cheese Ring, in an ancient and very secluded stone circle. The two campers thought that they had found an idyllic hideaway on the moor and settled down in their tent for the night.

In the early hours they were both woken up by a horrible 'inhuman' screaming sound and a very bright blue-white light that lit the whole surrounding area. The light was directly above them and was too bright for either of them to look at directly. The sound seemed to be coming from the same source as the light. Suddenly the sound and the light disappeared and the campers found themselves in pitch darkness. Terrified by the experience, the two men huddled in the tent with a torch, not daring to venture outside. Eventually, the batteries of the torch ran out, but the two men stayed awake, petrified with fear.

At first light one of the men cautiously ventured outside and immediately screamed with horror. Right next to the tent were the remains of a sheep. The front legs were missing and the spine was twisted out of shape, the carcass was devoid of all flesh and there was no blood. The only part of the fleece that remained was a small tuft on the top of the head. Unsurprisingly, the two campers quickly packed their belongings and left the area as fast they could.

I have read reports of eerie screams on Bodmin Moor, which have been attributed to big cats, and they have been known to pick a carcass clean. However, they do not illuminate areas and they are not airborne.

Another strange incident occurred on Bodmin Moor on 23rd August 1995. A man was driving near the moor at about 2220 hours and saw a cluster of lights as he turned off the main road. The lights appeared to be by the roadside, and as he approached them in his car, a black triangular craft, with red lights at each point and the centre, flew right over his vehicle. The witness stated that the craft was so low he felt he could have touched it. He claims that the craft emitted 'a loud engine noise'. There have been many reports of black triangular craft across the whole of the UK.

Like Exmoor and Bodmin Moor, Dartmoor too has its share of ABC sightings, and in March 1988 local newspapers reported a mystery jet-black cat had been seen prowling around a field, close to the centre of Tavistock. Also in March, a walker on Dartmoor said he came within a hundred yards of a large ginger-haired cat that was the size of an Alsatian dog. However, it appears that the big cats have a preference for Exmoor and Bodmin Moor, where the habitat is clearly ideal for them.

The ABCs have often been blamed for animal mutilation cases, especially where sheep have been killed, but it is my opinion that the big cats kill for food and devour almost the whole carcass, picking the bones clean. They do not perform precise excisions and leave the body largely intact.

In September 2001 in Great Dalby, Leicestershire, the carcass of a dead sheep was found in the branches of a tree, eighteen feet up. The suggestion was that a big cat had taken its prey into the tree so that it could devour the dead sheep at its leisure, a normal practice for certain big cats like leopards. However, eighteen feet up a tree seems rather high to me, and why was the carcass still relatively intact? There is another possible explanation for this – perhaps the dead animal was dropped onto the tree. If this was so we can rule out big cats and many other explanations put forward for the bizarre deaths of sheep.

On the 27th February 2003 Member of Parliament Norman Baker, representing the Lewes constituency, asked the Secretary of State for the Environment, Food and Rural Affairs how many sightings had there been since June 2001 purporting to be big cats and could the figures be analysed by county. He also asked what steps had been taken to investigate the sightings, with a view to ascertaining if a big cat was actually present in a particular area. The Secretary of State, Mr Morley, gave the following written reply:

> *Big cats, such as tigers, lions, cheetahs, leopards or puma, are not native to the UK and are not naturally found in the wild in this country. There are widespread and frequent reported possible sightings but, despite investigations the department is not aware of any confirmed instances of big cats of unknown origin being found out of captivity in England in the last 20 years. The lack of hard evidence (such as captured animals, corpses or photographs) is hard to reconcile with the number of*

reported sightings, unless people are genuinely but frequently mistaken with their identification.

The department does investigate claims of big cat sightings where there is potential risk to possible livestock predation. Where livestock deaths are involved and it is likely that hard evidence could be obtained to identify the predator, a field visit may be conducted. However, the department does not systematically record all alleged sightings.

Since June 2001, the department's Rural Development Service (RDS) have had 22 cases of alleged big cats reported to them connected to possible livestock predation and where there was potentially hard evidence to follow up, there have been field visits in relation to these reports. The counties for these reports were, Buckinghamshire, Cornwall, Devon (3), Essex (3), Kent, Norfolk, North Somerset (2), North Yorkshire, Oxfordshire, Shropshire, Staffordshire, Suffolk, Surrey (2), Warwickshire, West Midlands and Wiltshire. In many cases the details of the report provide insufficient circumstantial evidence to justify the expense of a field visit. However, should a field visit be deemed necessary, a trained wildlife biologist carries out detailed searches for various types of evidence such as examining the body in the field for evidence of how it had been killed or checking for footprints, in none of the field visits could any evidence be found to confirm the presence of big cats.

Release of the big cats into the wild is prohibited under the Wildlife and Countryside Act 1981 and possession of these species is regulated under the Dangerous Wild Animals Act 1976. If there is believed to be a public safety issue, for example from an escaped big cat, then this is a matter for the police.

The attitude of DEFRA appears to suggest that there is no significant problem with big cats and indeed, despite the resources available to it, they have failed to uncover any hard evidence that there are any big cats in the wild. This stance by the government department does, perhaps, indicate a little indifference and, dare I say it, complacency on their part, as there are definitely big cats out in the wilds of Britain some of which are occasionally attacking livestock.

Alien big cats are a fascinating enigma that appeals to the majority of us, suggesting the untameable, the lone underdog (if you will excuse the expression!), an escapee in a foreign land and the finely tuned beauty of nature's feline predators. We may love the romance conjured by these creatures, but they are not responsible for the sheep mutilations.

43

Black Dog and the Lydford Beast

One of the enduring legends of Dartmoor is that of the black dog, a spectral hound that haunts the eerie, misty moorland and its track ways. The black dog has different connotations and is sometimes portrayed as the ghost of a faithful canine servant. However, it is more usually associated with a malevolent spirit and witchcraft. The legend of black dog and the bleak atmosphere of Dartmoor at night was the perfect setting for Sir Arthur Conan Doyle to write the Sherlock Holmes classic *The Hound of the Baskervilles.* I can vouch for the fact that on one night carrying out a surveillance operation on Dartmoor, that particular piece of fiction seemed frighteningly real!

There are numerous stories about the enigmatic black dog and I would like to give two examples of the legend. A Dartmoor farmer claimed he was chased across the moor by a large black dog. As the man ran for his life it seemed inevitable that the beast would overtake him and kill him. The man was exhausted and terrified as he ran and half stumbled to a crossroads. The terrifying hound bounded towards him, at this point the black dog disappeared in an explosive flash and the force of this frightening event threw the farmer to the ground. The black dog had completely disappeared. It should be noted that in folklore, crossroads are places associated with the devil.

Another little story from Dartmoor concerns a local titled lady of no virtue. Lady Howard of Tavistock was wicked in life and it is said that her tormented soul appears in the form of a large black dog. Every night the hound has to run beside a coach made of bones, driven by – yes, you've guessed it – a headless coachman, to Okehampton Castle where the black dog must pluck a blade of grass in its mouth and take it back to Tavistock. Legend has it that when she has cleared the grass from Okehampton Castle, Lady Howard's soul will rest in peace. Well, there doesn't seem much chance of that, does there?

What are we to make of the following account in which a farmer from

Lydford on the north-western edge of Dartmoor came face to face with a beast that was straight out of local folklore and legend?

The *Tavistock Times* dated 16th April 1982, carried the bizarre story of a local farmer Mr Knowles, who had a farm at Inglebrake near Lydford. Under the headline 'Eerie creature seen by Lydford farmer' the *Times* described how Mr Knowles had been out at 3 a.m. checking on a ewe that was about to lamb. He spotted 'the black creature' which he described as approximately four or five feet long, built like a greyhound, but with the back legs and face of a colt. Its eyes reflected no light from the powerful torch he carried. The *Times* stated that BBC Television confirmed they were not filming *The Hound of the Baskervilles.* Mr Knowles was quoted as saying, *'The funny thing was when I shone my torch in its face, its eyes didn't shine at all. I've heard that stags' and hinds' eyes don't shine back, but I haven't seen other animals like that.'* Mr Knowles speculated that the animal may have been blind.

A month after the sighting Mr Knowles gave a fuller account of the incident. He had been sitting in his kitchen for most of the evening with the intention of going out to check on a ewe that was about to lamb. He had fallen asleep and the time had moved on to three o'clock in the morning. Mr Knowles picked up his torch, which was extremely powerful and called to his dog to join him. Surprisingly the dog would not move and cowered under the table. Mr Knowles had never encountered this kind of reaction before from the animal and presumed that the dog did not want to go out into the cold. The sheepdog was always by his side, but no amount of coaxing could persuade the dog to join him outside so, with the faithful dog still cowering under the table, Mr Knowles went out by himself.

The sheep that were lambing were kept in a large field close to the farmhouse and as Mr Knowles entered the field he scanned the area in front with the beam from his torch. As he neared the top half of the field, he thought he saw a 'big, black calf'. He was mystified by this as there weren't any calves supposed to be in that field, therefore he supposed it must be a dog of some kind. The animal appeared to be taking no notice of Mr Knowles whatsoever, despite the fact that the powerful torch beam was directed straight onto it.

It was at this point that Mr Knowles, who was now only ten yards from the animal, realised it was not a dog, he described the creature as follows: *'Body long, with hind legs more like a colt or calf, hock fairly high up. Long body with drooping stomach and long tail curved between back legs, possibly a little white marking near the front legs. It resembled a colt in size and stance, tail long and like a greyhounds as was the coat, short hair, not fur. The animal looked very strong and muscled, fit, broad pad feet, a big animal.'* Mr Knowles further stated that the animal looked to be in excellent condition.

At this point, Mr Knowles was walking parallel to the creature and when it neared the corner of the field and turned, he came face to face with it. The torch beam was now full on the face of the creature. Mr Knowles described what he saw as follows: *'Face long, pointed ears turning forward, one crumpled one pricked, barrel type nose with dark markings where the eyes should have been.'* At no time did the creature open its mouth.

The creature continued to be oblivious to the presence of Mr Knowles and approached to within ten feet of him. At this point the creature stopped and raised its head. With the torch beam full on its head, Mr Knowles was shocked to see that the animal had a *'snout – just like a pig'* which was wet, quivering and moving from side to side *'sniffing air, exactly as a pig would do.'*

After a few seconds of 'sniffing the air' the animal appeared to catch the scent of Mr Knowles and looked straight at him. As the creature confronted him, Mr Knowles was shocked to see that the animal had no eyes, only a black line where the eyes might have been. At no time were any eyes visible and there was no light reflection to indicate the presence of eyes. Because of this, Mr Knowles assumed the creature must have been blind.

The creature and Mr Knowles maintained a stand-off for a couple of minutes. As he continued to look at the strange animal, Mr Knowles thought about what he should do. Eventually he raised his arms and shouted at the creature in order to provoke a reaction. Initially, the creature appeared unperturbed, then simply turned and, in Mr Knowles' words, *'seemed to bound in a flowing gait, rather like a foal cantering. In three bounds it reached the corner of the field.'* At this point the creature tried to jump onto the six-foot wall that surrounded the field, but missed its footing and fell backwards. Mr Knowles, showing no regard for his own safety and realising that only the capture of the beast would prove conclusively what he had seen, ran towards the animal, thinking he might catch it. However, the creature quickly made a second attempt and succeeded in getting on top of the wall whereupon it jumped down into the adjacent field. The creature disappeared into the night and Mr Knowles had no further sight of the animal. It should be noted that the sheep in the adjoining field remained undisturbed by the events.

Incredibly, Mr Knowles claimed that at no time did he feel afraid, despite this shocking encounter in the middle of the night on Dartmoor. I can only feel he must have had nerves of steel!

Mr Knowles stated that he had lost a lamb around the same time of the encounter and that the animal had been killed allegedly by a massive bite to the neck, in fact the bite marks were so large he could put his finger through the holes. In addition, the lamb's rib cage had been crushed to pulp. He stated that from his extensive experience (Mr Knowles was sixty-five years of age) no dog, badger or any other known animal could have inflicted these injuries. Mr Knowles was convinced that the creature he saw was real and had somehow managed to keep itself away from humans. His father denounced the reality of the 'beast', stating that its manifestation was witchcraft, later refusing to discuss the matter further.

There appears little doubt that Mr Knowles saw something very strange that night and the fact that he had the creature in close view for nearly ten minutes seems pretty conclusive. He did not volunteer the story to the *Tavistock Times* and he was hardly the kind of individual who would concoct such a story. So what did he see? We may never know. However, there is an interesting legend from that area of Dartmoor. The notorious Judge Jeffreys, the infamous hanging judge of the seventeenth century, held assizes at nearby Lydford Castle, and was said to haunt the surrounding area in the form of a black pig!

It is interesting to note that during the early part of the same year the Lydford beast was seen, 1982, there was a series of mysterious sheep killings in nearby Peter Tavy. The victims were all lambs and were apparently savagely slaughtered and torn apart (though not devoured). Despite all-night surveillance by two local farmers, the attacker, or attackers were never found.

44

UFOs and Strange Activity on Dartmoor

In Part I I related a number of interesting reports of UFOs or craft of unknown origin that were seen around the western edge of Dartmoor during 1977/78. We shall now review further anomalous activity around the same area since 1979.

Despite the huge area of desolate moorland that forms the Dartmoor national park, there are many reports of strange aerial activity either close to or over the moor, both at night and in the daytime. The British army carries out manoeuvres and other practice activities on Dartmoor day and night. However, the reports I am going to present here are unlikely to be anything to do with the Ministry of Defence. From all the numerous reports I have in my possession I have selected only those from the western edge of Dartmoor, covering Lydford in the north-west down to Princetown and Ivybridge in the south-west. The reason for selecting this particular area is because of its close proximity to Postbridge, scene of the 1977 pony deaths, and Moortown, scene of the Dartmoor sheep deaths. I should also mention that I have details of a huge number of UFO sightings from the Plymouth area, which is less than ten miles from the edge of Dartmoor that I have selected.

I think we should ignore chronological order and start with a frightening experience on a remote Dartmoor road in 1982. Under the headline 'Mystery object scares CB users away from Moor' the *Tavistock Times* reported that a man speaking to a lady friend on a CB radio (the precursor to mobile phones) became aware of what he thought was a car headlight. As he turned and looked around he saw it was an egg-shaped craft, with the bottom cut off and a fin on its side. The craft had a ring of small lights around the bottom and was directing a beam of light downwards. It was only forty feet up in the air and approximately one hundred yards away. The craft was visible for nearly ten minutes and the lady he was speaking to, CB call sign 'Morning Glory', confirmed that the man, named only as Michael, was quite alarmed by the experience. Other CB users who used that particular place for good reception were allegedly staying away from the area. The

Tavistock Times included a rough drawing of the craft, done by Michael for Joan Amos. The newspaper report was couched in references to CB radio, such as handle (name), breaker (CB user) and rig (CB radio); such terminology is now quaintly out of date. The article unfortunately omitted some important details about the encounter. Joan Amos had reported the story and from her original notes and witness statement we can obtain a fuller picture of the incident.

The witness, Michael, who at the time was thirty-three years of age, lived at Crapstone, a village that was less than a mile west of Yelverton. On the Friday 12th March 1982 he was walking by the side of the B3212 Yelverton to Princetown road at The Pond near Sharpitor, a place much favoured by CB radio users because of the good reception. The time was 0245 hours and he was talking to a lady friend (CB handle, Morning Glory) when he became aware of a light approaching, which initially he thought was a car. Because he could hear no sound, Michael turned round and looked behind to see what the source of the light was. To his utter amazement, he saw that the light was coming from the sky and was only about forty feet in the air and about one hundred yards away. He described the craft thus: *'There was a series of lights about forty of them, quite small. They seemed to be turning around and one huge beam was coming out of the bottom. It looked like an egg with the bottom cut off with what looked like a fin on the side.'* The craft was grey in colour and completely silent.

The beam lit up a pony that was on the side of the road (Michael incorrectly describes it as a horse, which would be an unlikely animal to be found wandering on this part of the moor). The pony lifted its head up to see what it was. There is a version of this incident which states that the pony was rearing up in fright and being pursued by the strange craft. However, Michael makes no mention of such a reaction in his statement. The UFO was visible for ten minutes, before the lights on it went out and the craft went towards Plymouth Sound, eventually disappearing from view.

Corroboration of this incredible encounter came from the lady who was listening to Michael for the duration of the sighting. Her recollection of what Michael said was given to Joan Amos as follows: *'There's some strange lights in the sky, it's queer – very bright, not moving, lots of lights, not coloured, stationary – It's still there, sitting up there in the sky. Lights were coming from underneath – no sound. It's changed position, going away.'* Constance commented that Michael sounded quite frightened and that was not like him.

This amazing encounter is highly unusual in that it has a secondary witness, many miles away, to the main witness's reaction to the event. It is also unusual for the close proximity and the duration of the sighting. In the circumstances, Michael could hardly have mistaken what he saw for any conventional craft.

Let us now go back to the previous year, 1981, and a classic sighting at Merrivale, which is right next to Moortown, a place with which we became very familiar in Part III. In February 1981 a member of a group, visiting Dartmoor on a school day trip, saw a cigar-shaped object over Merrivale. The object moved behind Heckwood Tor and emerged from the other side, it then stopped, pivoted into a vertical position, then descended out of sight. The witness viewed the object for three minutes. The astounding part of this sighting, apart from it being in daytime, is the fact that the UFO descended out of sight.

A few months later Sue Elwell from nearby Whitchurch saw a green fireball crossing the sky at nine-thirty on a summer's evening.

On 10th August 1981 Joan Amos saw a strange aerial object descending over Peter Tavy in broad daylight, this is her written account:

> *Two thirty pm sitting in my garden at Peter Tavy leaning right back in my deck chair. I was sunbathing, but a dark cloud obscured the sun, I looked up to see how big the cloud was, when suddenly to the left of the cloud I saw a quick moving object, that first appeared dark and then silver as it caught the sun it was descending very fast then went into a wispy cloud and disappeared. I watched intently waiting for it to come out on the other side, but it did not, then the cloud dispersed and the sky was blue, high and blank at that spot, there was no sign of the object it had vanished. It did not go anywhere, as I didn't take my eyes off that patch of sky for about a quarter of an hour. It had just disappeared. I was wearing Rapide Reactolite glasses which enable me to see perfectly, even in bright sunlight.*

In the same year, 1981, a fisherman had an unnerving experience at Lee Mill, Dartmoor. Although this event took place many years ago I am withholding the name of the witness, who was a company director at the time of the incident. On Friday 30th July 1981, just after midnight, the witness was fishing for trout in the river Yealm near Lee Mill, on the south-western edge of Dartmoor. He became aware of a light in a field opposite where he was fishing. The shaft of light was approximately one hundred yards away and was a very intense blue with a halo of diffused light around it. The shaft of light was about two hundred feet high and about two to three feet wide. The witness was amazed by the intensity of the colour of the light. The witness initially assumed that the light was being shone from the ground up into the air. However, he soon realised that the shaft of light was coming from the sky. The light began to move in the general direction of the witness and approached at an angle of forty-five degrees to the river. The witness claimed that he heard a *'whistling hiss'* from the shaft of light as it got closer.

The light moved straight towards the witness, entering the river which was approximately sixteen feet wide at this point. As it did so, the water around the light began to reverberate and the witness could see that the light illuminated the river bed. The light reached the middle of the river then stopped.

The light began moving again and came out onto the river bank, only a few feet from the witness. The beam of light moved into a position directly overhead and the witness found himself kneeling inside the beam of light. What he thought was a solid beam was in fact a ring of light. Looking up, the witness, who had not seen what was emitting the shaft of light, saw that the light was coming from a cylinder. Inside the shaft of light the witness stated that the beam appeared conical, although when he saw it from outside it appeared straight-sided. The witness also said that the hair on the back of his head stood on end.

By now the witness was in a state of terror, and after five or six seconds inside the beam, he bolted to a nearby tree. The shaft of light remained still momentarily then began to move around as if looking for the witness who, by now, could stand no more. The witness grabbed his fishing tackle and ran for his life. As he ran, terror-stricken, through a field to his car, he fell down. As he did so he looked back and saw that the light was no longer there.

The witness drove directly to Crownhill police station and reported the incident. Unfortunately the police accused him of making the whole thing up, much to the chagrin of the witness who elected to say no more. The fisherman was further annoyed when, the following morning, the incident was reported on local radio, giving his name and address. He telephoned the police and complained in the strongest terms about the betrayal of confidence and that contrary to the radio report he had not reported seeing a UFO. The witness stated that shortly after the experience, he was dehydrated and had 'pins and needles' all over his scalp. The terrifying incident lasted no more than one minute.

The police contacted the man a few days later and said that they had made exhaustive enquiries to local military installations, coastguards and meteorologists and that no explanation could be found. During this conversation the police made the astonishing revelation that this was the fourth identical incident received by the Devon and Cornwall Constabulary that year!

Another interesting sighting in this area took place on 11th or 12th September 1993, when a self-employed builder was travelling from Ivybridge back to his home in Mary Tavy. The time was approximately ten o'clock in the evening and the witness, Mr William Reed, was approaching the village of Wotter, which is situated on a moorland road leading to Yelverton when he saw an extraordinary box-shaped craft, approximately forty-five degrees to his left. The craft, which had white lights on it, was travelling in the direction of Ivybridge. Mr Reed stopped his car further down the road, but was unable to get a further look at the bizarre craft.

Was this craft the same as the massive L-shaped craft seen on the southern edge of Dartmoor by three witnesses in September 2000?

At 2145 hours on 11th September 1993, Mrs Sue Friend and her sister were travelling from Tavistock to Peter Tavy when they saw a very bright orange sphere over Dartmoor. The object rose up and came down again in the direction of Cox Tor and was visible for about ten minutes.

Perhaps this is just a coincidence, but around the same date, on 12th September 1993, a Tavistock resident, Mr Raymond Cornforth, reported a strange silent craft flying over the town just after midnight. The craft appeared to have two separate fuselages *'like a catamaran'* and the witness saw two rows of lighted windows. In addition there were what he described as red and white strobe lights on the object. The craft was travelling north-east (towards the moors) at an altitude estimated at one thousand feet. There were five other witnesses to this event.

There appears to have been a lot of strange aerial activity around 11th and 12th September and in these three cases the witnesses appeared to have seen different types of craft.

The previous month, in August 1993, there was another strange sighting at Bere Alston, near Yelverton. Mrs Phylis Taylor was milking two of her goats when she noticed a strange formation of lights. Being used to seeing a wide variety of aerial activity in the night sky, Mrs Taylor was intrigued by the close grouping of the lights that she and her husband witnessed for fifteen minutes.

On an unspecified date in October or November 1993 a witness saw an egg-shaped craft on the outskirts of Tavistock. It was afternoon and the sighting lasted five minutes.

Back to 1984 and further UFO activity over Tavistock. On 24th April 1984, a married couple saw two strange objects over the town and I quote from the statement submitted by Mr Banks:

On Tuesday the 24th April at exactly 21:00 hours I observed two flying objects, brightly lit in the night sky over Tavistock. The objects circled to the south of the town then flew, in formation, towards the north-east. I observed them for approximately ten minutes, both with the naked eye and through binoculars. Fifteen minutes later, I observed two bright specs of light to the south-west and high in the sky. They were travelling erratically and at varying speed and did not conform to gravity.

Mr Banks also stated that no sound came from the objects.

Milton Abbot is a small village just a few miles north-west of Tavistock and on the evening of 10th May 1985, Mrs Ruby Palmer saw a rather strange craft. While reading late at night, Mrs Palmer heard what she first thought was a plane. She went to the bedroom window, looked out and saw a craft of unknown origin that was shaped like a 'goldfish'. There was a row of brilliant lights across the centre of the craft and smaller lights all around the edge and rear fin, the object gave off a humming sound, which Mrs Palmer described as almost like an airship. Mrs Palmer stated that the craft was travelling in a south-easterly direction (towards Tavistock) and was visible for about forty-five seconds.

During 1987 and 1988 Mr Michael Gliddon of Exeter saw some strange aerial traffic going to, and coming from Dartmoor. In the summer of 1987 Mr Gliddon and a neighbour saw some strange objects, which he described as being like 'starfish', travelling from Exeter airport towards Dartmoor. In the same year he saw three silver balls travelling towards Sidmouth (east), the sighting was on a Saturday afternoon. On 30th October 1988 the same witness saw a round luminous green object, travelling from Dartmoor in the direction of Exeter.

I wonder if the luminous green object seen by Mr Gliddon had any connection with the next incident? On the night of 27th July 1988 two youth club members Stuart (name withheld) and Brendon (name withheld) were on a night hike on Dartmoor, in an area around Great Nodden and Arms Tor, which is just to the north of the village of Lydford. The following statement was made by Stuart, who was a Territorial Army reservist at the time of the incident:

Brendon and I were sitting on the track at grid reference 543879 (Landranger ordnance survey map sheet 191, 1:50,000 scale). Our attention was drawn in the dark by four luminous lights behind and to the left of us, in the area of grid reference 535870. The green lights were made hazy by cloud cover, started to go to the left and rapidly moved rightwards so fast that they all seemed to be on at the same time. This gave the impression that an invisible object was emitting the lights, as it seemed like no aircraft of natural origin that I know of could have given the same display.

This 'light show' continued for between fifteen and twenty seconds. We hit the deck and the time I noted was 01:10 hours. On my instructions Brendon and I moved off to go down the steep side of Great Nodden with Brendon ten metres ahead. Halfway down at grid reference 540874 the same pattern of lights appeared again above cloud cover on the slopes of Arms Tor to the right of the Tor as we looked at it. The lights stayed on for around fifteen to twenty seconds again, if not a little longer. Brendon and I then moved down to the stream where we rendezvoused. I then gave him a quick brief on keeping our distance back up over Arms Tor. Spacing was set for five metres, and I can remember saying 'shit, this is the real thing' and all the evasion skills I had learnt were against something I had never seen before.

On the way up Arms Tor we were separated by our camouflage and the dark. At what I would guess would be just the other side of the stream the lights appeared again for about fifteen to twenty seconds. Halfway up the Tor I was forced to take cover by a single same type of green light flashing across the sky parallel to the ground. It had a starting point, flashed across the sky for a shortish distance, stopped, then started the pattern again but very rapidly, a little like a spot on an oscilloscope leaving a trace.

Just short of reaching the main rocks on top of Arms Tor I was relieved to meet up with Brendon. We moved to the top of the Tor and kept an air watch for ten minutes. We made some food in a cleft in the rock and shielded any light with a poncho. We made our way back to camp at first light.

I was only a little worried on my own moving up the Tor at night a) because the moon was casting light over the ground as it half broke from beneath the cloud cover, and b) because I knew Brendon and I were on our own if anything had happened.

This very detailed statement with its precise grid references was corroborated by Brendon, who claimed the lights came from a massive oval shape *'the size of Wembley stadium'* and that he felt that they were being watched. There may be further confirmation of the strange green lights from the following account. Other youths at the base camp also saw lights in the area at 0020 hours.

On the night of 28th July 1988, Mrs Shiela Jasper and her husband Stanley had arrived at their home in Brentor, just south of Lydford, after driving across Dartmoor from Kingsbridge. The time was 0115 hours and I quote directly from their statement: *'My husband and I saw this object in the sky, thin cloud was partially covering the centre, but five green lights were flashing in an up and downward movement each beam being of an equal distance apart, covering an area of approximately one mile from south to east.'*

This would position the object over Dartmoor and a mile or so south of

Great Nodden. There is a possibility that the dates given in these two reports may not be one day apart and were on the same night, as the timing of each sighting, around 0110 hours, could suggest that the witnesses saw the same object at the same time.

A possible explanation for the UFO sightings was the rehearsal for the Armada laser show at Plymouth, which is about thirteen miles from where Brendon and Stuart had their encounter. I find this explanation of a laser show quite unsatisfactory given the detail of Stuart's statement and the topography of the area.

In 1978 four patients at Tavistock hospital saw a rather strange craft one morning. Here is another report from a patient at the hospital, this time in 1990. The witness has requested anonymity. The witness awoke very early on the morning of 21st September 1990 and looked out through the window at the large number of stars in the sky. However, she soon realised that there were hundreds of 'stars' or bright lights in a massive round shape. After watching for a while, some of the lights went off, revealing what appeared to be a sort of 'landing strip' in the sky. Thirty seconds later the whole thing completely disappeared.

On 21st April 1993 at Yelverton, two witnesses reported seeing a bright silver 'torpedo' that flew towards the witnesses, changed direction and flew off. The sighting was at two fifteen in the afternoon and the object was visible for about forty seconds.

Was this craft seen again on 24th July 1993 at Bideford? Situated on the north Devon coast, Bideford is some distance from Dartmoor. However, it may have some correlation with another sighting of an identical object on the same day. At 7.30 on the evening of 24th July a witness saw a silver cigar-shaped object over Bideford. The witness viewed the strange object for five minutes and managed to capture eight seconds of video footage before the craft disappeared from view.

An hour and fifteen minutes later, at Ivybridge on the south-western edge of Dartmoor, four witnesses saw a cigar-shaped craft moving very slowly. They had the craft in view for forty minutes and claimed it was identical to the craft of unknown origin seen and videoed at Bideford earlier that evening. If the craft was indeed the same one, then it is likely that it flew in a straight line across the western part of Dartmoor.

On November 10th 1993 at 1615 hours, two white cigar-shaped craft were seen by a witness at Peter Tavy.

Our next report also comes from Peter Tavy and concerns a sighting there on 7th December 1994. At about 1850 hours on 7th December Paul Sample was returning to Peter Tavy after working in nearby Tavistock. He became aware of two 'stars' that were approaching the village, very slowly. He alerted his grandmother, the redoubtable Joan Amos, who came out into the still night air to view the objects, which appeared stationary. The object or objects appeared to be hovering over the nearby A386 main road. The objects began to move slowly towards the village of Peter Tavy and as they got closer it was apparent that there was a single object with two large orange 'headlights' and two or three smaller white lights on it. The object flew across the village very slowly and in a northerly direction (over the moors). As the object passed directly over the two witnesses, a low humming sound was heard. At this point the lights on the object went out for a few seconds, before reappearing.

Again at Peter Tavy, another interesting report. At 1500 hours on the 22nd December 1994 a witness saw a transatlantic jet high in the sky. Behind it, as if fixed to the jet, was a huge white, box-shaped craft. The square-shaped craft was many times bigger than the jet. The witness said that the jet was completely dwarfed by the 'flying box', which in comparison to the jet was like an Oxo cube to a dot. The witness viewed this incredible spectacle for five minutes after which the huge craft suddenly disappeared.

On Saturday 4th March 1995, two young people were returning to their mobile home in Chillaton, near Tavistock after a night out with friends. The time was 0530 hours and as they gazed up at the clear night sky they saw a fast-moving object. The object had flashing green, yellow and red lights and appeared oval in shape. The object came down to within a couple of hundred yards of the witnesses and began to hover behind some trees. For nearly twenty minutes the object with its multiple flashing lights, hovered so low that the ground around it appeared to be illuminated. Finally, it moved away and disappeared into the distance.

On Saturday 7th April 2007 Mr Stephen Edgcumbe was walking his dog at the Merrivale army firing range, not far from Peter Tavy and situated in a remote part of Dartmoor. The time was about 1430 and Mr Edgcumbe took the opportunity to try out his new camera, a Canon Eos 350D. Aware that there were no red flags flying on the range, indicating there was no firing for the day, a fact later confirmed by an army spokesman, Mr Edgcumbe took a number of pictures, but did not download them until some weeks later.

When the images were on his computer, he found one had captured an image of an unknown dome-shaped craft flying over the moor. Mr Edgcumbe is not the first person to have inadvertently photographed a strange craft and there have been other examples of such images taken in the south-west.

I have suggested the possibility that animal mutilation attacks may be some kind of sampling programme carried out by alien entities. If this so then the following account may be further evidence of this.

In September 1993, a man who had walked on Dartmoor for more than thirty years made an amazing discovery. While walking across a remote and largely inaccessible part of the moor, he came upon an area of disturbance. Large granite boulders, some weighing more than half a ton, had been uprooted and some had disappeared altogether. There were no signs of footprints or tyre tracks. The area was almost circular and measured forty-eight metres north to south and thirty-five metres east to west. In the middle of the circle was a depression approximately one metre deep and grass was visibly flattened. The walker had never seen anything like it before and was at a loss to explain how this could have occurred in such a remote area of Dartmoor.

I will finish this chapter with a very strange encounter near Yelverton. The incident was investigated by Bob Boyd of PUFORG (Plymouth UFO Group). Bob has investigated many UFO incidents in the south-west.

At 2250 hours on 12th June 1990 a Devonport dockyard worker was driving along an unclassified road from Bere Alston towards the main A386 at Yelverton. The road was unlit and about a mile from the nearest buildings. As the witness approached the A386 from Crapstone (known locally as the Rock) he noticed a six-foot tall silver-suited figure with a 'bucket' on his head, walking normally *'in a determined manner'* towards him.

The figure took no notice of the car and the 'bucket' appeared to have no eyeholes or openings. The witness, who was a former policeman, thought initially that the figure might be someone dressed for a fancy dress party. However, he was intrigued enough to turn his car round at the next junction, some thirty yards away, and drove back along the road for sixty yards, before turning right onto another unclassified road, leading towards Yelverton. He drove a further fifty yards without seeing the figure again. Wondering where the figure could have gone to, the witness turned his car round so he could resume his journey to work. As he did so he saw the silver-suited figure again, this time by a large natural outcrop of granite, from which the area got its name, the Rock.

The witness stopped the car and turned his spotlight on the figure. Despite the powerful beam of light, the figure appeared completely unperturbed. The witness sat in his car for several minutes watching the strange silver-suited figure *'acting in a definite manner'*. After a while, the witness became afraid, he started his car and drove past the figure to get onto the main road.

The witness drove straight to work and upon arrival, at 2315 hours, reported the incident to the Devonport M.O.D. Police. The M.O.D. Police contacted Plymouth police, who sent a patrol car to the Rock to investigate – nothing was seen and the patrol car reported back at 2345 hours.

This extraordinary encounter raises some interesting questions and it is unfortunate that the witness (who refused to be identified, although known to Bob Boyd) would not elaborate further on the details he submitted to the police. How was the figure able to move when his head was covered with the 'bucket' which had no eyeholes? What was it doing in such a determined way? What made the witness, who was an ex policeman, go back for another look at the figure? Why did the witness become afraid as he watched the figure in the glare of his spotlight? I wonder if there is any connection between this silver-suited figure and the silver-suited figure seen outside a pub at Peter Tavy in November 1978 (see Part I)?

I do not think that the reduction in reported sightings since 1995 suggests a downturn in UFO activity, merely a decrease in reporting. There is something plainly important about this western edge of Dartmoor that attracts the amount of activity I have detailed here and in Part I. Is it the remoteness of the area, or its close proximity with Plymouth and the numerous naval installations there?

Dave Gillham and myself have video footage of the extraordinary light flashes seen on 14th May 2006, which we now know are from craft of unknown origin. This activity has been going on for a long time and I have to ask – what is attracting this large amount of anomalous aerial activity to this part of Dartmoor?

45

Britain's Biggest Secret

The United Kingdom has many dark secrets and I believe the darkest of them all concerns the animal mutilation problem.

You may wonder why it is that despite the coverage this problem has received in the USA, we have not had a single documentary on the subject on any terrestrial UK television channel. Are they afraid of causing panic? I have to ask this question – if it's considered in the public interest for a current affairs programme to screen graphic images about the war in Iraq and Afghanistan, child prostitution, violence in hospitals, the effects of foot and mouth disease etc., then why not a programme about the animal mutilation problem?

The BBC produce a programme called *Country File* that deals with a range of rural issues. Strangely, this programme has chosen to ignore the animal mutilation problem. In 2005 they did a report on the Beast of Bodmin and interviewed a farmer who had a dead lamb which had its tongue removed. Needless to say 'the beast' was accused of the attack. At the time I thought it unlikely that a puma or any other ABC would kill a lamb and only remove the tongue, so I took the opportunity to write to the producer of *Country File* and ask if I could be put in touch with the farmer concerned. Unfortunately I did not receive a reply.

However, during 1998 and 1999, researcher David Cayton was the subject of a feature for a BBC Television programme produced in Manchester. Many hours were spent filming and the final result was a five-minute slot on the programme *The Big End*, screened nationally late on a Sunday night. During the production of this feature the BBC attempted to get a MAFF spokesperson to discuss the issue of animal mutilations with David Cayton, outside their Barton Hall facility. Unsurprisingly, MAFF declined the offer. However on 11th December 1998 they faxed a statement to the BBC from Stuart Dobbs of the MAFF press office, the statement read as follows:

The series of animal mutilations have been very distressing for the farmers involved and the majority of these incidents have been reported to the police as very serious

> *offences and are being dealt with by them at present. As a result it is not for the Ministry of Agriculture, Fisheries and Food to pass comment on these incidents, as they are being handled by the relevant authorities.*

This statement is important as it clearly shows that MAFF were aware of the problem and that it was ongoing as indicated by the use of the word serial. As we shall see shortly, the pretence that all animal mutilation attacks are referred to the police is a lie.

David Cayton placed a series of adverts in *Farmers Weekly* and the long-established journal contacted Cayton for information about the animal mutilation problem and promised a two-hundred word article by their reporter Johann Tasker. The information, including photographs and pathology reports, was sent to *Farmers Weekly* and David awaited the promised article. Some months later, on 26th March 1999, David received a letter from David Cousins, Features Editor for the *Farmers Weekly*. The apologetic letter contained the following comment:

> *It certainly makes disturbing reading, but I feel that it is a little too sensational for our readers. If definite proof can be found we would certainly be interested in running something, but I guess that is some way off.*

I wonder if this apparent 'cooling' on the animal mutilation article was by choice or the result of pressure from the magazine's owners or indeed MAFF.

Three weeks after placing his advert in the *Farmers Weekly*, David Cayton received a telephone call from MAFF at their Barton Hall establishment. The caller was very officious in her tone and demanded to know the identity of the pathologist that David had seconded to his investigations. David politely declined to disclose the information, whereupon the caller followed up with a second question.

'Is this to do with the aliens?' shortly followed by, *'not that we know anything about that.'*

The MAFF official then berated the farmers for giving their dead animals to David, for 'unofficial private experiments'. Needless to say David was swift to correct them, stating that the animals were being examined, not experimented on. The lady from MAFF then claimed that BSE regulations prohibited such private investigations. David replied that he was unaware that there was any BSE risk with sheep or lambs. Not to be outdone, the MAFF spokesperson claimed that *'farmers should bury or incinerate any dead animal within forty-eight hours'*. This directive had never been issued to any farmers at that time. The call ended with a demand for David's home address, which he gave freely expecting, no doubt, an officious letter as a follow up. Surprisingly, there was no letter forthcoming.

There is an interesting account I would now like to relate regarding the activities of MAFF. I would suggest that the activities described in this next case are continuing today under the auspices of DEFRA and form part of their ongoing programme of suppression. Details of this case were kindly passed on to me by David Cayton and I have withheld the names of those involved.

In October 1998 a farmer in Northamptonshire discovered two of his sheep dead in a field. Curiously, both had identical wounds. The farmer, his stockman and a gamekeeper friend studied the bodies and were shocked to note that the sexual organs had been removed and the rectums were cored out. Furthermore, there was no blood on or near the bodies – this was a classic mutilation case.

The carcasses were removed from the field where they were found and placed in a barn overnight. The following day the farmer went to Leicestershire on business and was away all day. During the morning two men in a BMW estate car called at the farm and asked to see the farmer's stockman. Both men displayed green MAFF identification cards and claimed they had come to remove the two dead sheep. The stockman assumed that they had made prior arrangements with the farmer, who had forgotten to inform him that they were coming to collect the dead sheep. Because of this the stockman acceded to their request and helped load the bodies into the BMW. Unfortunately the stockman, who was no doubt intimidated by the officials, failed to make a note of the names of these two 'officials'.

On his return, the owner of the farm was not too pleased with this intervention and asked a friend, whose brother was a local chief inspector of police, to look into the matter and make a formal complaint to MAFF. The farmer was claiming that the two dead sheep had effectively been stolen from his farm.

The Chief Inspector contacted MAFF and was told by the official he spoke to that they had not sent the two men to collect the dead sheep. The Chief Inspector countered the denial by saying that the stockman had been shown MAFF identification cards and that as a formal complaint of theft had been made it was now a police matter. The Chief Inspector requested that a more senior member of MAFF should speak to him.

Another official came to the phone and, contradicting what his colleague had said, stated that the farmer would be compensated for the loss of the two sheep, adding that it was not a police matter. It should be noted that despite this promise of compensation, no payment was forthcoming. The Chief Inspector, perhaps not used to this kind of official prevarication, informed the MAFF official that he was duty bound to pursue the matter, unless the farmer withdrew his allegation.

The MAFF official repeated his threat that the matter should go no further and told the Chief Inspector that his superiors would be notified in the event that he persisted with the matter. Needless to say this high-ranking policeman did not take kindly to this threat. However, it was not long before the Chief Inspector was indeed instructed by his superiors to drop the matter and cease his enquiries into the alleged theft.

There are some interesting questions that are raised by this case such as, how did MAFF know about the dead sheep, which had been dead only twenty-four hours? Only the farmer, his wife, the stockman and the farmer's friend knew of the two dead sheep.

Whilst puzzling over this curious fact, the farmer remembered an incident that occurred on the night of the killings that may have been connected to the MAFF visit. On the night in question the farmer had seen a bright light over the field where the sheep were kept. The time was about 2030 hours and twenty minutes later he noted two dark-coloured helicopters flying very fast over the same field. What was the origin of this activity? We know that black helicopters are often noted at animal mutilation sites. Were the authorities monitoring an alien incursion in the area?

I have been told by animal mutilations researcher David Cayton that a source had informed him that during the UK premiership of Margaret Thatcher, a special unit was set up within MAFF (now DEFRA), to monitor the animal mutilations in the UK. It is alleged that the unit was disbanded by the John Major administration – I don't think so!

Animal mutilation attacks are invariably treated as satanist or occult assaults by the UK press (this cover story has also been much used in the USA). The animal mutilation problem has achieved fleeting appearances in the UK national press and such articles that have appeared rarely confront the issue that the perpetrators may be from outside this Earth, and never seem to be followed up. My interview with a major south-west newspaper about the Moortown sheep attacks typifies the reluctance of newspapers to meet this issue head on. It's fair comment to say that they would not wish to cause panic, but why did they not explain their decision not to print the interview? I have not had a response to my communications with either of the reporters concerned.

I have already shown the lengths to which DEFRA are prepared to go, in order that they can harass or control research into this sinister subject. I was warned that vets and scientists willing to assist in research of this problem would be 'warned off' if their identities became known and, sure enough, that has happened to me and to others. Why is the UK government trying to hinder research into this problem?

DEFRA has sixteen regional laboratories throughout the UK and they are part of the Veterinary Laboratory Agency. All the regional VLAs report to the two Veterinary Surveillance Centres at Hatfield, Hertfordshire and Leahurst, South Wirral, the centre that had my mobile phone records interrogated.

One of the sixteen regional laboratories is VLA Preston, otherwise known as Barton Hall. This facility had its mask of secrecy removed by researcher David Cayton during his involvement with BBC television for *The Big End* programme. This facility was built in the late 1970s (at a time when the animal mutilation problem was gaining some momentum) and occupies the site of a former Royal Air Force base. Official signs designate the establishment as an animal health centre. I am sure that it is not the only VLA facility that has an animal mutilation section.

It is worth recalling the incident concerning the Vietnamese pot-bellied pig, found dead and decapitated near Lannescott Mines in Cornwall, referred to in Part II. The RSPCA became involved in the case and arranged for a post mortem on the victim. The examination was carried out by the MAFF facility at Truro, which is now known as VLA Truro. When the lady owner of the pig requested details of the post mortem report she was somewhat brusquely told, *'There's nothing in it – so what do you want it for?'* The MAFF spokesperson stated that a dog had killed the pig. Hmm, some dog that could wrench a seven-foot door off its hinges!

The DEFRA facility at Sand Hutton off the main York to Scarborough road is another laboratory built on Ministry of Defence land. The Central Science Laboratory at Sand Hutton employs over five hundred scientists and laboratory technicians and is involved in a variety of research projects. Despite the huge facilities within this complex, it would appear that the animal mutilation problem is being monitored from Leahurst Campus at Neston, near Liverpool.

What of the police in all this intrigue? We have already heard about their possible involvement in accessing my mobile phone records and the curious visit of a police inspector to a smallholding on the Shropshire–Wales border making inquiries about a dead sheep.

The upper levels of the police are controlled by the policy makers at ACPO, as evidenced by their involvement in my Freedom of Information appeal, and I suspect that the police in the UK are merely pawns in the game being played by Britain's government to suppress investigation of these killings. Remember my request to the Tavistock police for access to the Moortown sheep attacks file? The police were content for me to see that file, so long as I went through the proper channels. It was when my application under the Freedom of Information Act reached the level of headquarters that I began to experience 'difficulties'.

I have been given unsubstantiated information that there have been human mutilation attacks in the United Kingdom and that they have been covered up. Official figures state that on average around two hundred and twenty thousand people disappear in the UK each year. The vast majority of these are either found, or return of their own accord. If only a quarter of one percent are never found, then five hundred and fifty missing persons seems like a rather large number to me.

If there are human mutilations then someone in the police must have knowledge or experience, of such an attack. Would they come forward if they did? I doubt it. However here is a strange case that has come into the public domain.

On 6th June 1980 Polish-born Zygmunt Adamski, who lived in Tingley near Leeds with his wife Lotte, walked to a local corner shop at the end of his road, to buy some potatoes. It was the last time he was seen alive. Mr Adamski was missing for five days before his body was found by a coal merchant's son Trevor Parker, in a hollow on top of a large pile of coal in Todmorden, Lancashire some thirty miles away. According to Mr Parker, and the police constable who accompanied him, the body looked as if it had been placed gently in the hollow. The police were baffled as to how the body could have been dumped on the top of the coal heap.

Mr Adamski's body had burns from an unknown corrosive substance on his scalp, neck and the back of his head. He was found wearing a jacket but no shirt and his watch and wallet were missing, although there was five pounds in his pocket. The body was very clean, 'as if he had stepped from a shower'.

Consultant pathologist Dr Alan Edwards stated that death was caused by heart failure, possibly due to *'a severe shock or fright'*. Fifty-six-year-old Adamski had no connections with Todmorden and had never visited the place. He drank little, did not gamble and kept himself to himself. This background is at odds with some strange claims made in the local *Halifax Courier* that Adamski had been seen drinking in various pubs in the Todmorden area and had also been seen 'wandering' about the countryside prior to his death. The police were unable to find a motive for the death and enquiries suggested that Adamski had no enemies.

Mr James Turnbull, the West Yorkshire Coroner who presided over the inquest into Mr Adamski's death, made an astonishing statement to the press:

> *As a trained lawyer I have to rely on facts. Unfortunately we have been unable to uncover any facts which may have contributed to his death.*
>
> *I tend to believe that there may be some simple explanation.*
>
> *However, I do admit that the failure of forensic scientists to identify the corrosive substance which caused Mr Adamski's burns could lend some weight to the UFO theory.*
>
> *As a coroner I cannot speculate. But I must admit that if I was walking over Ilkley Moor tomorrow and a UFO came down I would not be surprised. I might be terrified, but not surprised.*
>
> *I cannot believe that all the thousands of reports of this sort of phenomenon – covering almost every country in the world and going back through the ages – result from human error.*

We should savour the candour of Mr Turnbull's statement to the press – believe me, you will not hear many coroners, or officials, talk with such open-minded honesty.

There was a strange twist to the Adamski case involving PC Alan Godfrey, who was one of the two policemen who attended the scene when the body was found. PC Godfrey had an encounter with a UFO in Todmorden a few weeks later and the significance of the bizarre death of Zygmunt Adamski became overshadowed by the experiences of the police constable.

There are some incredible aspects to the Adamski case such as the failure of forensic scientists to identify the corrosive substance found on the body and how did the body get dumped in a hollow at the top of the coal heap thirty miles from his home? I find it unbelievable that, given strange circumstances of his death, the Home Office agreed to the repatriation of Adamski's body to his homeland Poland less than a month after the body was discovered.

A final disturbing aspect of this case occurred in 1981 when researcher Graham Birdsall investigated the case. Mr N. Mortimer, who lived in the Todmorden area, assisted Birdsall in his investigations and it appears that the police were none too happy with his involvement. Mr Mortimer was visited at his home by a senior police officer who strenuously denied that UFOs were involved in the incident and that it would be wise for Mr Mortimer to forget the whole matter.

The secrecy remains and DEFRA continue to use their wide-ranging powers to threaten and coerce farmers, vets and researchers. They will not admit there is a problem and they will not admit that they are not in control of a situation that as yet may only be the beginning of a greater wave of savage, unstoppable attacks by unknown predators. No wonder the mutilation problem is Britain's biggest secret.

46

Veterinary Analysis

There have been hundreds, if not thousands, of post mortem reports on mutilated farm animals and I would suggest that very few give a precise cause of death. Invariably, the findings are speculative as to how the animals were killed.

I would like to review three post mortem reports from the USA, Canada and the United Kingdom. Each is different, but will give the reader an idea of the veterinary pathologists' examinations and findings.

Farmer James Waterhouse was checking his stock on Sunday morning, 11th May 1980 at his farm in Washington County, Iowa, when he found the remains of a bull calf, with the mother nearby, clearly distressed and bellowing. The dead calf was lying on its left side and the ground was dry and firm. There were no signs of a struggle or any tracks and there was no blood. The body was approximately twenty-five yards from a creek. The eyes had been removed and there was some residue blood in the sockets. The tongue had been removed, though not with the precision of a classic mutilation, and the teeth were coated with blood. Some blood had been smeared on the right shoulder of the calf and the genitals had been removed with some precision. The calf had last been seen alive on the evening of Friday 9th May. Mr Waterhouse contacted the authorities, who arrived at 0430 hours. By this time the body was showing a slight amount of bloating, though there was no rigor mortis.

It is worth mentioning that Mr Waterhouse and his neighbours had witnessed several unidentified helicopters flying over or near the property before the date of the attack.

Because of the suspicious circumstances surrounding the death it was decided to subject the carcass to a full pathological examination. A special agent of the Iowa Department of Public Safety Division of Criminal Investigation arranged for the dead calf to be transported to a laboratory where a necropsy was carried out by two highly qualified pathologists.

During the examination, observed by the special agent, he noted the pathologists' comments that the attack had been carried out with a very sharp instrument and was definitely not the work of natural predators. One of the pathologists showed special interest in the removal of the eyes and stated that it was a very neat job, further commenting that it would have been difficult for him to duplicate the same removal.

The carcass was extremely autolysed (the process whereby the cells are destroyed by their own enzymes). It appeared as if the animal had been dragged a distance on its side and there was a subcutaneous blood clot in the jugular which suggested a possible intravenous injection.

The tongue was absent (excised) and the margin of the remaining stump was somewhat jagged with clotted or dried blood on its surface. There were high numbers of maggots present in the mouth making more critical evaluation difficult. Both eyes were absent, while the eye lids remained intact and appeared normal.

The scrotum and testicles had been removed and there was a round or ovoid hole in the skin where they had been. The hole measured approximately six to seven inches in diameter with the edges of the skin being very uniform and smooth. The carcass appeared to contain a normal amount of blood which ruled out exsanguination (a common feature of animal mutilations).

A black (ultra-violet) light was used to examine the external surface of the animal for fluorescent material, and some traces were found on the left hip and shoulder area. The material appeared to be only on the tips of the hair, in very small amounts, and could be rubbed off easily with the fingers.

No poisons were discovered in the contents of the stomach – further analysis was not possible due to the advanced autolysis.

The pathologists concluded that the preliminary laboratory results did not provide sufficient information to determine the cause of death. However, they agreed that death was probably the result of human intervention, suggesting that the removal of the tongue was virtually impossible for a natural predator, in addition to citing the possible injection into the jugular.

There are some interesting points about this necropsy that I would like to comment on. The rather rough excision of the tongue was not done with the usual precision experienced in many classic mutilations, yet the expert removal of the eyes is puzzling. Scanning the body with a black light (ultra-violet) suggests that the pathologists may have had previous knowledge of mutilation cases, where strange substances have been detected on animal skins under ultra-violet light. It has been speculated that these 'marker' substances have been used to identify potential victims. The pathologists ruled out the possibility that the killing had been done by natural predators and suggested that humans were responsible.

The next case comes from British Columbia, Canada and the necropsy, carried out less than twelve hours after the animal had been killed, was done at the request of the Royal Canadian Mounted Police, who were investigating the incident.

Robert and Lillian Ternier ran the TLR Ranch near Armstrong, British Columbia. On 3rd July 1981 they found a three-year-old Hereford cow dead and mutilated. The cow had been alive and well when checked during the late evening of 2nd July and the killing had taken place in a field just fifty yards from a busy road and within eighty yards of the nearest house. The right upper lip and part of the nostril were missing, as was the udder and external genitalia. The excision appeared to have been carried out with a sharp instrument. The post mortem report, which was carried out by a very experienced pathologist at a local veterinary clinic, is summarised as follows:

The animal had been found lying on its left side in a grassy field and, surprisingly, the eyes were intact. This was very unusual considering the number of magpies and crows in the area. There was no sign of a struggle or any movement by the animal in the immediate or surrounding area. The upper right lip, including a portion of the right nostril and part of the lower right lip, were missing. The entire udder had been removed up to the abdominal wall with the exception of one of the rear teats. The vulvar labia were missing and approximately one inch of tissue around the orifice had been removed. Other marks on the exterior included two or three small abrasions on the breast skin; these were superficial and did not penetrate the skin. There was very little haemorrhage in the areas of missing tissue described above and there was no haemorrhage from the other body orifices. Rigor mortis was present but not complete. There was no bloating of the carcass and the body was fresh and in good condition.

The entire abdominal viscera were normal, with nothing unusual being observed. Examination of the uterus showed signs of a very early pregnancy. On opening the thoracic cavity (the area between the neck and abdomen), the lungs did not collapse. The lungs were showing considerable autolysis and had some foamy material in the minor airways. The trachea had pin-point haemorrhages on the front of the larynx. The heart was enlarged, completely full of clotted blood, as were all the great vessels. The region from the larynx, including the trachea, down to the breast region was extensively bruised with small, peculiar gelatinous blood clots throughout. No skin punctures or foreign bodies were found despite a vigorous search.

The pathologist made the following observations:

1. The apparent ease and rapidity of death suggested by undisturbed grass at the site.
2. The missing tissue, probably removed by a sharp instrument.
3. The almost professional dissection of the udder.
4. The absence of any significant haemorrhage at the mutilation site.
5. The absence of predators, particularly magpies.

The pathologist concluded that the animal died very suddenly of unnatural causes.

The pathologist concerned commented afterwards that he'd done a few hundred autopsies in his many years of practice, but he had never seen anything to compare with this attack. Perhaps this is why he made a telephone call to the Provincial Veterinary Pathology Laboratory in Abbotsford, British Columbia, to consult further on his findings.

The third examination report was done in England in 2006 and because of the circumstances involving this case I regret that I have to withhold not only the identity of the veterinary pathologist who carried out the post mortem but also the farmer's details.

The case involved the deaths of six sheep in a field next to a barn. The deaths were treated as suspicious and the animals had apparently been killed during the night. It appeared that the bodies had been laid out in a rough circle arrangement and had been dead about twenty-four hours. Two specimens from the six victims were selected for post mortem examination.

Cheviot X Ewe No 1

The ewe identified by ear tag UKxxxxxx/xxx weighed 38 kilos and was in good body condition. There was a severe degree of autolysis associated with the carcass, the abdomen was severely swollen and the anus was protruding.

There was noticeable green discolouration in the groin area and a vesicle containing sanguineous fluid extended from the side of the udder to the angle of the thigh. There was extensive subcutaneous haemorrhage present over the mandibles, extending into the angle of the jaw, the neck and the right side of the head, as well as over the skull and shoulder blade, pelvis and sacrum. Less extensive haemorrhage was present over the ventral thorax. Subcutaneous emphysema was also present in some locations.

Gas was present in the area overlying the muscles of the medial thighs and the diaphragm was grey in colour (suspected due to autolysis).

The liver had a pale, 'cooked' appearance and was markedly friable and autolysed. A good fill of food was found in the second stomach (suggesting the animal had been eating shortly before death), which was distended with gas. The small intestine also was swollen with gas and autolysed, and soft faeces were found in the large intestine.

Haemorrhagic fluid was present in the nasal chambers and sinuses and there was absorption and congestion of the tracheal mucosa, with varying degrees of congestion throughout the lungs. Marked absorption of fluid into the lining membrane of the heart was evident.

The kidneys were markedly autolysed and grey in colour.

The brain appeared autolysed. No haemorrhages were present.

No gross lesions were visible in the lymphoreticular system. The endocrine and genital systems were not examined.

Cheviot X Ewe No 2

The ewe weighed 40.5 kilos and was in good bodily condition. There was a severe degree of autolysis associated with the carcass and the abdomen was distended. The right ear had been cut and there was a band of haemorrhage extending one millimetre beneath the wound, suggesting the cut had occurred before death. No tag was present.

Extensive green discolouration of the skin was present in the groin and over the medial thighs. Extensive subcutaneous haemorrhage was present, over 0.5 centimetres deep in places, over the skull, muzzle, mandibles, angle of the jaw and the proximal ventral neck. Haemorrhages also were present over the cranial aspects of the shoulder blade, the pelvis and sacrum, the right hock and down the left foreleg to the carpus. Emphysema of subcutaneous tissues also was present.

As in the first ewe, there was gas in the area overlying the medial thighs. The diaphragm was autolysed, being discoloured grey with gas bubbles present.

The liver was grey/brown, with a cooked, autolysed appearance. Some adhesions were present between the abomasums, spleen and anterior abdominal wall.

As in the first ewe, a good fill of food was found in the second stomach and normal stools were present in the rectum.

The nasal chambers and sinuses were congested and contained sanguineous fluid. Marked imbibition/congestion of the tracheal mucosa was present and there was variable congestion throughout the lungs.

There was absorption of sanguineous fluid into the lining membrane of the heart and gas bubbles were present in the serosa of the great arteries and veins.

Fluid adhesions were also present on the spleen.

The kidneys were markedly autolysed, friable and grey in colour.

The brain was autolysed. No haemorrhages were present.

The endocrine and genital systems were not examined.

No Salmonella organisms were found in the small intestinal contents from both ewes.

The pathologist observed that the most striking finding from the post mortem examination was the extensive haemorrhage over the heads, pelvis and sacrums of both ewes. The cause of this was unclear and there was no evidence of fractures or intra-abdominal or intracranial haemorrhage. Some of the congestion seen could have been due to the advanced state of decomposition of both carcasses and this also may explain partially the sanguineous intrathoracic fluid found, although the latter may have been traumatic origin. Unfortunately, he considered that due to the degree of decomposition, further investigations were limited and it was likely that a conclusive diagnosis would not be possible, despite the suspicion that the findings were traumatic in origin.

The injuries to these two ewes were very similar and both bodies exhibited signs of advanced decomposition and bloating. Both livers had a 'cooked' appearance and were friable (crumbling to touch). What had been done to these animals to cause this?

Ewe No 2 had its right ear removed, and in the opinion of the pathologist, the removal had taken place while the animal was still alive!

The severe congestion by sanguineous (blood like) fluid was put down to the advanced state of decomposition.

The extensive haemorrhaging on the heads, pelvis and hip had no explanation, but it was suggested that the origin of the injuries was traumatic.

Both these animals had been dead approximately twenty-four hours and the advanced decomposition is a puzzle. The farmer, who had spent a lifetime farming sheep, was completely baffled by the state of the bodies, which were found on a bright but cool morning.

We have three intriguing post mortem reports and there is only speculation as to the cause of death. However, there are numerous questions raised by these reports and anomalies in the circumstances surrounding the deaths of these animals.

So what of the mutilators? They carry out their attacks with method and precision (and impunity!). The mutilations often vary, but invariably conform to the list of injuries that are now synonymous with these sinister attacks. Furthermore, some of the mutilation attacks appear to employ the Rokitansky technique. This technique of pathological examination was devised by Baron Carl von Rokitansky (1804–1878) and involved the removal of major organs in-situ. I would suggest that no natural predator is capable of employing this technique and that a human would need some advanced knowledge, skill and technology to replicate the mutilators' procedures.

47

What Happened to the Dartmoor Ponies?

Had it not been for John Wyse and his small team carrying out their investigation looking for trace elements of a UFO landing at Hollocombe Bottom, it is extremely unlikely that any details relating to the Dartmoor ponies incident would ever have come into the public domain. When an alert newspaper editor saw the local story about dead ponies and UFOs it was a dream story, made for the tabloid press, and the ensuing headlines were predictable.

However, this was mid-July 1977 and the first myth surrounding this sinister incident had been created. Anyone who picked up on the story from the newspaper reports assumed that the date it happened was 13th July 1977, the time that the story broke into the national press. Consequently, a false trail was laid for researchers not prepared to dig deeper and visit the area first-hand.

There are only two ways to get to Hollocombe Bottom, the hard way and the even harder way, and I have tried them both. From Postbridge there is a pathway leading towards Broad Down, a stone wall leads up into the hills and at times the climb is almost perpendicular. Keeping left of the wall as it ends before Broad Down, another stone wall snakes off towards Lower White Tor. When the wall peters out you arrive at the top of Hollocombe Bottom, nestling below Lower White Tor. A stream zigzags from the moor and cascades gently down a succession of small waterfalls into the lower part of the small valley. The walk, if you can call it that, is just under two miles and is pretty exhausting.

There is a more direct route that can be taken from the pottery at Powdermills, just off the B3212. This way is more complex, but much shorter. Nonetheless, it is quite a trek and the distance from the B3212 is only about half a mile shorter. The first thing that struck me about this remote location was the distance from the main road and any human habitation – Postbridge is approximately two miles away. Who or what would come to this remote valley and carry out these mass killings?

It is evident that this incident passed many researchers by and the scant investigation by *Bufora* in 1978 was the only published report to cover the deaths, but they too got the date wrong.

What of John Wyse and his Torbay UFO group? I have a copy of a sketch map that John Wyse did for Joan Amos, which suggests they discussed the case. However, the cover up had already been very effective and it appears that the redoubtable Joan was unable to uncover anything of significance regarding this case. Unfortunately, I have been unable to locate Mr Wyse or any of his four-man team, to see if they can contribute something to the investigation – perhaps this book will stir some memories and prompt one of them to contact me.

Let's review the facts about this incident. The fifteen ponies and one sheep were killed on 10th or 11th April 1977 and were discovered on Easter Monday 11th April 1977 by Mr Alan Hicks, his wife and two children, who were out walking on the moor. Despite reporting the incident to the police and RSPCA as soon as they returned to Postbridge, nothing appeared in the press until the first week of June, two months after the incident.

This was a massive story for the *Tavistock Times*, who despatched photographer Jim Thorrington and reporter Tom Utley on a two-mile trek to Hollocombe Bottom. I believe that Thorrington and Utley were sent to the crime scene as soon as the *Tavistock Times* got wind of the incident, so why did the story not appear until the first week in June? I cannot believe that the *Times* news desk was not aware of this incident the week it actually occurred, week commencing 11th April 1977. The gap between the date of the incident and the front page headline on Friday 3rd June 1977 has no reasonable explanation. I do not believe that Thorrington and Utley would have walked to that remote place, carrying equipment, unless they thought it was a very big story.

The photographs taken by Jim Thorrington are key to giving us a clue as to what happened. Similarities between the classic shot of the dead pony with its bleached skull twisted backwards, Bellever Tor in the distance, and the picture of the Apaloosa mare called Lady in 1967, are unmistakeable. These photographs provide a clear link and possibly a reason for the cover up of the Dartmoor pony deaths.

The Ministry of Agriculture, Farm and Fisheries (MAFF) sent their own vet to the scene, which if nothing else shows that they were very concerned about the killings. MAFF, or DEFRA as it now is, allegedly have no records of the incident. Why send a vet on a near two-mile hike to examine some dead ponies? However, with the gathering momentum of animal mutilations in this country and the USA, I find it hard to believe that all details of this incident aren't under lock and key in some government office, together with details of other similar cases.

The involvement of the army in this incident is unclear. That the army were involved is without doubt. I have two witnesses who have confirmed the involvement of troops in this incident. What were they doing there? Was the army alerted by 'other' activity at Hollocombe Bottom? Was the army presence connected with an investigation of the crime scene, whereby their role was to seal off the area while scientists combed the area for clues?

The army use large parts of Dartmoor for training purposes and this no doubt includes survival training. However, we can discount the assumption that the ponies were killed by hungry 'squaddies' desperate for some meat. The bodies of the ponies were twisted and mangled and were not shot. The evidence for this came from John Wyse and his team. They scoured the area with metal detectors and found no metal traces at all, so we can discount shooting by hungry troops or anybody else for that matter.

Joanna Vinson and Ruth Murray of The Dartmoor Livestock Preservation Society have provided important information. Joanna Vinson and Ruth Murray visited the crime scene for several evenings in a bid to find clues to the deaths. They were unable to come up with a plausible explanation although Ruth Murray favoured the theory that the ponies were the victims of a spiteful, broken relationship. I have to ask what happened to the forensic specimens, taken by Ruth Murray and referred to by local press reports. In my telephone conversations and written correspondence with Joanna Vinson there was no mention of a dead sheep among the fifteen ponies and, to be fair, Joanna was unable to be precise as to how many bodies remained at Hollocombe Bottom, during her evening visits.

The apparent violent manner in which the bones of the victims were smashed or broken is deeply puzzling. In my opinion it does suggest that the bodies were either dropped from a great height or were violently hurled down into the valley. Could the following newspaper article from the *Wales on Sunday* on 10th September 1989, provide a clue?

> *Scientists Cowed by Mystery Sea Find*
> *Scientists counting fish from a submarine made a bizarre find deep below the ocean surface – a sunken cow.*
>
> *Tory O'Connell, a biologist with the state department of Fish and Game, said she and the pilot of the two-seat submarine saw the carcass for several seconds as they cruised about 20 miles west of Baranof Island, Alaska, 690 feet under the sea.*
>
> *The researchers did not offer theories for how the cow ended up on the ocean floor. Its condition indicated it had not been there for long, O'Connell said.*

I would suggest the possibility that the cow might have been abducted and dropped by mutilators into the ocean.

Looking at the evidence I have accumulated I am of the opinion that the deaths of the fifteen ponies and one sheep were the result of an animal mutilation attack by an alien culture whose motives are, as yet, unclear. I believe the government, through the Ministry of Agriculture Fisheries and Foods, acted swiftly to investigate the killings and effectively suppressed news of the incident until their investigations were complete. I cannot believe that the mutilation mayhem being carried out in the USA was not of great concern to the UK government, who did what they could to hide from the public domain all knowledge of this and numerous other cases since.

There is a final enigma regarding this disturbing and sinister case. What does the BBC television producer, whose friend rang a BBC Radio phone in with such a tantalising description that this was a major British government cover up, know about this incident? What information does she have that puts this incident in the most secret category? I hope that if she or her friend ever read this book they will contact me and provide what may be the final piece in the jigsaw.

48

Who or What Carried out the Moortown Sheep Attacks?

From the day I visited Dartmoor, that fateful Friday 1st April 2005, and my concerns that the January killings were not the occult ritual they were claimed to be, I have been gradually convinced by an ever-increasing volume of evidence that the majority, if not all, the Moortown sheep deaths have nothing to do with human activity.

The seven sheep inexplicably killed on 2nd January 2005 created a myth that persists to this day, that the killings had an occult motive and were ritualistic in their execution. The facts do not bear this out. The bodies were not laid out in a 'star' shape as alleged and the bizarre nature of these killings influenced those who saw the bodies lying on the hillside. Seven bodies, seven-pointed star, equals occult! When I asked Chris and Adrian Cole to do a rough map of the bodies it was apparent that there was no 'star' shape. When I saw the digital camera pictures of the crime scene taken by Frank Yeo, it was obvious that while the bodies were spread roughly in an elliptical form, there was definitely no 'star' shape. Where was the altar? Where was the occult paraphernalia?

How had the sheep been corralled in two separate areas while they awaited their fate? Chris Cole was experienced enough to know that they had been kept in the two holding areas for at least twenty minutes. There was no sign of any tracks or post marks for temporary fencing, yet the sheep appeared to have remained docile and calm as they were systematically slaughtered. Experienced sheep farmers will tell you that when going to an abattoir for slaughter, sheep instinctively know the fate that awaits them and will often become agitated and 'mess' themselves. Witnessing the executions, why did the seven sheep not act in similar fashion?

The lack of blood at the scene is also very curious and I find it frustrating that the tongues were not all checked for possible excision. However, the vet noticed the strange bruising, possibly indicating that the sheep had been prodded with a sharp instrument or stick.

We should not forget the eighth sheep that was rescued from a nearby culvert. This sheep also had the strange bruising and was clearly traumatised by the experience. This animal, which had a very lucky escape, bolted across a cattle grid and would not eat for more than twenty-four hours despite being next to a herb garden. If only this survivor could speak!

The long gap between the January 2005 killings and the attacks on 14th and 15th October 2005 gave me a chance to speak to the farmer concerned and identify some of the typical injuries that are consistent with the animal mutilation problem. In the event I was fortunate that my prediction that an attack on or about the full moon would be highly likely and of the removal of the tongues in the six victims gave my warnings a strong credibility. If there had been any doubt about the January attack, then there was no doubt about these two attacks carried out on Friday and Saturday 14th and 15th October.

The role of the police was an important factor in the October killings. The attendance of a scene of crime officer, on Sunday 16th October, and the numerous photographs that were taken prompted my application for the case file under The Freedom of Information Act. The photographs released under my appeal are astonishing and prove that the killings are indeed linked to similar attacks in the USA.

The incredible events of 14th and 15th May 2006 do not provide the 'smoking gun' for this series of mutilation attacks. Dave Gillham and I obtained some very, very important footage during that night and we were witness to the activities of an unknown intelligence. Unfortunately, we can only be sure that on that part of Dartmoor there is an intelligence, most probably alien in origin, that either visits the area for some unknown purpose or is resident there and operating at a speed and in a spectrum outside human capability. For all we know the activity seen by Dave and I could be just one of many different races that could be operating in or visiting the area, perhaps even monitoring the activities of the mutilators.

The fourth attack on 26th June 2006 was unexpected as it occurred outside the full moon window. Three sheep, including one lamb, had been killed and this attack was to have a major bearing on the whole investigation. By the time Dave, his son and I reached the crime scene on Wednesday morning, only one body lay in situ. The dead animal looked as if it had been struck down as it was walking and the missing tongue and eye told a familiar story. This corpse was to prove very important because a thin strip of tissue had been removed from the lower jaw. The cauterised, serrated cut edge was my first sight of the classic 'cookie cutter' mutilation, so prevalent in USA cases. We had a further clear link to the mutilations in the USA.

One of the three bodies had been removed by the farmer at my request and was to prove no less significant than the body we had examined on the moor. I removed the second body to a vet in the West Midlands and only I knew the identity of that vet. The cursory post mortem revealed that the anal sphincter had been removed and that the tongue had been excised by a smooth cut to the back of the mouth. One eye had been completely removed and a two centimetre hole had been made on the underside of one leg, directly into the abdominal cavity. While the information received from the vet was highly significant other matters were to overtake the investigation.

It is apparent that there were other agencies interested in the investigation I was carrying out and the subtle way DEFRA obtained my mobile phone records to get the name of the vet before approaching me through the local Environmental Health Officer, show the high-level monitoring of the animal mutilation problem.

The killing of two lambs on 7th July 2006, one in a field close to Moortown Farm house, the other near Tavistock golf course, created further confusion. The killing near the golf course seemed particularly audacious as the area is well used by people walking their dogs. No one saw or heard anything. The second killing was in a field that is not easy to access and within close proximity to the farmhouse. An astonishing aspect of this particular killing is the fact that the victim was selected from a flock of some one hundred and twenty sheep. Why did they select this one animal? The moon phases do not appear to have been a factor in these two attacks and as the mutilators became more active, the full moon could no longer be relied on as a potential time for attacks.

On 21st August 2006 there was another killing in a field near Moortown Farm. The victim had been killed in broad daylight on a busy working farm – how had they managed that? It is interesting to note the low flying military aircraft that appeared to be photographing the Barn Hill and common area on 16th August.

Then 29th August saw another killing, this time on the common near Pork Hill car park. This animal, like the previous victims, had its tongue excised, one eye removed and possible rectal coring. There was a most sinister and disturbing element to this killing. The farmer brought the dead animal back to the farm in her Land Rover and when she checked the body a couple of hours later she was shocked to find an enormous pile of dead blow flies next to the body. What had the mutilators put on the body to kill the flies?

On 30th August three sheep were killed in a field on the other side of the

B3357, approximately a quarter of a mile down Pork Hill. The cause of death was not established and the killings were attributed to dogs. Curiously the bodies were not torn as one might have expected in such an attack. There is some doubt as to whether these three deaths were the work of the mutilators.

The month of September 2006 saw a huge increase in attacks and killings and I have recorded twenty-three victims during the eight days between 10th September and 17th September. The reason for this escalation is unclear although the massacre appeared to bring a temporary cessation to the attacks. One of the strange features of the September attacks was the rapid decomposition and bloated appearance of the bodies. Why did the two bodies I examined have such a high level of electromagnetism, eight times higher than normal?

The state of the livers in two of the September victims caused comment from two vets and there were 'abnormalities' noted. I wonder if a case from New Mexico in 1979 has any relevance? On Friday 19th January 1979 three horses were killed, two of which were mutilated, in an area south of Carlsbad, New Mexico. A foal had been removed from one of the victims and four days later on 23rd January another horse was killed and mutilated. The horse that had not been mutilated in the first attack was also disfigured by the mutilators, who carried out their attack despite all-night surveillance by the owner of the ranch.

A local veterinarian, revealed that in his opinion the horses died of *'acute toxic hepatitis'*. The vet did not offer any further speculation on the deaths. An experienced animal mutilation investigator, who researched the incident, pointed out that severe liver deterioration had been noted in other mutilation cases. I am not sure how three seemingly fit horses can die the same night of acute toxic hepatitis. However, it appears to me that the deterioration of an animal's liver may be another symptom of the mutilator's activities.

A further seven sheep were killed on Barn Hill sometime during 16th and 17th July 2007. This attack was attributed by some to dogs. However, Mary Alford, the owner of these animals, was adamant that the sheep had been killed as previous victims and that the seven deaths were an additional statistic of this disturbing series. How dogs could have removed the tongues of these animals is not clear..

On 4th November 2007 a lamb was abducted from a field on the Alfords' farm and killed and mutilated on Barn Hill. The curious thing about this attack is that the mutilators took the animal from a field and transported it half a mile to the place where its body was left. There was much activity at Moortown Farm for a social event on the evening in question. Why did the mutilators take a risk by transporting the victim to Barn Hill? It is clear that the area where so many of the bodies have been found is of some importance in this mystery.

The last recorded attack was during 13th and 14th November 2008, when a neighbour of Mary Alford found one of her sheep dead in a gorse bush near the track and next to, coincidently, the place where Dave Gillham and I used to park on our surveillance nights. The animal bore the classic signs of a mutilation attack (its tongue had been precisely excised by a smooth cut to the back of the throat). Given the location of the body, which appeared to have been dropped into a gorse bush, was this some sort of bizarre message from the mutilators to Dave and myself?

It is difficult to say with certainty that there have been no further attacks. I am curious about the involvement of the military and it is possible that dead animals are being removed from the area before they can be discovered.

One of the most disturbing facts to come out of this series of killings is that some of the hapless victims of these horrendous attacks are still alive when the mutilations are carried out. What evidence do I have for such a statement? A government veterinary officer. I quote from his report: *'The right ear had been cut and there was a band of haemorrhage extending one millimetre beneath the wound, suggesting the cut had occurred pre-mortem.'* Veterinary pathologists in the USA have made similar findings in mutilation cases.

A possible motive for the series of mutilation attacks on Dartmoor arose in November 1997, when ex-government minister Patrick Nicholls, MP for Teignbridge in Devon, called for a public enquiry into the effects of a series of germ warfare tests carried out in an area between Lyme Bay and Devonport. The tests were carried out in the 1960s and did not conclude until 1977 (the year of the fifteen pony deaths). This scandalous testing programme involved the release of a 'cocktail of bacteria', such as E.coli 162, over a corridor across Dorset and Devon to simulate a biological attack. The agency responsible for this horrifying scheme was the Defence and Evaluation and Research Agency, who claimed the tests would have no harmful effects.

In a disgracefully short debate, Mr Nicholls argued that there was no evidence to support the Defence Evaluation and Research Agency view that the bacteria release was harmless. Mr Nicholls cited the case of the Dorset village East Lulworth, on the coast of Lyme Bay, where all the girls in twenty-two families had gone on to have miscarriages or give birth to children with defects. Regrettably, no public enquiry was forthcoming.

Could it be that the selective serial attacks on sheep in the Dartmoor area are part of a monitoring programme by entities studying the environmental effects of these human tests?

Whatever entities carried out the Moortown sheep killings they have a technological superiority and an indifference that is truly chilling. Daytime, night-time, they carry out their attacks with precision and impunity; they cannot be stopped. Their motives are unclear and the only hope the farmers have is that the programme of sampling, for that is what it appears to be, will soon be complete and the mutilators will move to another location to carry out their bizarre attacks. I believe we are faced with an alien culture that is responsible for the killings and I, and the farmers, would like to know what the government of the UK is doing about it.

49

Need to Know

In his book *Need to Know – UFOs, the Military and Intelligence*, Timothy Good makes reference to the animal mutilation problem in Central, North and South America. He states that despite the usual suspects of satanic cults and natural predators being suggested for these attacks, the scientific evidence proves otherwise. In an interview in 1984, with Dr Pierre Guerin of the French Institute of Astrophysics, Good was told, *'The testimonial facts are always doubtful, because the material facts, independent of the witnesses – in the case of the mutilations – are of a superior degree.'*

The animal mutilation attacks appear to provide trace elements of a presence on our planet of an alien culture whose technology and motives are difficult for us to understand. There is compelling evidence that the alien entities that may be responsible for these attacks are also the occupants of some of the craft of unknown origin or UFOs that have been so widely witnessed around the world. If this is so, then two of the most enigmatic mysteries of modern times have scientific substance and should be considered, not as paranormal subjects, but as mainstream scientific investigations.

I am disappointed that animal cruelty is an issue that can motivate a large number of people in Britain, yet the animal mutilation problem appears to be too extreme for them. The connection with UFOs and alien entities does not help, as I believe a second barrier to acceptance is created. It is one thing to come to terms with the appalling cruelty involved in these crimes, quite another to accept that an alien culture or even our own government may be responsible.

This problem is not an ongoing problem for farmers in the way that foot and mouth and BSE are a problem. The mutilations are not an occupational hazard that has to be accepted by farmers, pet owners or anyone else. In addition, don't be fooled into thinking that the long period of time, some forty years, during which animal mutilations have been recorded is any way comforting. I do not believe that time has the same relevance for the entities that may be carrying out these attacks.

The worldwide problem of animal mutilations requires an international initiative to investigate it. It is apparent that only in the USA is there a large private resource available for researching this problem, while in the UK only a handful of researchers like myself are devoting our time and very limited resource, in order to learn more about this disturbing issue.

The clandestine nature of investigations by the British government suggests that the problem is very high on the agenda, but I believe it is the responsibility of government, animal welfare groups and individual researchers to make people aware of the animal mutilation problem before something unthinkable happens and the public are presented with an overnight catastrophe that they are collectively unable to deal with.

I would close with these words, slightly amended, and attributed to the Irish-born British politician and philosopher, Edmund Burke:

The only thing necessary for evil to succeed is that good people do nothing.

Appendix 1

26th July 2006
Telephone Conversation with Environmental Health Officer (EHO)

MAF – Hello, is that Mr EHO? My name is Freebury and I understand you have contacted a vet requesting details about me.

EHO – *Excuse me Mr Freebury while I pick up my other phone. (I heard a click before the conversation continued.) Yes Mr Freebury, I understand you had a post mortem carried out on a sheep.*

MAF – That's correct, yes.

EHO – *I have been asked to look into this as my responsibilities involve the movement of animals to and from the area.*

MAF – I would like to know actually, how you came by the information about the vet that carried out this post mortem?

EHO – *I had a request from the Ministry Regional Vet for information relating to the circumstances surrounding the post mortem carried out on this sheep, especially as it had been transported across several counties, to the borough in order for the post mortem to be carried out.*

MAF – Right, right.

EHO – *The Ministry Regional Vet wished to know the circumstances and contacted me as this was in my area.*

MAF – Yes, right, right.

EHO – *The movement of dead animals is obviously of some concern to us and this is why I have been asked to look into the matter.*

MAF – Mm, right.

EHO – *The Regional Ministry Vet has powers under the Animal Health Act to ensure* *that there are strict controls on the movement of dead animals. Moving a dead sheep from Devon to the West Midlands is plainly an issue that raises some concerns.*

MAF – Mm, right. So could you just tell me when you received the email from the Regional Ministry Vet?

EHO *– I received the email from the Regional Ministry Vet on Friday asking me to contact the vet.*

MAF – Right, right.

EHO *– The Regional Ministry Vet has obviously got concerns and that is why I contacted the vet to ask what your interest was.*

MAF – What is quite interesting is that first of all I am quite sure that the Regional Ministry Vet knows precisely what it is that I'm looking into. I'm investigating a series of unexplained killings and beyond that I'm not prepared to say at this stage.

EHO *– Animals?*

MAF – Animals? Yes. I am staggered that they could have found out the identity of the vet, which makes me think! And I can assure you that what I'm actually doing is basically carrying out my patriotic duty.

EHO *– We cannot allow the unauthorized movement of dead livestock around the country willy nilly as there are all kinds of issues involved, such as the spread of foot and mouth and other highly infectious diseases.*

MAF – Mm, well I have to say that I have the full approval of the farmer and the animal was contained in two containers. And, yes, I am aware that obviously one has to be careful when dealing with dead livestock, in fact, any animals. This animal was one of three that died in very mysterious circumstances. The other bodies were actually left on Dartmoor, mm, which you could say constituted a risk as well.

EHO *– That's quite right.*

MAF – But, mm.

EHO *– Have the police been involved in all this?*

MAF – Well, the farmer has actually gone to the police on this and they have been unable to help at all.

EHO – *So you have become involved in all of this and that is why you have had the post mortem done.*

MAF – Yes, yes I mean I presume you've had a copy of the report [post mortem].

EHO – *Could you explain the details of the post mortem to me?*

MAF – There are certain things about this report that are quite important and certainly kicks into touch the police and the media claims that these are occult killings. And I don't know if you have read the report, that there was a two centimetre hole through one of the legs that went into the upper body cavity, through which material was being taken. This is extremely unusual. Also, the anal sphincter had also been removed and this again is highly unusual. And this killing puts it directly mm, in the same category as those in America of a similar nature. They are being put down as occult killings but I have to tell you that they are not.

EHO – *How long have you been investigating this?*

MAF – I have been investigating this now for eighteen months and there are several farmers involved. And they've all lost stock and the police, basically, have drawn a blank.

EHO – *Could this not be down to the occult or Satanists?*

MAF – Absolutely not, no, there is a sampling aspect to this, as if something is sampling the livestock.

EHO – *I see, that's very interesting.*

MAF – Yes, I certainly don't wish to cause any trouble or transgress any laws or regulations, but I really don't think that there has been any risk in this particular instance.

EHO – *Well, I'm inclined to agree.*

MAF – I don't know whether you've written to me at all on this issue at all because the vet told me on Friday [21st July] that you were in touch.

EHO – *Yes, I have written to you.*

MAF – I do not think that ...

EHO – *Have you received my letter?*

MAF – No, no, I have not received a letter yet.

EHO – *Well, the post is a bit slow! If you get my letter you can disregard it because we've already had a discussion on the points raised.*

MAF – Right, right.

EHO – *I will let the Regional Ministry Vet know what we've discussed and pass on your comments.*

MAF – Mmm. I mean, have you had to forward a copy of the post mortem yet? Have they requested it yet? I mean, if they wish they can contact me direct on this, there is no problem with that.

EHO – *Is this just happening in Devon?*

MAF – No, no, this is happening in various parts of the country. There is a pattern to this across the country and I'm sure the Regional Ministry Vet is probably aware of this problem.

EHO – *I see. If I need to contact you is there a number I can get you on?*

MAF – OK. Please ring on my landline, there is no problem you can ring me any time. I have an answer phone and I'll always get back to you.

EHO – *Thank you for ringing Mr Freebury.*

MAF – Ok, Mr ——. Thank you for your time. Bye bye.

Call terminated @ 1141 hours 26/7/06
Duration of call : 11 minutes 24 seconds

Comments – This transcript has been reconstructed from a recording made of the conversation, notes and memory.

Bibliography

Andrews, Ann and Jean Ritchie *Abducted* – Headline Book Publishing, Great Britain 1998

Fitter, RSR *Collins Pocket Guide to British Birds* – Collins, London revised edition 1966

Wilkins, Harold T *Flying Saucers on the Moon* -- Peter Owen Ltd, London

Keel, John A *The Mothman Prophecies* – Hodder and Stoughton, revised edition, Great Britain 2002

Delgado, Pat *Crop Circles Conclusive Evidence?* – Bloomsbury Publishing Ltd, Great Britain 1992

Downes, Jonathan *Monster Hunter* – CFZ Jonathan Downes 2005

Downes, Jonathan *UFOs over Devon* – Bossiney Books Ltd, Launceston 2000

Plymouth UFO Research Group – *UFO's over Plymouth*

Paget, Peter *The Welsh Triangle* – Granada Publishing Ltd, Great Britain 1979

Neal, Alan *Ley Lines of the South West* – Bossiney Books Ltd, Launceston 2004

Moulton Howe, Linda *Glimpses of Other Realities – Volume I: Facts and Eye-witnesses* – LMH Productions, USA 1994

Moulton Howe, Linda *An Alien Harvest* – LMH Productions, USA 1989

White, Paul *Ancient Dartmoor an introduction* – Bossiney Books Ltd, Launceston 2000

Smith, Frederick W *Cattle Mutilation – The Unthinkable Truth* – Frederick W. Smith, Freedland Publishers 1976

Vallee, Jacques *Messengers of Deception* – And/Or Press, USA 1979

Brierly, Nigel *They Stalk by Night* – Yeo Valley Productions – Devon 1989

Other Sources

Articles

'Down on the Farm' Investigation into Animal Mutilations including post-mortem evidence by David Cayton – *UFO Magazine* Jan/Feb 1999

'*High Heat*' by David Perkins – *Western Spirit Magazine* – May 1998
'Down on the Farm' An update on Animal Mutilation Research by David Cayton – *UFO Magazine* Nov/Dec 1999
Joan Amos Archive
Flying Saucer Review Archive
Zygmunt Jan Adamski: Some further points worth noting – Earthlink April 1983 taken from Graham Birdsall article in *Awareness* magazine winter 1981
Video report of Chepstow sheep deaths by David Cayton and Robert Hulse
Stigmata Magazine published by Tom Adams